Debating Higher Education: Phi Perspectives

Volume 6

Series Editors
Ronald Barnett, Institute of Education, University College London, London, UK
Søren S. E. Bengtsen, Danish School of Education (DPU), Aarhus University, Aarhus, Denmark

Debating Higher Education: Philosophical Perspectives.

Higher education has become a huge matter globally, both politically and socially, commanding massive resources, national and cross-national decision-making, and the hopes of many. In parallel, over the last four decades or so, there has been a growing interest in the academic literature in grappling with technical issues in and around higher education. In particular, work has developed drawing on philosophical perspectives and social theory. This is evident right across the world, especially in the journal literature and in research students' doctoral theses. In effect, we have witnessed the formation of a new sub-discipline, a shorthand of which is 'the philosophy of higher education', and which includes perspectives drawn not only from philosophy and social theory but also feminism, ethics, geopolitics, learning theory, and organizational studies.

Through this book series – the first of its kind – the editors want to encourage the further development of this literature. We are keen to promote lively volumes which are informed about changing practices and policy frameworks in higher education and which engage seriously and deeply with matters of public interest, and are written in an accessible style.

Books will take a variety of forms, and will include both sole-authored and multi-authored formats. Importantly, each volume will have a dialogical flavour, engaging explicitly in dialogue with contemporary debates and their contending positions and, where practicable, especially in volumes with many contributors, will themselves exemplify dialogue.

The editors are keen that the series is open to many approaches. We wish to include work that focuses directly on the university as a social institution and on higher education as an educational process; on the idea of the university and on higher education as a sector with political and policy frameworks; on students and learning, and on academics and academic knowledge; and on curricula and pedagogy, and on research and knowledge processes.

Volumes will examine policy and practical issues including, for example, internationalisation, higher education as a set of 'public goods', access and fairness, and the digital era and learning as well as more conceptual and theoretical issues such as academic freedom, ethics, wellbeing, and the philosophy of social organizations.

The editors very much welcome informal inquiries at any time.

Ronald Barnett, UCL Institute of Education – ron.barnett@ucl.ac.uk; Søren S.E. Bengtsen, Aarhus University – ssbe@tdm.au.dk

More information about this series at http://www.springer.com/series/15094

Søren S. E. Bengtsen • Sarah Robinson
Wesley Shumar
Editors

The University Becoming

Perspectives from Philosophy and Social Theory

Editors
Søren S. E. Bengtsen
Danish School of Education (DPU)
Aarhus University
Aarhus, Denmark

Sarah Robinson
Center for Educational Development
Aarhus University
Aarhus, Denmark

Wesley Shumar
Department of Communication
Drexel University
Philadelphia, PA, USA

ISSN 2366-2573   ISSN 2366-2581 (electronic)
Debating Higher Education: Philosophical Perspectives
ISBN 978-3-030-69630-6   ISBN 978-3-030-69628-3 (eBook)
https://doi.org/10.1007/978-3-030-69628-3

© The Editor(s) (if applicable) and The Author(s), under exclusive license to Springer Nature Switzerland AG 2021
This work is subject to copyright. All rights are solely and exclusively licensed by the Publisher, whether the whole or part of the material is concerned, specifically the rights of translation, reprinting, reuse of illustrations, recitation, broadcasting, reproduction on microfilms or in any other physical way, and transmission or information storage and retrieval, electronic adaptation, computer software, or by similar or dissimilar methodology now known or hereafter developed.
The use of general descriptive names, registered names, trademarks, service marks, etc. in this publication does not imply, even in the absence of a specific statement, that such names are exempt from the relevant protective laws and regulations and therefore free for general use.
The publisher, the authors, and the editors are safe to assume that the advice and information in this book are believed to be true and accurate at the date of publication. Neither the publisher nor the authors or the editors give a warranty, expressed or implied, with respect to the material contained herein or for any errors or omissions that may have been made. The publisher remains neutral with regard to jurisdictional claims in published maps and institutional affiliations.

This Springer imprint is published by the registered company Springer Nature Switzerland AG
The registered company address is: Gewerbestrasse 11, 6330 Cham, Switzerland

Acknowledgements

The volume has emerged from the joint endeavours of the members of the *Philosophy and Theory of Higher Education Society* (PaTHES). The chapters are selected from keynotes and paper presentations delivered at the first two annual Philosophy and Theory of Higher Education Conferences titled 'The Purpose of the Future University', held at Aarhus University in 2017, and 'Student Being and Becoming in the Future University', held at Middlesex University in 2018. We thank the organisers of the two conferences and all the contributors of this volume for turning their material into the present volume chapters.

We also wish to extend our thanks to Springer Editor Annemarie Keur and Editorial Director Nick Melchior for their support and guidance throughout the process. Thanks also to former series editors Professor Paul Gibbs and Professor Amanda Fulford for supporting the volume proposal, and Professor Fulford for being part of the early stages of the development of the volume. A special thanks goes to series editor Emeritus Professor Ronald Barnett for his enduring support and valuable feedback and advice throughout the entire formation of the present volume.

Søren S.E. Bengtsen, Sarah Robinson, and Wesley Shumar

Contents

1	**Introduction – The University Becoming** Søren S. E. Bengtsen, Sarah Robinson, and Wesley Shumar	1

Part I Higher Education and Its Societal Contexts

2	**The Philosophy of Higher Education: Forks, Branches and Openings** Ronald Barnett	15
3	**Higher Education and the Politics of Need** Benjamin Baez	29
4	**Education as Promise: Learning from Hannah Arendt** Jon Nixon	51
5	**Can Academics Be Trusted to Be Truth-Tellers More Than the Rest of Society?** Paul Gibbs	67

Part II Student Being and Becoming

6	**Higher Education: Learning How to Pay Attention** Sharon Rider	81
7	**In Search of Student Time: Student Temporality and the Future University** Søren S. E. Bengtsen, Laura Louise Sarauw, and Ourania Filippakou	95
8	**A Kantian Perspective on Integrity as an Aim of Student Being and Becoming** Denise Batchelor	111
9	**An Entrepreneurial Ecology for Higher Education: A New Approach to Student Formation** Wesley Shumar and Søren S. E. Bengtsen	125

Part III The Idea of the Future University

10 Philosophy for the Playful University – Towards a Theoretical Foundation for Playful Higher Education 141
Rikke Toft Nørgård

11 The Migrant University 157
Ryan Evely Gildersleeve

12 The Student as Consumer or Citizen of Academia and Academic Bildung 173
Mariann Solberg

13 Creating Experimenting Communities in the Future University 185
Sarah Robinson, Klaus Thestrup, and Wesley Shumar

14 Coda: *Perpetuum Mobile* 201
Ronald Barnett

Index 205

List of Contributors

Benjamin Baez Department of Educational Policy Studies, Florida International University, Miami, FL, USA

Ronald Barnett University College London Institute of Education, London, UK

Denise Batchelor Surrey, UK

Søren S. E. Bengtsen Danish School of Education (DPU), Aarhus University, Aarhus, Denmark

Ourania Filippakou Department of Education, College of Business, Arts & Social Sciences, Brunel University London, Uxbridge, UK

Paul Gibbs East European University, Tbilisi, Georgia

Ryan Evely Gildersleeve Morgridge College of Education at University of Denver, Denver, CO, USA

Jon Nixon Middlesex University, London, UK

Rikke Toft Nørgård Aarhus University, Aarhus C, Denmark

Sharon Rider Department of Philosophy, Uppsala University, Uppsala, Sweden

Sarah Robinson Center for Educational Development, Aarhus University, Aarhus, Denmark

Laura Louise Sarauw Roskilde University, Roskilde, Denmark

Wesley Shumar Department of Communication, Drexel University, Philadelphia, PA, USA

Mariann Solberg UiT The Arctic University of Norway, Tromsø, Norway

Klaus Thestrup Aarhus University, Aarhus, Denmark

Chapter 1
Introduction – The University Becoming

Søren S. E. Bengtsen, Sarah Robinson, and Wesley Shumar

The university is moving on uncertain terrain. As we are writing this introduction, we are coming close to completing the first year of the pandemic (but possibly not the last). As a consequence, and due to the massive changes and restrictions, the last year has seen a disruption of some of the recent global drivers within higher education, such as student (and staff) mobility, internationalization, and professionalization of higher education. On the other hand, we have seen a major increase in, and push for, the digitalization of the university as many courses, conferences, and projects have had to move either partly or entirely online. Further, habitual research practices have been influenced as well. Collecting empirical data, field work, and the use of university facilities such as laboratories, media labs, office facilities, and libraries have, for periods of time, been either closed off altogether or have been open with restrictions to physical access and on numbers of people allowed.

Universities and academics around the world have felt the repercussions of the pandemic both in relation to institutional infrastructure and leadership, course planning and organization, research and learning environments, exams, and research practices – but also in relation to connections to the surrounding society through disrupted career plans, agreements with external partners, and societal outreach projects. The already existing multiple demands for academic work and higher

---

S. S. E. Bengtsen (✉)
Danish School of Education (DPU), Aarhus University, Aarhus, Denmark
e-mail: ssbe@edu.au.dk

S. Robinson
Center for Educational Development, Aarhus University, Aarhus, Denmark
e-mail: srobin@au.dk

W. Shumar
Department of Communication, Drexel University, Philadelphia, PA, USA
e-mail: shumarw@drexel.edu

© The Author(s), under exclusive license to Springer Nature Switzerland AG 2021
S. S. E. Bengtsen et al. (eds.), *The University Becoming*, Debating Higher Education: Philosophical Perspectives 6,
https://doi.org/10.1007/978-3-030-69628-3_1

education to provide and promote in-depth disciplinary knowledge, highly advanced knowledge and research expertise, generic competences and transferrable skills for the current and future job-market, and the formation of students to become democratic world-citizens have been further pressured and added to by the conditions of the pandemic which may result in a 'torn curriculum' (Bengtsen 2020). It is certainly the time to, yet again, ask the questions 'what is the university becoming?' and 'what does it mean to become the university today and in the future?'

The current situation, however, also seems to foster a still growing canopy of emerging ideas of possible university futures some already clearly visible, while others remain unclear. We see, for example, new forms of student agency on the rise through numbers of student unions and associations for junior academics in precarious employment. We also see a growing number of journal publications, books, and conferences focusing explicitly on the current and future situation of universities and the role and purpose of higher education. These many and various suggestions of possible university futures may have been accentuated by the current pandemic situation, but they are not defined by it nor limited to it. The current situation accentuates especially three strands of university becoming, which have been on the rise throughout at least the last two decades, from the turn of the millennium and up until today. These three strands include discussions about the integrity of the university, the possibility of reclaiming the idea of the university, and new forms of university becoming. We shall briefly outline the three strands in the following and argue that the current volume places itself particularly within the last strand but with connections and nerve-systems entangled with all three.

The Integrity of the University

The academic and scholarly discussions of the past, present, and future meaning and purpose of the university and higher education could rightly be said to take off and pick up momentum with the series of book publications by Ronald Barnett, beginning with his first book *The Idea of Higher Education* (1990). By the middle and end 1990s, Readings (1997) joined the debate and voiced a rising concern that the university "no longer participates in the historical project for humanity that was the legacy of the Enlightenment" and asked if we were entering the "twilight" of the university (1997, p. 5). Readings warns of the fetish of 'excellence' that turns universities away from a passion for depth-knowledge and critical thinking into corporations driven by market forces. Around the same time as Readings, Shumar (1997) provides a precise forecast of the increasing capitalization and consumerism of universities and higher education.

The concern about the slow erosion of the integrity of the university has also been discussed in relation to the failing public and political trust in universities (Gibbs 2004) and the institutional struggles with issues of fake news and knowledge creation in a post-truth society (Peters et al. 2018). The major concern within this strand of thinking and discussion is that the university is losing its integrity as an 'institution of truth' (Rider 2018), which endures as a safe-zone, or buffer-zone, between the interests of the state, the market, and the individual. In this mode of thinking, the university make out a cultural realm and value, which cannot be purchased, financially manipulated with, or swayed by ideology.

Within this strand of the university's becoming we find a clear historical or genealogical thread reaching back (and forward) and connecting the current and future university with the past. The historical aspect of the integrity strand is important as it connects our own time and epistemic, societal, and cultural concerns with "the memories, stories, and lives of our ancestors and *their* thoughts, *their* societal engagement and visions for a higher education." (Barnett and Bengtsen 2018, p. 4). The integrity of the university reminds us that the university is old, almost 1000 years, and that its "roots go deep into the history and culture of the Western world, and its being goes beyond the present and timely institutions and buildings of today." (ibid.). Such voices are often heard from the defenders, or perhaps stewards, of the university's becoming who strive to harness what Collini (2012, p. 86 and 87) terms the "spiritual legacy" of the university, to "incarnate a set of 'aspirations and ideals' that go beyond any form of economic return." Becoming a university is just as much about connecting back to the origins and traditions of the institution as it is about connecting with current, and future, societal and political agendas.

To understand and critically assess what the university has become, one must be able to contrast its current situation with its near and distant past institutional iterations and societal manifestations. In order to know who we are, we need to know where we come from and how we have journeyed to get here. The integrity of the university does not mean holding fast uncritically to certain institutional or curricular customs or habits, but, on the contrary, to be able to know what we are changing and what is being changed by whom in our institutions and not least why.

The integrity of the university's becoming not only includes its internal culture and the higher education curriculum, but reaches beyond the institutional realm and into the wider societal and cultural value systems. As Nussbaum (2010, p.15) points out, "producing economic growth does not mean producing democracy" and nor "does it mean producing a healthy, engaged, educated population in which opportunities for a good life are available to all social classes." Nussbaum reveals a great paradox at the heart of the integrity of the university.

On the one hand, she argues that pure models of education for economic growth "are difficult to find in flourishing democracies since democracy is built on respect for each person, and the growth model respects only an aggregate." (Nussbaum 2010, p. 24). However, and worryingly, we see "education systems all over the world are moving closer and closer to the growth model without much thought about how ill-suited it is to the goals of democracy." (ibid.). Nussbaum's point illustrates that the university's becoming is inextricably linked to instrumental demands of the global economic system rather than the well-being of the societies in which it is found.

To uphold the integrity of institutional, academic, and curricular values also cannot be separated from the wider cultural integrity of the societies we live in now, and in the future. The university's becoming is, indeed, "a truly collective enterprise (...) [that requires] cooperation, collaboration, and a communal spirit" (Bengtsen and Barnett 2020, p. 17) both within the universities themselves and through the social contracts they form. The integrity of the university is about, continually and with a cultural as well as a historical awareness, the critical discussion of what it means to stay true to the core values of the university – and what these values are. The part the university plays is an evaluative role in the sense of advising and projecting preferable future paths for the society and its members. Not that the university can answer this question for the society, but it becomes the place where this debate takes place.

Reclaiming the Idea of the University

The second strand of the university's becoming, which arguably has been particularly vocal and visible over the last 10 years, is one of strong societal and cultural engagement and world-embracement and to strive for the common good (Marginson 2016) and the public good (Nixon 2011). Here, we find an understanding of the university fully submerged and entangled within societal, political, and cultural realms. Barnett (2018, p. 17) has promoted the understanding of an ecological university, which "points to the interconnectedness of all things in the world (and even beyond)." Even though the focus is on forming new social contracts with the policy community, external partners within professional sectors and the industry, and the wider civic stakeholders and the public, the aim is also to reclaim the university ethos and its position within the world.

Being an interconnected university does not mean being compliant and to uncritically provide societies and policymakers with the services and solutions they might call for. As Barnett (2018, p.166) underlines, "the ecological university is not a university that plays safe", on the contrary, "it is its own agent". The ecological university comes to itself bringing "critique into the world" and in this way "advancing the *critical society*" (ibid.). The perspective is not on the relationship between the university and society. The university *is* (part of) society.

The university's becoming within this strand is less about reconnecting with its own internal ethos and integrity and more about transgressing traditional institutional, intellectual, and disciplinary boundaries. Here, we find advocates for a strong transdisciplinary higher education curriculum (Gibbs 2017) and an open and creative institution (Peters and Besley 2013). At the same time, the ecological ethos challenges the silos of the disciplines established in the wake of industrial societies in the nineteenth century, and the of notion protectionism and segregation visible in the walled-in campus and curriculum. As Nixon (2011, p. 130–131) argues, a "futures curriculum for higher education would require a bolder and riskier mediation between the claims of established specialist areas and those of new and emergent fields of study." Such a curriculum would encourage students to risk crossing disciplinary and intellectual borders and to be "open and receptive to new ideas and practices, collaborative and confident in working with others, and capable of seeing their own area of specialist expertise in a wider context." (ibid.). Reclaiming the university is also about reclaiming certain student (and teacher and researcher) attitudes – of curiosity, sincerity, and wonder.

The second strand of the university's becoming is not only about claiming a role and responsibility in relation to the creation and sustaining of the public good, but also contributing to the fight for social justice (McArthur 2014) and epistemic justice (de Sousa Santos 2016) within and from the margins of our curriculum, institutions, and societies. Reclaiming the university also means claiming social, gender, and ethnic equality and equity in relation to higher education access, recognition, and acknowledgement – in the classroom, across academic positions, and within the curriculum itself.

As McArthur (2018, p.158) underlines, social justice is at the heart of the public good as social justice is "about critique and transformation: understanding the injustices and distortions in the existing social world, and arguing for a better one beyond it." (McArthur 2018, p. 158). When reclaiming the university, and building our university futures, we must be aware of the "hidden distortions or pathologies that stand in the way of people achieving genuine freedom and the capacity for a 'good' life." (ibid.). Reclaiming the university means decentring the university socially and culturally. Decentring brings with it the realization of lost, or never recognized and acknowledged, peripheries. As Sørensen (2019, p. 109) points out, "marginality has epistemological value *per se*. Being marginal adds to the epistemic sensitivity, especially when it comes to perceiving injustice, inequality, reification, alienation, difference, etc." (Sørensen 2019, p. 109). The university's process of future becoming aims not for the centres of power and traditional social or cultural hegemonies but speaks for the silent, the silenced, the forgotten, and those *without* power. Within the political interest of the university's becoming, there is a strong ethical awakening rising up against destructive asymmetries and revealing new collective momentum.

The University Sprawling

Especially within the last 5 years we have seen a burst in conferences, seminars, special issues, and edited volumes (the present one included) on a great variety of new perceptions and understandings of where the university and higher education is heading. Some of the bulk of these intellectual and conceptual synergies is published within this book series (e.g., Barnett and Fulford 2020; Bengtsen and Barnett 2018), and related (Stoller and Kramer 2018), and in the recently established journal *Philosophy and Theory in Higher Education* (e.g., Bengtsen and Barnett 2019; Gildersleeve and Kleinhesselink 2019). A true myriad of new ideas and imaginaries have emerged exploring new alleys and pathways for the university's becoming. Some of these are mere glimpses, while some present well-developed core concepts, while others seem like visions of academic prophecy. The third strand of the university's becoming manifests a rising collective momentum and community-based pulse around diverse and cross-disciplinary discussions around the philosophy and theory of higher education and university futures.

In the wake of recent powerful and hugely important fully developed theories of the university's becoming, we, at the very moment, live amidst, and within the emergence of, a 'thousand tiny universities' (Grant 2019). One of the important common denominators within this sprawling of ideas and concepts is, as Grant (2019, p. 23) describes it, to "incite thought about the university outside the fatalistic binary that places the global neoliberal university as the dominating one and the old Western collegial university (say) as its subordinated other." As Grant stresses, such binaries threaten to trap us "in an unhappy mix of fury and nostalgia, nostalgia which might be mobilising but is just as likely to be pacifying." (ibid.). We sense the university is heading towards a new state of becoming and trying out its feet in different waters politically, societally, and culturally. Most likely, these many and different ideas and practices will settle into new strongly developed theories of universities and higher education. We hope this volume contributes to both – to boost the diversity and variation in different perspectives on universities and higher education *and* to conceptually strengthen and refine emerging theories.

Interestingly, we start to see discussions of a 'new' public good, or common good, springing not (only) from the universities as institutions but from societal and cultural spaces, which may, for a while, take the form of a university. The university, here, is not only associated with certain buildings, curricula, degrees, and academic communities but becomes a social and cultural force or awakening which pushes forth – and possibly becomes attached to institutions and sustainable communities. We find reports, theorizing efforts, and critical discussions of these forms of the 'new public good' in the notions of the citizen scholar (Arvanitakis and Hornsby 2016) and the common in higher education (Szadkowski 2018). Also, the social embeddedness and cultural nestedness of the university and higher education are central themes in the works of Shumar and Robinson (2018, 2020), Barnett (2018), and Wright (2016). The third strand of the university's becoming relocates the process of becoming from traditional institutional spaces and into in-between spaces, where the public and common good is foregrounded and the university serves more the role of the catalyst than the society-educator.

A good example is found in Schildermans (2019) and Schildermans Simons and Masschelein (2020), in their work on universities in refugee camps, where the university becomes a communal force within civic society and literally rises from the ruins of the old to form a new public and common good. The linkage back to Readings's (1997) use of ruins as an imagery and metaphor becomes explicitly discussed and related to actual ruins and a ruined societal infrastructure. The university's becoming does not take place from within the centre of societally and culturally lit-up spaces, but from the very margins and peripheries of society, where "it is life in exile that is investigated and that requires responsibility." (Schildermans et al. 2020, p. 39). This form of university "is not a resolution to [a] contradiction" and it "does not take away the question by giving an easy response" nor "does it allow to take refuge in the imaginations of edenic pasts or salvific futures" – it is, on the contrary, *"staying with the trouble."* (Schildermans et al. 2020, p. 40). The university's becoming is now not only present within disciplinary silos, research laboratories, lecture halls, libraries, and fenced-in campus areas around the world. It is between us, like a wild-growth, a plant in rocky soil, insisting on its own becoming despite all kinds of hardships. Also, the university's becoming is visibly and tangibly linked to our social and cultural becomings. They are one.

The Structure of the Book

Each chapter in the volume gives its own view on what the university is becoming. The chapters, together, form a canopy of the university's current and future becoming from leading scholars around the world within the field of philosophy and theory of higher education. The book has been divided into three parts, each with chapter-clusters that speak into similar aspects of becoming.

Part 1 is titled 'Higher education and its societal contexts' and focuses on the wider political, social, and cultural contexts surrounding and merging with the university.

In Chap. 2, titled 'The Philosophy of Higher Education: Forks, Branches and Openings', Ronald Barnett discusses the university's becoming in relation to ecology, social justice, well-being, and the public good. Barnett discloses the many different historical, societal, political, cultural, and educational root systems and undercurrents that form and shape the present possibilities of the current and future university's becoming. Through metaphor, Barnett addresses the many branches growing from the university trunk and considers the weight and multiple demands, going often in different directions, spreading the branches of the university tree.

In Chap. 3, titled 'Higher education and the politics of need', Benjamin Baez engages in a critical analysis and discussion of the neo-liberal regimes shaping the university's process of becoming today. Baez points out how political, economic, and educational agendas are becoming still closer woven together in our societies, and not for the benefit of the university. Baez challenges the predominant discourses of utility in relation to higher education debates and strategies, and promotes an alternative higher education economy built around excess and the freedom from usefulness and necessity.

In Chap. 4, titled 'Education as Promise: Learning from Hannah Arendt', Jon Nixon, through the lens of Hannah Arendt, discusses how the university's becoming is shaped through the linkage between generations and their societal and cultural value and belief systems. By activating the powerful Arendtian concepts of plurality, promise, and natality, Nixon argues that generations link to each other both through a promise of heritage but also one of unpredictability and new beginnings.

In Chap. 5, titled 'Can academics be trusted to be truth-tellers more than the rest of society?' Paul Gibbs argues that universities should foster academics who make judgments on what can be trusted and hereby seek to become truth-tellers. The university has to become (or stay) trustworthy and truthful in current societal, political, and cultural spaces, where truth and professional trust is being challenged and undermined from many sides. Gibbs argues that the university's process of becoming relies on deep existential foundations of overcoming self-deception and manipulation. The university's epistemic and moral aims are bound together.

Part 2 is titled 'Student being and becoming' and focuses on the inner life of universities as institutions for higher education and academic community building. Part 2 discusses themes around higher education formation, integrity, temporality, and the ability to pay attention.

In Chap. 6, titled 'Higher Education: Learning How to Pay Attention', Sharon Rider explores the nature of 'deep problems' in our universities and higher education curriculum. Rider argues that the ability to tackle deep and foundational issues in our thinking, institutions, and societies, relies on the ability to pay attention. Learning to pay attention does not mean to get the answers right but to be able to contain uncertainty and doubt and to develop critical thinking. When we learn to pay attention, we manage to move ourselves out of confusion and into clarity and discover a sense of autonomy that is rarely experienced in contemporary higher education.

In Chap. 7, titled 'In search of student time: student temporality and the future university', Søren Bengtsen, Laura Louise Sarauw, and Ourania Filippakou discuss how the notion of time in higher education has been assimilated into neo-liberal discourses about performativity and consumerism. The authors critically discuss alternative ways forward that are concerned with how to build academic communities around conceptions and practices around time as lived and integrated into curricula and formation trajectories. Time is not exterior to but is part and parcel of the thinking and learning process where the university's becoming emerges.

In Chap. 8, titled 'A Kantian perspective on integrity as an aim of student being and becoming', Denise Batchelor, through the optics of Kantian ethics, analyses and discusses the ethical dimensions of higher education learning trajectories and processes of becoming. Batchelor discloses the importance of understanding academic integrity and moral responsibility as part of higher learning, and she calls for greater awareness of the importance of humanism and ethical conduct as the foundation to any ambition of higher learning and formation.

In Chap. 9, titled 'An entrepreneurial ecology for higher education: a new approach to student formation', Wesley Shumar and Søren Bengtsen explore the meaning of value in higher education, and also how higher education itself is, and has been, assessed and valued. The argument takes its starting point in the context of economic value promoted by current neo-liberal policies and shift towards the focus and importance of societal and cultural value of higher education. Higher education is particularly adept at foregrounding social and cultural value found in the periphery and margins of societies often unrecognized by the majority norms.

Part 3 is titled 'The idea of the future university'. With the departure in current higher education practices and institutional contexts, the chapters critically discuss and imagine possible university futures.

In Chap. 10, titled 'Philosophy for the Playful University – Towards a Theoretical Foundation for Playful Higher Education', Rikke Toft Nørgård argues for the need of, and the possibilities for, a more playful higher education within a marketized and gamified university. Nørgård argues for a shift from performativity towards playfulness, which is not separate from higher education and academic work but found at the heart of these activities. Through a playful higher education, the curriculum opens up to the creativity, originality, empathy, community spirit, and fellowship that are needed to build sustainable institutional and societal futures.

In Chap. 11, titled 'The migrant university', Ryan E. Gildersleeve argues that universities and higher education need to adapt better to the constantly changing societal and cultural contexts and population. Using examples from immigrant and biopolitical contexts, Gildersleeve argues that the future higher education system and curriculum, in order to become sustainable, should better integrate and represent diverse societal identities and biological life-forces. Gildersleeve rethinks the meaning of movement and mobility in the future university.

In Chap. 12, titled 'The student as consumer or citizen of academia and academic Bildung', Mariann Solberg analyses and discusses the higher education curriculum through the lens of Bildung, or formation. Solberg takes her departure in the Scandinavian higher education context, where the understanding of Bildung finds itself at a crossroads between academic consumerism and citizenship. Solberg argues that in order to build responsible and sustainable societies and university futures, the road towards academic citizenship has to be chosen, and chosen soon.

In Chap. 13, 'Creating experimenting communities in the future university', Sarah Robinson, Klaus Thestrup, and Wesley Shumar argue that furthering global interconnectedness and cross-national and cross-cultural communities is one of the prime tasks of the future university. Through examples from practice, where digital technologies have been integrated into the course programme, the authors show how experimenting and creative communities may emerge across otherwise diverse and remote institutional, societal, and cultural settings.

References

Arvanitakis, J., & Hornsby, D. (Eds.). (2016). *Universities, the citizen scholar, and the future of higher education*. London: Palgrave Macmillan.
Barnett, R. (1990). *The Idea of higher education*. Berkshire: Open University Press.
Barnett, R. (2018). *The ecological university: A feasible utopia*. London/New York: Routledge.
Barnett, R., & Bengtsen, S. (2018). Introduction: Considering the thinking university. In S. Bengtsen & R. Barnett (Eds.), *The thinking university. A philosophical examination of thought and higher education* (pp. 1–12). Cham: Springer Publishing.
Barnett, R., & Fulford, A. (Eds.). (2020). *Philosophers on the university. Reconsidering higher education*. Cham: Springer.
Bengtsen, S. (2020). Building doctoral ecologies and ecological curricula. Sprawling spaces for learning in researcher education. In R. Barnett & N. Jackson (Eds.), *Ecologies for learning and practice. Emerging ideas, sightings, and possibilities* (pp. 146–159). London/New York: Routledge.
Bengtsen, S., & Barnett, R. (Eds.). (2018). *The thinking university. A philosophical examination of thought and higher education*. Cham: Springer Publishing.
Bengtsen, S., & Barnett, R. (2019, November). (Eds.). Imagining the future University. *Philosophy and Theory in Higher Education*, Special Issue, 1:3.

Bengtsen, S., & Barnett, R. (2020). The four pillars of philosophy in higher education. In N. Davids (Ed.), *Oxford research encyclopedia, education*. Oxford University Press. https://doi.org/10.1093/acrefore/9780190264093.013.1467.

Collini, S. (2012). *What are universities for?* London: Penguin Books.

de Sousa Santos, B. (2016). *Epistemologies of the south: Justice against Epistemicide*. London/New York: Routledge.

Gibbs, P. (2004). *Trusting in the university: The contribution of temporality and trust to a praxis of higher learning*. New York: Kluwer Academic.

Gibbs, P. (Ed.). (2017). *Transdisciplinary higher education. A theoretical basis revealed in practice*. Cham: Springer.

Gildersleeve, R. E., & Kleinhesselink, K. (2019, April). The Anthropocene in the Study of Higher Education. *Philosophy and Theory in Higher Education*, Special Issue, 1:1.

Grant, B. (2019). The future is now: A thousand Tiny Universities. In Bengtsen, S., & Barnett, R. (Eds.). Imagining the future University. *Philosophy and Theory in Higher Education*, Special Issue, 1:3, pp. 9–28.

Marginson, S. (2016). *Higher education and the common good*. Melbourne: Melbourne University Press.

McArthur, J. (2014). *Rethinking knowledge in higher education. Adorno and social justice*. London: Bloomsbury.

McArthur, J. (2018). When thought gets left alone: Thinking, recognition and social justice. In S. Bengtsen & R. Barnett (Eds.), *The thinking university. A philosophical examination of thought and higher education* (pp. 155–166). Cham: Springer Publishing.

Nixon, J. (2011). *Higher education and the public good: Imagining the university*. London/New York: Continuum.

Nussbaum, M. (2010). *Not for profit: Why democracy needs the humanities*. Princeton: Princeton University.

Peters, M. A., & Besley, T. (Eds.). (2013). *The creative university*. Rotterdam: Sense Publishers.

Peters, M. A., Rider, S., Hyvönen, M., & Besley, T. (2018). *Post-truth, fake news: Viral modernity and higher education*. Cham: Springer Publishing.

Readings, B. (1997). *The University in Ruins*. Cambridge, MA/London: Harvard University.

Rider, S. (2018). Truth, democracy, and the Mission of the university. In S. Bengtsen & R. Barnett (Eds.), *The thinking university. A philosophical examination of thought and higher education* (pp. 15–30). Cham: Springer.

Schildermans, H. (2019). *Making a University. Introductory notes on the ecology of study practices*. PhD dissertation. Faculty of Psychology and Educational Sciences. Laboratory for Education and Society. KU Leuven.

Schildermans, H., Simons, M., & Masschelein, J. (2020). From ruins to response-ability: Making a University in a Palestinian Refugee Camp. In N. Hodgson, J. Vliege, & P. Zamojski (Eds.), *Post-critical perspectives on higher education. Reclaiming the educational in the university* (pp. 27–41). Cham: Springer.

Shumar, W. (1997). *College for sale: A critique of the commodification of higher education*. New York: Routledge Falmer.

Shumar, W., & Robinson, S. (2018). Universities as societal drivers: Entrepreneurial interventions for a better future. In S. Bengtsen & R. Barnett (Eds.), *The thinking university. A philosophical examination of thought and higher education* (pp. 31–46). Cham: Springer Publishing.

Shumar, W., & Robinson, S. (2020). Agency, risk-taking, and identity in entrepreneurship education. In Bengtsen, S., & Barnett, R. (Eds.). *Imagining the future University*. Special Issue. Philosophy and Theory in Higher Education, 1:3, pp. 153–173.

Sørensen, A. (2019). Social ethos and political mission. University of the Margins. In Bengtsen, S., & Sørensen, A. (Eds.). *Danish Yearbook of Philosophy*, Special Issue titled Revisiting the Idea of the University, 52:1, pp. 104–138.

Stoller, A., & Kramer, E. (Eds.). (2018). *Contemporary philosophical proposals for the university: Toward a philosophy of higher education*. Cham: Palgrave Macmillan.

Szadkowski, K. (2018). The common in higher education. A conceptual approach. *Higher Education*. https://doi.org/10.1007/s10734-018-0340-4.

Wright, S. (2016). Universities in a knowledge economy or ecology? Policy, contestation and abjection. *Critical Policy Studies, 10*(1), 59–78.

Søren S. E. Bengtsen is Associate Professor in higher education at the Department of Educational Philosophy and General Education, Danish School of Education (DPU), Aarhus University, Denmark. Also, at Aarhus University, he is the Co-Director of the research centre 'Centre for Higher Education Futures' (CHEF). Bengtsen is a founding member and Chair of the international academic association 'Philosophy and Theory of Higher Education Society' (PaTHES). His main research areas include the philosophy of higher education, educational philosophy, higher education policy and practice, and doctoral education and supervision. Bengtsen's recent books include *The Hidden Curriculum in Doctoral Education* (Palgrave Macmillan, 2020, co-authored with Dely L. Elliot, Kay Guccione, and Sofie Kobayashi), *Knowledge and the University. Re-claiming Life* (Routledge, 2019, co-authored with Ronald Barnett), *The Thinking University. A Philosophical Examination of Thought and Higher Education* (Springer, 2019, co-edited with Ronald Barnett), and *Doctoral Supervision. Organization and Dialogue* (Aarhus University Press, 2016).

Sarah Robinson is Associate Professor in the Center for Educational Development at Aarhus University, Denmark. She is an Educational Anthropologist interested in the role of higher education and the purpose and future of the university. Her research spans curriculum reform, policy in practice, ethnographic methods, teacher agency and enterprise education. She has a strong international profile and has published in *The Thinking University; A Philosophical Examination of Thought and Higher Education* Springer (Bengtsen and Barnett 2018) and *The Idea of the University: Volume 2 – Contemporary Perspectives*. Peter Lang (Peters, M. A., & Barnett, R. 2018), as well as being a co-author on *Teacher Agency; An ecological approach* Bloomsbury (Priestley, Biesta & Robinson; 2015). Sarah is on the board of the Philosophy and Theory of Higher Education Society (PaTHES) and arranges conferences, webinars, and online discussions that bring together a range of international scholars interested in Higher Education and its reforms. Currently she is working to design 'a pedagogy for change' by combining an exploration of academic identity with learning from enterprise education.

Wesley Shumar is professor in the Department of Communication at Drexel University. His research focuses on higher education, mathematics education, and entrepreneurship education. His recent work in higher education focuses on the spatial transformation of American universities within the consumer spaces of cities and towns. From 1997 to 2018, he worked as an ethnographer at the Math Forum, a virtual math education community and resource centre. He continues to do research into the use of online spaces to support mathematics education. He is author of *College for Sale: A Critique of the Commodification of Higher Education*, Falmer Press, 1997, and *Inside Mathforum.org: Analysis of an Internet-based Education Community*, Cambridge University Press, 2017. He co-edited, with Joyce Canaan, *Structure and Agency in the Neoliberal University*, Routledge/Falmer, 2008. He also co-edited, with K. Ann Renninger, *Building Virtual Communities: Learning and Change in Cyberspace*, Cambridge, 2002.

Part I
Higher Education and Its Societal Contexts

Chapter 2
The Philosophy of Higher Education: Forks, Branches and Openings

Ronald Barnett

Introduction

The main title of this book is 'The University Becoming'. It is an intriguing title. 'Becoming' is a philosophical concept, and the university has been an object of philosophical study for over two hundred years, but the idea of 'the university becoming' has only recently emerged in the literature. That idea and its inquiry began to take off in a serious fashion in the 1980s and 1990s as part of the recent emergence of the philosophy of higher education as a field of study, and that field is now flourishing. The field has split into two main trunks, as it were, concerning separately the ideas of 'university' and 'higher education', with a number of branches opening out.

On the 'university' trunk appear concepts and issues of academic freedom, institutional autonomy and the 'spirit' of the university, as well its 'public good' and its 'public goods'. Here, too, would be found the concepts of management and leadership (how might they differ?) and the emerging idea of the university as a corporate agent. On the 'higher education' trunk, one branching that can be spotted is that between 'higher education' understood as referring primarily to educational processes – where issues of teaching, curricula, learning, students' development and experiences, and what it is count *as* higher education, are prominent – and 'higher education' as having a system and an especially societal aspect, where issues of social justice come into play (e.g. who should pay for higher education? And who should be permitted to study in institutions of higher education?).. Since these two trunks and some of their branches can be spotted, a question opens immediately: are there links between the two trunks – 'university' and 'higher education' – or are

---

R. Barnett (✉)
University College London Institute of Education, London, UK
e-mail: ron.barnett@ucl.ac.uk

© The Author(s), under exclusive license to Springer Nature Switzerland AG 2021
S. S. E. Bengtsen et al. (eds.), *The University Becoming*, Debating Higher Education: Philosophical Perspectives 6,
https://doi.org/10.1007/978-3-030-69628-3_2

they separate from each other? On this relationship depends the idea of the university's becoming, as to whether it is a unitary idea or whether it is a multiplicity.

I want to take the space of this chapter to address this matter and also to stake out a particular position about the matter of the university's becoming. My argument will be that higher education contributes to the university's becoming (but does not exhaust it) and that the university's becoming is largely that of a university perpetually in motion on the Earth and for the Earth.

I should perhaps offer a note on the writing technique adopted in this essay. It will draw on resources of metaphor – specifically that of trees and their multitudinous branches. It will take note of the base and the roots of the trees as well as reaching into the airy upper branches. I shall depict the ideas of university and of higher education as two connected tree trunks, and the text will fly from trunk to trunk and branch to branch. In all this, the main object is quite simple: to place us in a position sufficient to do justice to the university's becoming while being sensitive to it being a complex matter that is always in motion.

Metaphors for Higher Education

The idea of 'the university becoming' is provocative. If the university is to become, is it that it has never come before? The modern university has grown out of nine-hundred-year roots in the Middle Ages in Europe and was preceded by institutions of learning in Egypt, India, Persia, China and so on. Has the university not been with us for quite some time? It has assuredly passed through various stages, various incarnations indeed. But perhaps the university can become itself in a way not readily possible in the past. Now, it can start to live up to its own rhetoric about itself, its openness and its sense of the unity of knowledge and its proclamations about its service to society. And it can start to live up to this rhetoric in a way never before because now a *plane of optionality* has opened in front of the university. The university now has choices before it, and, for the first time, it can *become* itself, even if its becoming is a never-ending challenge and task – and with each university striving perpetually to become itself and realise itself (in its own way). That at least is a set of claims that I wish to advance here.

The matters here are complex in the technical sense. They run into each other and open out in haphazard ways. Being a university in the twenty-first century is, to a significant degree, an open matter, possessing qualities of unpredictable *emergence*. The patterns exhaust our ordinary language, and we can justifiably reach for metaphors. Deleuze and Guattari (2007) warned us against arborescent metaphors as being too static. 'We're tired of trees', we were told (ibid:17). Rather than a tree that continues to branch, we were urged to take on the rhizome as a metaphor. The tree and branching analogy was overly linear and predictable: what is needed – in a world of Kafkaesque unpredictability and waywardness – was a metaphor that offers formlessness. Hence, the metaphor of rhizome: 'any point of a rhizome can be connected to anything other' (ibd:7).

The rhizome metaphor has an application to higher education, whether that phrase is understood in its educational sense (the student receiving a 'higher education') or in its systems sense (universities simultaneously in national and global systems (plural) of higher education'). In its educational sense, the phrase 'higher education' points to significant elements of unboundedness, uncertainty and even troublesomeness. There is a haphazardness here that is both epistemic (the forms of knowledge and experience that confront the student are presented as open) and experiential (the student has a welter of experiences that are open and even bewildering). In its systems sense, higher education – as collectivities of institutions of higher education (typically 'universities') – are moving in fluid global spaces and are subject to forces and encounters as well as openings and possibilities.

So understood, it is perhaps *liquid* metaphors – of fluids, pools and streams – that are attractive. The university, it may be said, may be likened to a squid, for it possesses a hard shell, can traverse the globe and quickly and yet – with its tentacles – can reach into the smallest crevices and with much delicacy. It is a fluid object moving in a fluid medium. But I want to go back to that earlier metaphor of a tree with its branches. The idea of the tree may yet bear fruit here, helping us in understanding higher education as a set of educational processes and the university qua institution – and their interrelationships.

In the introduction to this chapter, I suggested that the field confronting us has two trunks marked as 'university' and 'higher education'. They grow out of the one set of roots, but their girths are dissimilar. There is a major and a minor trunk. The major trunk is that of higher education as a *level* of education. This scholarship concerns itself with the nature of the educational journey that students might undergo and the kind of development that they might experience as persons. Key concepts here include those of 'virtues', 'wisdom', 'citizenship' and the notoriously difficult concept of *Bildung*. It opens to a number of branches. One of these is the curriculum, issues which include whether there might be a 'liberal education' that transcends disciplines and how the relationship between teaching and research might be conceptualised. Another sizeable branch is that of pedagogy, and the pedagogical relationship. Might a pedagogy be such as to promote happiness or fun?

A yet further branch concerns the disciplines that find their place in the higher education that students experience. The idea of troublesome knowledge is instructive here (Meyer and Land 2005). It seems to straddle both curriculum (what is to be taught?) and pedagogy (how might it be taught?); and it provokes philosophical interest as to whether troublesomeness is *epistemic* in nature, residing in properties of disciplines, or whether troublesomeness is phenomenological, being felt by (some) students in (some) pedagogical situations. Further, is troublesomeness a *necessary* feature of higher education, an enduring element of what it is to be in the milieu of a genuinely higher education, *or* is it simply a moment contingently to be experienced and worked through by individual students as best as they may?

The minor trunk these days is that of the very idea of the university. This idea used to constitute a much stronger line of inquiry than it has been of late, though there are signs of new growth, with many ideas of the university being recently suggested (Barnett 2013: 67–70). It has had a long innings, stretching back over two hundred years, when what it was to be a university was of central significance to major philosophers in Germany. A strong branch was that of matters of knowledge and universality, while another more recently has been that of the relationship of the university as an institution in the wider society, giving rise to matters of academic freedom, the public good and the connections between the university and the public sphere.

Self-evidently, these many lines of inquiry are offering openings as new forks, and further branchings emerge. Might there be a unity here, a central trunk with some girth holding the field together, or are we in the presence of a pollarded growth, with just continual and apparently unconnected outcrops occurring? Adopting a philosophically realist approach, I shall opt for the former possibility and suggest that there is much to hold the field together.

As I pursue this inquiry, I want also to keep in view the main quarry, that of the idea of university becoming. In understanding the conceptual relationship between higher education and the university, where – if anywhere – might this concept of university becoming come into play? As we shall see, in teasing out the way in which the idea of university becoming can come into view, we shall also gain insights into the whole field of the philosophy of higher education and *its* possibilities.

Universities and Higher Education: A Real Situation

Some very quick scene-setting is in order. There are around twenty thousand universities in the world which are educating around two hundred million students. Programmes of study may be full-time or part-time, on campus or at a distance, making little or very heavy use of digital transmissions, synchronous or asynchronous, intimately related to research but not necessarily so, and enjoyed by students attending both from the host country and from many countries. Further, programmes of study may be directly connected to particular situations in the labour market or may be structured with no such consideration in mind, an aspect that is made more complex still by the co-presence in most higher education systems of both private and public institutions. Moreover, programmes of study will be bound to reflect local, national or regional traditions in the pedagogical relationship and the student experience, and even in the type and manner of research being undertaken.

Reminding ourselves of these basic empirical features of universities may prompt the thought that any effort to think in general terms about either the concept of higher education or of the university must run into the sands. There are – it may be felt – no general concepts that can hold water across disparate systems of higher education. Each system, each institution, and each programme of study deserve to be examined empirically, without any assumption being made that there might be universal features that could be said to have application across all such settings. That would be a premature judgement.

As this is being written, the world is plagued – more or less literally – by a virulent virus. The episode is testimony to a world that is even more interconnected than is often recognised. Perhaps every group of entities and features of the world is implicated as the virus passes on its deadly path, and they include animals; human beings (both their biological, social and psychological aspects); knowledge systems; public institutions; transport and distribution systems; national and international policymaking; economics; health systems; spatial relationships at micro, local and global levels; professional practices; traditions and cultures; and socioeconomic matters. There are horizontal and vertical *inter*connections here. Invisible particles have effects on national populations and, at the same time, abstract knowledge systems (for instance, in statistics and mathematical modelling) too can and do have effects on natural systems at all levels. Reduction as a means of understanding, that is any attempt to dissolve entities either downward *or* upward, would be illegitimate (Harman 2018: 43).

If we draw upon the 'holy trinity' that Bhaskar saw as lying at the centre of his critical realism (Bhaskar 2010: 150), we may say that the coronavirus crisis points us vividly to *ontological realism*, *epistemological relativism* and *judgemental rationality*. But we can go further. For the crisis has reminded us – if it was necessary – that the world is constituted by *multiple and layered assemblages* from microparticles to global systems (DeLanda 2013). There are multiple ontologies present since each class of entities has its own natural state of being, which may differ profoundly. Secondly, we bring to bear on this virus many frameworks of understanding, both informal (in the traditions, lifeworlds and cultures of peoples) and formal, in systematic knowledges, in the advancement of which universities play a major part. Let us depict this not as epistemological relativism (Bhaskar's term) but epistemological *diversity*. Thirdly, there is present here not only *judgemental rationality* but also judgemental *power* and even judgemental *ir*rationality. It may well turn out that some of the planning decisions in dealing with the coronavirus are the result of *distorted* knowledge processes, in which academic disciplines are at war with each other and in which those that wield the greater resources temporarily triumph.

The coronavirus crisis is, therefore, telling for the university's becoming. The first lesson it teaches us is precisely one of the interconnectedness of the world, an interconnectedness that is dynamic and always in motion (Nail 2019); and it is an interconnectedness that possesses features not always recognised. Knowledges are affected by the world, and knowledge can and does affect the world: the cognitive world and the natural world have powers over each other.

The university is *within* this maelstrom, not outside of it peering at it. The world, the whole world, all of the entities in it, is acting upon the university; and the university can act, and is acting, upon the world. The coronavirus is a striking example of this fact, for it has wreaked havoc with universities right across the world, posing all manner of quandaries. Just what are the responsibilities of a university that has padlocked its gates? The university likes to see itself as an agent of its affairs, but here we have a reminder – if it was needed – that much like every other entity in the world, it is fragile – and so is every entity, human and non-human, within it. And, in all of this fragility, universities are at the centre of efforts to confront and understand, and even disarm, the coronavirus.

The first lesson here, then, arises from a recognition of the layered and multiple ontologies that constitute the world, and it is that the university should possess a degree of modesty for it is but a node in an interconnected and layered world. Despite their powers, the university's knowledges are going to be limited in what they might accomplish. Western knowledge about the coronavirus – established much of it in universities – may well struggle to have grip in traditional cultures with their own knowledges and ideas of medicine. Moreover, university knowledges cannot be independent of the world but will be affected by it, even while they can exert powers in the world.

The second lesson springs from a recognition that the university is characterised by epistemological diversity, but it is an epistemological diversity that exhibits a major fault. That it is epistemologically diverse poses questions as to the *lack* of relationship with the real world, in all its ontological depth and complexity. The university has formed over time – especially over the last two hundred and fifty years or so – such that different intellectual fields have arisen which, until very recently, were largely isolated from each other. Such boundedness of knowledges must be suspected of being inadequate in illuminating the world, in all its ontological interconnectivity.

The current coronavirus is again testimony to the point. Part of the difficulties that nations are finding in responding to the virus is that it is ontologically interconnected, such that its various manifestations are interconnected but the different knowledges – for example, in transport systems, health systems, economics, virology, professional studies, statistical techniques, political science, social psychology, moral philosophy and history – are unable or, at least, find it difficult to speak to each other. Our modern *epistemological diversity* does not match – and is no match for – *ontological interconnectedness*.

The second lesson then is that the academic world has to find ways of enabling much greater levels of travel across the borders of disciplines. I said a moment ago that the intellectual fields of the present age have been largely isolated from each other 'until very recently'. A largely unremarked *virtue* of the digital age is that it has encouraged – if unwittingly – a much heightened fluidity in intellectual life. Now, with search engines, links, and the sheer serendipity of the internet, ideas, concepts and theories are percolating *across* disciplinary borders and with much bending of dominant meanings. As well as it being an unintended instrument for heightening exclusions in society, the internet is acting as a *positive* disrupting force. It is enabling disciplines to raid items in each other's domains. The question arises, thereby, as to whether universities can do more to promote this jackdaw behaviour to become a systematic feature of academic life.

Epistemic Injustice: A Local Matter

A third point is that, for all their extraordinary variety, the knowledges of universities in the present age now comprise something of a closed universe. There is an understandable interest these days in depicting the academic epistemologies of the world as an emblem of the colonising tendencies of the 'Global North' in its dominant posture towards the Global South (de Sousa Santos 2016). Especially indigenous knowledges or more regional knowledges (of Africa, of South America) are not merely downplayed but are implicitly characterised as not counting as real knowledge. Work from those regions – and analogous regions *within* Western counties (in Australia, New Zealand, Canada and so forth) – is consequently felt as unworthy of gracing the major international journals which form the basis of rankings of academic work (such as the World of Science and Scopus).

There is doubtless some merit in these suggestions as to the presence of epistemic injustice (Fricker 2010), but largely unnoticed is it that epistemic injustice is to be found *within* the dominant knowledges of the world. 'Cognitive capitalism' (Boutang 2011) favours particular knowledges within those found (even) in the Global North (a somewhat unfortunate and imprecise term, not least since it is never made clear as to whether China is included or, indeed, where China is to be placed in this 'colonising-colonised' epistemic geography, but let that pass). It is not even that the so-called STEM (science, technology, engineering, mathematics) disciplines are favoured but that there are selections *within* that grouping while others are hovering into view. Now, it is the disciplines with techno-power and biopower that are especially favoured – chemistry, biochemistry, statistics, mathematics, microbiology, virology, computing, neurology, engineering, informatics, neuropsychology, behavioural psychology and population studies.

The point here is that what counts as knowledge always expresses societal values: there are judgements *within* the judgements to the effect that certain disciplines and their spokespersons have authority, whereas other disciplines and their potential spokespersons have very little (Gellner 1969); and the latter are rarely invited into the broadcasting studios. Epistemic injustice is to be seen *within* the universities of the Global North and within the audit procedures of global academia and their inner judgemental categories. If we must use the term colonisation, then let us use it fully and acknowledge that its tendencies are to be found *within* the Global North as well as beyond it. The power/knowledge (Foucault 1980) complex is alive and vividly present within the academic life of universities across the world.

There are, therefore, elements of closure that have come to characterise academic knowledges. Precisely because certain knowledges attract high evaluations, a self-assurance descends on the fields in question. There may be elements of reflexivity, and it will be claimed that all is tentative, subject to peer review and contestable, and open to revision. But the power and elevation bring in their wake a self-understanding of position in a knowledge hierarchy. The cluster of disciplines that have biopower understand that they now possess economic, political, informational and cultural power denied to those who study medieval history (cf Peters

2013). Moreover, it is understood that high marks flow to empirical work, statistical work and mathematically based work. Large populations and mega-data count. Quantities are more powerful than qualities.

It is against the background of these global shifts in what counts as knowledge and the relative value to be accorded to different forms of knowledge (*within* the knowledges of the Global North) that we have to place the so-called crisis of the humanities. It is a so-called crisis because it has been with us at least since the 1960s (Plumb 1964) and arguably since the 1930s. The ailments of the humanities are readily understandable, but they are not terminal. The patient may have been wheeled into a side ward but is still alive and, on occasions, shows signs of remarkable good health, at least in some countries and in some institutions. One is entitled to wonder, at times, if the patient has not become fond of his/her very status and happily wears the garb.

What is apparent is that the university continues, as it has for over two hundred years, to exhibit a conflict of the faculties (Kant 1992). It is just that the conflict plays out now in a sharper sense, with a new hierarchy and a new set of epistemic inequalities across the disciplines (in their capacities to secure resources and to gain a hearing). Far from philosophy being at the apex, it is now near the foot of the pyramid, if not – in most universities – excluded altogether.

It has frequently been observed, over the past half century, that the university has become fragmented: it is a 'multiversity' (Kerr 1995) and 'loosely coupled' at that (Clark 1983). Two readings are prompted. This fragmentation is all to the good. It strengthens the university, for now the university has multiple resources in responding to the world and in its development. It can go this way and that. It has more 'lines of flight' (Guattari 2016) open to it. The other reading is that the fragmented university is less than the sum of its parts. The conflict of the faculties weakens its possibilities in the world.

However, a yet third reading is possible, namely, that *both options are true simultaneously*. Its epistemological diversity provides it with multiple possibilities for attending to the world; for listening to the world; in speaking to, in and with the world; and in acting in the world, *but* its diversity is so riven with internal borders that its multiple voices either speak across each other as they jostle for position or that many of its voices are barely heard. As a result, across universities, we have neither Bhaskar's judgemental rationality nor even a judgemental irrationality but a judgemental Babel. The university's becoming seems further off than ever.

Becoming a University

The world is in motion, and universities are perforce not merely carried along by this motion but are contributing to it. In this motion, the world moves in multiple *and* opposed directions, at once bespoiling the planet and attempting to save it, having concerns for gross inequalities *and* heightening them, and wanting to spread education across the world and at all levels, *and* yet also wanting to restrict educational opportunities. This is a world at once of control *and* of letting be.

The university takes on and even helps to drive all of these antinomies and more. What is it for the university to become under these conditions? Derrida (2001) was quite misleading in speaking of 'the university without condition': the university cannot be without conditions (plural); it lives always amid conditions, and it has to do so. The contemporary philosopher, Bernard Stiegler, has tried to right Derrida's misreading: 'there is no university without condition' (2015: 170). There are both contingent and conceptual conditions of the university's becoming: both the here and now empirical facts of the case, in its national and cross-national settings, *and* the necessary conditions of what it is to be a university in the twenty-first century.

The conceptual conditions of the university can be stated with surprising ease; and there is just one central condition. It is to produce epistemological resources for the world, both in its research and in its teaching functions. But that immediately prompts tough questions: what is the *legitimate* range of these epistemological resources? Is poetry to be included? Are indigenous knowledges to be given equal billing alongside the knowledges emanating from the Enlightenment? What, in any event, *is* an epistemological resource? Is it merely that that enables society and its organisations and assemblies to proceed with confidence, with more power and control; is it to include reflexive resources that enable those knowledges critically to reflect upon themselves; is it to offer appreciative resources that enable humanity to understand, in humility, this total Earth, and with an ever-wider array of insight; and/or is it to provide resources of critique that furnish powers not only to comment critically on the world but actually to improve it?

A single answer to these questions suggests that the term being proposed here – *epistemological resource* – is itself resource*ful*. It offers many resources, and we may bring this out in a comparison with the term encountered earlier, that of cognitive capital. Cognitive capital is a powerful but a more restricted idea than that of epistemological resource. Cognitive capital is constituted by those knowledges that wield immediate power in the world – and not restricted to economic power for it might be political, cultural or societal power. In contrast, the term being suggested here, that of epistemological resource, offers an even larger umbrella and allows for diverse knowledges and powers of reflexivity, critique and insight – and even wisdom (Maxwell 2014). Moreover, whereas cognitive capital asks of any form of knowledge ('what power do you yield?'), the concept of epistemological resource asks of a way of understanding-the-world that it allows itself to be seen as part of a family of ways of illuminating the world, of valuing the world and of aiding the Earth's total well-being – and to be understood as one way of speaking to each other.

The concept of epistemological resource, therefore, seeks not to rank knowledges and to place them in a hierarchy of power or profit generation nor does it seek to demarcate, still less to relegate a way of understanding the world as not worthy of consideration. This assembly of knowledges has open doors and enfolds its members as a unity. Moreover, the chairs are arranged in a circular fashion, with no platform or top table. All are on a level. Becoming a university, therefore, is a matter of creating ways in which the university – as in an institution and in its educational processes – becomes epistemologically open, such that its enlarging knowledges come to constitute *resources in critical dialogue* for illuminating the whole world. This condition may seem innocuous, but it would actually constitute a revolution in what it is to be a university.

A University in Motion and so Subject to Risk

If, as observed, the world is in motion, so too, and worldwide, universities are in motion. There is a paradox here. Just at the moment that universities have become highly significant in their nations, with every government taking a close interest in its universities (whether private or public) and a typical university becoming often the largest employer in a town and gaining a visibility never experienced in the last nine hundred years, so they have become weaker in some ways. Politically, they are objects of suspicion; culturally, they are accused of being unduly liberal; economically, they are felt to be insufficiently supportive of a country's economy; and socially, they are critiqued for being insufficiently open to those from certain socioeconomic classes. Their vulnerability, however, goes further. The coronavirus has had large and highly damaging effects on universities – and extremely quickly at that. The university is in motion, and its movements in the world place it in a position of continuing risk.

Risk comes in various guises: it may be political, as where a state closes, or sends the troops into its universities, or decides not to provide support to particular disciplines; it may be economic, as where many universities in a national system suddenly lose a funding stream – perhaps there is a fall in the propensity of potential international students to travel abroad; or it may be cultural, as where universities uncritically take on board societal expectations that are markedly instrumental and, in the process, their cultural functions are foreclosed.

The three risks just identified are, as it were, *risks of imposition*. They are testimony to the university's vulnerable position in the world. And they are the kinds of risk that attract the attention both of senior management teams within, and commentators on, universities. Risks of imposition are readily apparent. They lie on the empirical plane of university's being in the world. They are commonly recognised, and empirical evidence can be produced – with little or greater difficulty – by which to assess the degree to which the risks are prevalent. To what degree is a university subject to closure by state authorities? What proportion of universities' income is threatened by a fall-off in international student numbers? To what extent is a university, in its policies, activities and pedagogical practices, marked by neoliberalism?

However, there is another class of risks that are deserving of our consideration, which we may term *risks of omission*.

This class of risks lies at a deeper level of a university's being in the world. Such risks come into view in answer to the question: 'How might universities legitimately disport themselves in the world?' A proper response to such a question will not be empirical in the first place but will be normative, springing from a set of values felt appropriate to universities. Moreover, such a response will be likely to bring into view a large set of potential claims, posited at different levels of abstraction. Not uncommonly, universities are being urged to heed, for example, considerations of social justice, gender, regional indigenous communities or ecological matters. At an even higher level of abstraction, universities may be encouraged to attend to 'what is of value in life' (Maxwell 2014: 22) or to 'certain questions [that] go unasked' (MacIntyre 2011: 174).

Such prompts speak *not* to what is directly in front of universities and which they are already confronting or are evidently about to confront but to what is *absent and yet possible* for universities. This realm of the possible is admittedly ambiguous. It could simply be referring to what is contingently possible. It is *possible* that Harvard University may lose its premier position in the world rankings of universities (and on some rankings just this has happened). It is possible that the number of students in the world could exceed 250 million by 2030. It is possible that the number of research papers produced by university academics could double over the next five years (even having seen an exponential growth in recent years). It is possible that, in some nations, their universities will contribute 5% of the gross national product in the foreseeable future. All these are empirical possibilities that amount to an extrapolation of their present situation.

Risks of omission, however, can point to a further and more significant class of what is possible for universities. Being matters of omission, they clearly cannot be derived through extrapolations from their present character. Rather, they call for imaginative discernment of the deep and 'real' possibilities. They are derived from a reading of the *potential* that is latent within a university, given its total resources (its values, its epistemological range, its reputation, its technologies) and their powers given plausible readings of the world. A favouring of any such possibilities will be shot through with values. Universities are extraordinary machines with potential to cause harm, but they also possess unrealised potential to assist in improving the world.

The phrase 'risks of omission', therefore, cuts in two ways. The possibilities in front of universities which have hitherto been omitted could be possibilities that *should* remain dormant. Universities *could* be used to heighten the surveillance society, deployed to further the despoiling of the Earth and used to cultivate only the technical competences of students, leaving them as inauthentic beings in a difficult world. They *could* develop learning analytics so as to effect a regime of tight surveillance and control over their students. Higher education *could* be turned into systems in which students become computerised adjuncts to the internet of things in the fourth industrial revolution. Nations and corporations and even academic fields *could* wield undue power in pressing universities in malevolent directions.

But risk can take another form. Universities can be so taken up with the exigencies of the moment that they unwittingly forego considerations of their potential – as indicated – 'to realize what is of value in the world' (Maxwell, ibid). There is risk in attending to the potential inherent in universities, but there is also risk in not doing so. Universities would, thus, be bereft in a sea of strong forces bearing in on them. They will have inadvertently reduced their own corporate agency (List and

Pettit 2011) and fallen short of their possibilities in the world. Far from *becoming*, from realising their 'ground state' (Bhaskar,), they would have regressed.

The distinction between risks of imposition and risks of omission allows us to make the following judgement in relation to our theme here. Risks of imposition relate to the matter of the university's being in this world. As a result of the impositions to which it is subject, the university's being runs the risk of being – and often actually is – thwarted, malevolently directed, and is injurious both to the members of universities and to the wider world. However, the picture with respect to risks of omission is more nuanced, not least since they include positive possibilities for the university's becoming. In almost all jurisdictions in the world, the university has options for its becoming, that becoming understood as heightening the levels of well-being in the world. So understood, the university runs risks of omission. If it fails even to attempt to realise its (positive) possibilities in the world, it will open itself even more to capture by the malevolent forces to which it is subject. Admittedly, this is a difficult position in which to be, for the university is always becoming in this way. Its tasks of becoming itself can never be completed.

Conclusions

The prospect of the university becoming itself more fully is on the cusp. It has unrealised possibilities in front of it, but it also has malevolent forces swirling around it. In teasing out this story, I distinguished as two connected trunks the idea of the university and the idea of higher education, understood either as a major educational system and as a set of educational processes. Strong branches were identified about the corporate agency of the university as an institution, about the very idea of academic development, about the kind of human formation that is appropriate to a 'higher' education, about the ideas of research and of scholarship and about the concepts of learning and of teaching. Smaller but still important branches can be seen in the concepts of academic freedom, leadership and critical thinking. In the roots of this tree lie fundamental concerns with knowledge, truth, social justice, values, reason and – not least in a digital age – time and space.

The metaphor of the tree is potent, but – like all metaphors – it is limited, and one limitation is that the metaphor is too static. Yes, it allows for growth and even for the branches to grow at different rates. It allows too for those branches to sway in the wind and for the trunks to be assailed from within and corrupted by a canker. However, a tree typically remains in a singular place, retaining its form over time. To do justice to the practical and institutional field of higher education, we also need mobile and liquid metaphors and metaphors that encompass greater space. Both the university – whether a single university, a national system or the worldwide set of universities – and the learning processes of higher education are in constant motion. This is a motion that ebbs and flows in and across the world. The digital age, geographical movements of students and staff, intersections of ministers of higher education and institutional leaders, the morass of national and international institutions concerned with knowledge policies and so on, all bear upon every university – and sometimes cataclysmically. Higher education can never be quiescent.

But yet wider turbulences disturb the university. It hears pleas that it should widen its view and direct itself to matters of ecology, social justice, well-being (of persons and the Earth itself) and the public good. Such pleas would pull the university into new and even difficult spaces. The university, therefore, is always in a state of becoming, and in this becoming, the university runs risks, both risks of imposition and risks of omission. Rightly, it will never satisfy the claims coming its way or, indeed, the responsibilities that it discerns for itself. It is always on the verge of flowering but never quite managing it. This will be disappointing to many, but it is the best that may realistically be hoped for.

References

Barnett, R. (2013). *Imagining the university*. London/New York: Routledge.
Bhaskar, R with Hartwig, M. (2010). *The formation of critical realism: A personal perspective*. London/New York: Routledge.
Boutang, Y. M. (2011). *Cognitive Capitalism*. Cambridge/Malden, MA: Polity.
Clark, B. R. (1983). *The higher education system: Academic Organization in Cross-National Perspective*. Berkeley, CA/London: University of California.
de Sousa Santos, B. (2016). *Epistemologies of the south: Justice against Epistemicide*. London/New York: Routledge.
DeLanda, M. (2013). *A new philosophy of society: Assemblage theory and social complexity*. London/New York: Bloomsbury.
Deleuze, G., & Guattari, F. (2007/1980). *A thousand plateaus: Capitalism and schizophrenia*. London and New York: Continuum.
Derrida, J. (2001). The future of the profession or the university without condition (thanks to the "humanities", what *could take place* tomorrow). In T. Cohen (Ed.), *Jacques Derrida and the humanities: A critical reader*. Cambridge: Cambridge University.
Foucault, M. (1980). *Power/knowledge: Selected interview and other writings 1972–1977*. New York/London: Harvester Wheatsheaf.
Fricker, M. (2010). *Epistemic injustice: Power & the ethics of knowing*. Oxford/New York: Oxford University.
Gellner, E. (1969). *Thought and change*. London: Weidenfeld and Nicolson.
Guattari, F. (2016). *Lines of flight: For another world of possibilities*. London/New York: Bloomsbury.
Harman, G. (2018). *Object-oriented ontology: A new theory of everything*. London: Pelican.
Kant, I. (1992). *The conflict of the faculties*. Lincoln/London: University of Nebraska.
Kerr, C. (1995). *The uses of the university*. Cambridge, MA/London: Harvard University.
List, C., & Pettit, P. (2011). *Group agency: The possibility, design, and status of corporate agents*. Oxford: Oxford University.
MacIntyre, A. (2011). *God, philosophy, universities: A selective history of the Catholic philosophical tradition*. Lanham, MA/Plymouth, UK: Rowman and Littlefield.
Maxwell, N. (2014). *How universities can help create a wiser world: The urgent need for an academic revolution*. Exeter: Imprint Academic.
Meyer, J. F. H., & Land, R. (2005). Threshold concepts and troublesome knowledge: Epistemological considerations and a conceptual framework for teaching and learning. *Higher Education, 49*, 373–388.

Nail, T. (2019). *Being and motion*. New York: Oxford University.
Peters, M. A. (2013). *Education, science and knowledge capitalism: Creativity and the promise of openness*. New York: Peter Lang.
Plumb, J. H. (Ed.). (1964). *Crisis in the humanities*. London: Pelican.
Stiegler, B. (2015). *States of shock: Stupidity and knowledge in the 21st century*. Cambridge/Malden, MA: Polity.

Ronald Barnett is an emeritus professor of Higher Education at University College London Institute of Education, where he was a dean and a pro-director. He is the past chair of the Society for Research into Higher Education (SRHE), was awarded the inaugural prize by the European Association for Educational Research for his 'outstanding contribution to Higher EducationResearch, Policy and Practice' and has been elected as the inaugural president of the Philosophy and Theory of Higher Education Society. He is a fellow of the Academy of SocialSciences, the SRHE and the Higher Education Academy, has published 35 books (several of which have been prize-winners), has written over 150 papers, has given 150 keynote talks across the world and is a consultant in the university sector. He has been cited in the literature over 20,000 times and can fairly be regarded to have established the philosophy of higher education as a serious field of study. For nearly 40 years, he has been advancing ideas and creating concepts and practical principles to transform universities and academic life for the twenty-first century. He has been described as 'the master scholar of the university'.

Chapter 3
Higher Education and the Politics of Need

Benjamin Baez

The Thesis: A Structure of Feeling

How might we think this present of the COVID19 pandemic and of what we might conclude will happen in/to higher education? The pandemic is of a somewhat universally shared present, of course, but like all presents, this one is not in any way settled, and what we can know now about what will happen in higher education after it, or even during it, cannot in any definitive sense be said to be certain. Yet, we *feel* certain something is happening now or will happen after. Does accepting the reality of uncertainty of any ongoing present foreclose positing hypotheses?

In *Marxism and Literature*, Raymond Williams noted how quick we are in our analyses of society to reduce what is currently happening to fixed and completed forms, essentially relegating the present to the past, and because of this, the past takes precedence over and against what is the active, ongoing, living present.[1] We must try to understand whatever present we're experiencing, of course, but to avoid the pitfalls of creating fixed forms for what is currently under formation, Williams suggests the need for cultural hypotheses that account for changes in "structures of feeling," or the changes in meanings and values as actually lived and felt. What we should look for are "characteristic elements of impulse, restraint, and tone; specifically affective elements of consciousness and relationships; not feeling against

---

[1] Raymond Williams, *Marxism and Literature* (Oxford, UK: Oxford University Press, 1977): 128–135, 128.

B. Baez (✉)
Department of Educational Policy Studies, Florida International University, Miami, FL, USA
e-mail: baezb@fiu.edu

thought, but thought as felt and feeling as thought."[2] All such cultural hypotheses, it must be stressed, must always come back to the living present for confirmation.

It is with such a view in mind that I say that there seems in societies (at least Western ones), as the start of possible emerging social formations, and even before COVID19, some changes in structures of feeling, or evidence of continuing expressions of concern, fear, and perhaps even antagonism, about the vast amounts of resources, economic and political, going to higher education, while economic inequities and new fascisms continue to rise worldwide. It is hard to say that these expressions reflect a new social consciousness or configuration of power, but they seem to reflect changes in feelings about higher education, which generally was accepted as important for addressing social inequality or political instability. In this paper, therefore, I will posit this cultural hypothesis: The incompatible arguments over expenditures in higher education are less important for themselves than for what they suggest are possible destabilizations of older dominant formations and dogmas associated with political economy, such as neoliberalism. Because the arguments about expenditures might point to emerging social relations, we might take this opportunity to propose new understandings of higher education. Thus, I propose in this paper that we should avoid thinking of higher education in terms of needs, and instead see it in terms of excess wealth, which can only be spent needlessly.

This cultural hypothesis about excess wealth is greatly informed by the work of Georges Bataille, who offers in *The Accursed Share* a perspective on political economy that requires us to repose questions about higher education.[3] Bataille proposes audaciously that political problems result from luxury, not necessity. In other words, political problems are ones of consumption, or, that is, they arise from the way societies spend their wealth. Given this understanding, I will make four major arguments, each making up a section of the paper. First, attending to the problems of the economy should raise questions about the expenditure of excess wealth, not utility. Second, competing claims about higher education appear to, but do not actually, deal with utility. Third, higher education should not be understood as a need, but as a luxury that must be spent uselessly; instead of diminishing it value, this understanding should allow us more freedom with which to think about educational problems. Last, in proposing an understanding of higher education as "useless," I hope to offer the possibility of a view of a sovereignty from utility, a freedom that sees the pervasiveness of, but also fragilities within, capitalism.

Excess and Utility: A General Economy

Let me say here a bit more about excess and utility. Bataille provides a perspective on political economy that offers solutions to political problems in accordance with conventional principles of social science, but he also proposes audaciously that the

---

[2] Ibid., 132.
[3] Georges Bataille, *The Accursed Share: An Essay on General Economy, Volume I*, trans. Robert Hurley (New York: Zone Books, 1988).

problem of political economy can be posed like this: The "sexual act is in time what the tiger is in space."[4] For Bataille, there is no growth but a luxurious squandering of energy (physical or political) in every form. The tiger represents the immense power of consumption of life. In the general effervescence of life, the tiger is a point of extreme incandescence, as is the sexual act, which is the occasion for a sudden and frantic squandering of energy resources, carried in a moment to the limit of possibility (i.e., it is in time what the tiger is in space). Thus, for Bataille, thinking about political economy "should run counter to ordinary calculations," and, thus, "it is not necessity but its contrary, 'luxury,' that presents living matter and mankind with their fundamental problems."[5] The problems of political economy, in other words, are actually ones of consumption of wealth.

In using the term "consumption," Bataille was not accepting traditional economic theories of utility and production. Conventional economics (especially neoclassical economics, which predominates globally) defines consumption as relating to needs (or wants) and thus in terms of production and utility.[6] Indeed, conventional economics sees all social phenomena in terms of utility. It ostensibly analyzes rational choice of scarce means or resources in relation to alternative uses (i.e., needs and wants).[7] Commodities satisfy human wants and are thus sources of wealth, Karl Marx told us, and their utility is determined by both their use value (to the laborer) or exchange value (to the capitalist).[8] Commodities are understood to be determined by their utility (necessity or pleasure), and thus the problem of modern economics has become understanding how consumers gain the maximum utility of commodities, given incomes and prices.[9] To the extent that the satisfaction of needs and the requisite income needed to attain satisfaction are in equilibrium, we have economic stability. Given this understanding, John Maynard Keynes could then say that it is natural for human beings to "increase their consumption as their income increases, but not by as much as the increase in their income."[10] Thus, we are now presented with the problem of accumulation. Human nature for conventional economics dictates that human beings will consume what they need to subsist and save the surplus for a variety of needs and wants.

---

[4] Ibid., 12 (emphasis in original).

[5] Ibid. (emphasis in original).

[6] See generally, Louis Althusser and Étienne Balibar, *Reading Capital*, trans. Ben Brewster (London: Verso, 2006, c. 1968), 165.

[7] See Milan Zafirovski, "Classical and Neoclassical Conceptions of Rationality: Findings of an Exploratory Study," *The Journal of Socio-Economics*, Vol. 37, no. 2 (2008): 789–820, 790.

[8] Karl Marx, *Capital, Volume 1: A Critical Analysis of Capitalist Production*, ed. Frederick Engels, trans. Samuel Moore and Edward Aveling (New York: International Publishers, 1967, c. 1861), 35–6.

[9] See E. K. Hunt and Howard J. Sherman, *Economics: And Introduction to Traditional and Radical Views, 4th ed.* (New York: Harper & Row, 1981), 102–3.

[10] John Maynard Keynes, *The General Theory of Employment, Interest, and Money* (New York: Prometheus Books, 1997, c. 1936), 96–7.

The logic of such economic thinking is one of a restricted economy. Bataille distinguishes a restricted from a general economy. A restricted economy is what we conventionally understand as *the* economy, one with isolatable operations (e.g., the production of automobiles or individual preferences). Concerns in a restricted economy include, among other things, welfare, goods (or the public good?), happiness, productivity, profitability, prices, and markets.[11] Bataille refers to the logic of such an economy as "classical utility," which is concerned with acquisition (production) and conservation (savings).[12] Under a general economy, however, phenomena cannot be easily isolatable; a general economy accounts for all economic and political energy on the surface of the earth.[13] For Bataille, human activity is not entirely reducible to production and conservation; there is also unproductive expenditures having no ends in themselves.[14] Attending to a general economy exposes, for example, the existence of tragedy, evil, abandon, sacrifice, destruction of wealth, unproductive expenditure, profitless exchange, the ritualistic, the sacred, perverse sexualities, and symbolic activities.[15]

Bataille, therefore, radically redefined consumption as the expenditure of wealth (seen from the view of a general economy), an expenditure that is non-recuperable, one that can only be wasted. All surplus energy, political and otherwise, must be wasted. Bataille views political economy as part of the total movement of energy on the earth. On the surface of the globe, energy is always in excess. Once the earth uses up the energy it needs for subsistence, it must expel the excess, and it often does so explosively. Similarly, beyond our immediate ends, our activity pursues the useless and infinite fulfillment of the universe. But surplus energy must be spent, and this expenditure constitutes the true measure of political existence, that is, societies are defined by how they spend wealth. Do they conserve at the expense of suffering? Do they privilege abstract future generations at the expense of historically present ones? Yet, it is production and accumulation that is privileged in capitalist societies; consumption has no meaning if it does not produce anything. Today, precedence is given to energy acquisition over energy expenditure; "glory is given to the sphere of utility."[16]

For Bataille, the fact of useless expenditure of wealth remains hidden to us because of the pervasiveness of the logic of utility promoted by capitalist practices. For example, within capitalist economy, the construction of a church is a needless consumption of labor (i.e., it is wasteful), as it has no utility that can be

---

[11] See Grahame F. Thompson, "Where Goes Economics and Economies?" *Economy and Society*, Vol. 26, no. 4 (1997): 599–610, 606.

[12] Georges Bataille, *Visions of Excess: Selected Writings, 1927–1939*, ed. and trans. Allan Stoekl (Minneapolis: University of Minnesota Press, 1985), 116.

[13] Bataille, *The Accursed Share, Vol. I*, 20.

[14] Bataille, *Visions of Excess*, 118.

[15] Thompson, "Where Goes Economics," 606.

[16] Bataille, *The Accursed Share, Vol. I*, 29.

commodified (it addresses itself strictly to intimate feeling).[17] Similarly, I would say, the humanities, or even any science, physical or social, that is not premised on promoting economic growth, might thus also be deemed wasteful under capitalistic logic. Yet these kinds of consumption might entail what Bataille calls a "destruction of utility," because they cannot be understood under its terms.[18]

While aspects of higher education are commodities that have utility for labor markets (e.g., business degrees, intellectual property), other parts clearly do not (e.g., friendships, protests, vandalism, academic freedom, most dissertations, alcoholic binge drinking, sexual liaisons between students, etc.). These other parts of higher education thus are not utilitarian in a direct sense; they may actually "destroy utility" to the extent that they are not easily reducible to its terms but direct themselves to intimate feeling, thought, or the useless expenditure of surplus energy. Yet, our reification of political constructions, reinforced by a discourse of utility that maintains them, prevent us from seeing that all but the satisfaction of physical needs results from the compulsion to expend excess wealth.

It is the discourse of utility, defining all phenomena in terms of a restricted economy, that masks the fact that surplus wealth must be spent needlessly. It thus generates anxiety, but only in terms of itself. It is certainly the case that for particular individuals, institutions, or nation-states, problems of satisfying needs arise, and the search for solutions brings about anxiety. In terms of a general economy—as opposed to the restricted one of, say, an individual, institution, or nation-state—when anxiety is allowed to pose problems, what is masked is the fact that it is the expenditure of wealth that generates most political problems. Any aspect of higher education, for example, can only present itself as a problem after our basic requirements of subsistence are met. Higher education as such, as a need, is without question a higher-order need, following Abraham Maslow's logic, which we can only perceive and reflect on after our basic needs of survival have been satisfied.[19] Higher education problems, therefore, can only arise from surplus. But, again, this possibility will be obscured by the pervasive anxiety generated by the discourse of utility.

Bataille states that the crucial analysis of political economy requires circumscription of the opposition of two political methods:

> [That] of fear and the anxious search for a solution, combining the pursuit of freedom with imperatives that are most opposed to freedom; and that of freedom of mind, which issues from the global resources of life, a freedom for which, instantly, everything is resolved, *everything* is rich—in other words, everything that is commensurate with the universe. I insist on the fact that, to freedom of mind, the search for a solution is an exuberance, a superfluity; this gives it an incomparable force. To solve political problems becomes diffi-

---

[17] Ibid., 132. Though, Bataille may be working with a contradiction here, since he stated earlier that Protestantism, especially its Calvinist strain, supported capitalist interests by promoting doctrines about hard work and individual initiative (see pp. 122–27). So, the construction of churches promoting such doctrines may indeed be deemed productive consumption under capitalist logic, if we are to recognize the need of any capitalist interest to reproduce itself.

[18] Ibid., 132.

[19] Abraham H. Maslow, "A Theory of Human Motivation," *Psychology Review*, Vol. 50, no. 4 (1943): 370–96.

cult for those who allow anxiety alone to pose them. It is necessary for anxiety to pose them. But their solution demands at a certain point the removal of this anxiety.[20]

There has been much anxiety over the financing of higher education, when seen from the viewpoint of particular individuals, institutions of higher education, or nation states, that is, when viewed from the perspective of a restrictive economy. It seems that public funding for higher education worldwide has decreased in proportion, if not in real dollars, and government officials increasingly tie such funding to job-related and other commercial activities. Colleges and universities have sought private sources of funding to replace lost revenues, and they have also attempted to shift the costs of education to the student and their families by increasing tuition and fees. At the same time that costs are being shifted to the student, national governments are demanding that institutions of higher education produce highly educated and skilled workforces in order to ensure future economic growth. All this generates anxiety only because we are taught to view higher education under a logic of utility.

The entire point of this paper, however, is to encourage us to reconsider arguments about the utility of higher education and to refrain from viewing it in terms of a restricted economy. We should avoid getting trapped in arguments about whether any claim about higher education is correct and instead direct our attention to the mechanisms of power that inundate us with such claims and that reinforce themselves by requiring their deployment in the first place. This is why I will refrain in this paper from engaging critically with other works claiming any purpose for higher education.[21] A discourse of utility ultimately requires one to think of and thus justify higher education as furthering particular needs at the expense of a freedom of mind to think outside conventional logic. My hope is to encourage readers to think about higher education, not just in terms of its necessity in a restricted economy but also as something that is, no matter the purpose conjured up for it, a luxury in a general economy.

---

[20] Ibid., 13–14, emphasis in original.

[21] I cite here just a small sample of such (more or less) competing philosophies of higher education, ones that collectively form a genre with a long history. See Ronald Barnett, *The Ecological University: A Feasible Utopia* (London: Routledge, 2017); Robert Maynard Hutchins, *The Higher Learning in America* (London: Routledge, 1995, c. 1936); Immanuel Kant, *The Conflict of the Faculties*, trans. Mary J. Gregor (Lincoln: University of Nebraska Press, 1979, c. 1798); Simon Marginson and Mark Considine, *The Enterprise University: Power, Governance, and Reinvention in Australia* (Cambridge, UK: Cambridge University Press, 2000); John Henry Newman, *The Idea of the University* (Notre Dame: University of Notre Dame Press, 1982, c. 1852); Ronald Nisbit, *The Degradation of the Academic Dogma: The University in America 1945–1970* (New York: Basic Books, 1971); Thorstein Veblen, *The Higher Learning in America* (New Brunswick: Transaction Publishers, 1993, c. 1918); Jennifer Washburn, *University, Inc.: The Corporate Corruption of Higher Education* (New York: Basic Books, 2005).

No Future: The "Need" for Higher Education

Higher education is conventionally understood as necessary for achieving some political goal. For example, according to a 2017 report sponsored by the World Bank, higher education for all nations is "instrumental in fostering growth, reducing poverty and boosting shared prosperity. A highly-skilled workforce, with a solid post-secondary education, is a prerequisite for innovation and growth: well-educated people are more employable, earn higher wages, and cope with economic shocks better."[22] This logic is one premised on an instrumentalist notion of utility (but, actually, is there another kind?) and is pervasive worldwide, though not unquestioned by those believing that higher education serves other purposes, such as enlightening minds, or ensuring democratic citizenship, or promoting social capital for elites, or socializing students into conventional notions of familyhood, or other progressive or conservative claims. But it seems probable to me that the economic depression experts say is resulting from the current pandemic will likely not expose to policymakers the need to question the logic of spending resources on higher education—economic, political, psychic—but will reinforce the presuppositions of World Bank's report: more resources for higher education.

Interestingly, after the pandemic is deemed to be over by our world's leaders, there will also likely be calls for cutbacks to higher education. Indeed, some universities in the United States are already instituting furloughs and other cutbacks.[23] The economic depression experts attribute to the pandemic will lead to a redeployment of claims about the value of higher education, which of its functions should become priorities and subject to more investment, and, where deemed wasteful, which of its functions should be eliminated or curtailed.[24] These concerns over the financing of higher education, like that of the World Bank's report, require colleges and universities to prove their value to governments in economic ways. That is, they are required to demonstrate using quantitative measures how much revenues for the economy they generate through their graduates, public service, and research (i.e., their "return on investment"). Critics seem concerned public higher education will further succumb to markets and be driven by the pecuniary interests of corporations and paying

---

[22] See World Bank, *Higher Education* (October 5, 2017), https://www.worldbank.org/en/topic/tertiaryeducation (Retrieved April 26, 2020).

[23] KGUN 9 On Your Side, "UArizona Announces Pay Cuts, Furloughs for all Faculty, Staff," April 17, 2020, https://www.kgun9.com/news/coronavirus/uarizona-announces-pay-cuts-furloughs-for-all-faculty-staff (Retrieved April 26, 2020). It is important to note here that the University of Arizona has an endowment worth over $1 Billion (US).

[24] For just a couple, though perhaps contradictory examples, of waste arguments, see Bryan Caplan, *The Case Against Education: Why the Education System Is a Waste of Time and Money* (New Jersey: Princeton University Press, 2018); Mark R. Reiff, "How to Pay for Public Education," *Theory and Research in Education*, Vol. 12, No. 1 (2014): 4–52.

"consumers" rather than the supposedly more altruistic interests of a general public.[25]

There will be debates about all this. These debates, however, will all be subtended by a discourse of utility, which requires such debates in order to reinforce its axiomatic logic. There will likely also be contestations of such logic in the form of nonutilitarian arguments or even varying levels of social unrest, contestations that suggest that the general acceptance of utilitarian logic is destabilizing. For the actual evidence does not support claims that education alleviates social inequity and political unrest. Social inequality and political unrest are rising worldwide even though there has been great investment in, say, higher education, which ostensibly alleviates such inequality and unrest by increasing national prosperity and thus individuals' incomes.[26]

The veracity of arguments about higher education and equality and political stability is thus very much in question. And yet these arguments persist. Veracity, therefore, cannot be the framework by which we can engage such arguments. Is our inability to see this contradiction between the arguments about the value of higher education and the social realities they purport to address the result of an ideology justifying the interests of the well-resourced classes? Ideology as a cause, however, seems to me yet too formed a conclusion, in the sense Raymond Williams warned about. We must think in terms of structures of feelings, but what exactly can we say about this contradiction? How might we reread these arguments about higher education? What do we *feel* is happening?

Capitalism and neoliberalism will insist on utility, of course. Yet, as I indicated before, there seems an increasing lack of consensus in these debates about the value of higher education. But we should avoid dealing with them on their own terms. These debates, when viewed with less anxiety, actually direct us to something beyond themselves. What structures of feeling might be reflected in these debates about the value of higher education? Are new social forms emerging, ones suggesting neoliberalism's dominance might be waning? What I can say with more certainty is that any unsettledness here means that we need not be tied to utility, that we can think beyond it. Thus, I have been suggesting in this paper one possible way out of utility: Let us think of higher education as, in the end, useless and even wasteful.

The economistic language that conventionally structures the current debates (and likely any future ones) about the value of higher education will be difficult to avoid, decipher, or even recognize, but it is important to consider this: We should see this language as commanding us to see education only as intelligible in terms of utility and necessity, thus restricting our ability to see it as otherwise. How might we refuse

---

[25] See generally, Sheila Slaughter and Gary Rhoades, *Academic Capitalism and the New Economy: Markets, State, and Higher Education* (Baltimore: The Johns Hopkins University Press, 2004).

[26] This logic is likely supported by the (previously?) universally accepted platitude that education produces human capital. See Gary Becker, *Human Capital: A Theoretical and Empirical Analysis with Special Reference to Education, third ed.* (Chicago: The University of Chicago Press, 1993), xxi. For an opposing argument, see John Marsh, *Class Dismissed: Why We Cannot Teach or Learn Out of Inequality* (New York: Monthly Review Press, 2011).

such a command and argue *in favor of* unnecessariness or wastefulness? In what ways might we experience less anxiety, and more freedom of mind, by seeing higher education as needless and wasteful? What aspects of higher education might we recognize, and what possibilities might emerge, if we think of higher education as only surplus energy, as an exuberance, or as an *excess* that can only be wasted? To think of higher education as a necessity is only to succumb to an anxiety generated by a discourse of utility that ultimately constrains thought and justifies social inequality. The concern with utility only makes us subservient to the imperatives of capitalist production, which may be unavoidable in the extended present in which we have trapped ourselves but no longer need to accept blindly.

The discourse of utility structures higher education, as it does all else that it captures, in terms of necessity, but it masks the fact that from the viewpoint of the overall wealth in the world higher education is an exuberance, an understanding that should allow us more freedom with which to think about problems in higher education. Releasing ourselves from a discourse of utility allows us a freedom of mind, as Bataille calls it, an exuberance that is most free from the anxiety over political problems. To be always anxious about problems obscures seeing all of higher education as really only possible because of excess wealth, which actually generates its major problems.

Thinking this way, for example, might allow us to see that in the state I live in, Florida, the very fact of surplus wealth is what permits the creativity necessary to establish and manipulate its performance-funding model that governs the 11 universities in the State University System.[27] When the state has less money, it tends toward uncreative and tired austerity policies, often times cutting off a percentage of each university's budget to make ends meet;[28] when it does have money, it tends toward playing funding games, pitting universities against each other for extra funds. Institutions of higher education similarly behave when they have surplus funds. For example, very few universities generate revenues from commercially

---

[27] Briefly, the Florida performance-funding model works by requiring the Board of Governors to withhold a proportion of each institution's budget that cumulatively equals the amount of new money allocated by the legislature for this purpose, thus creating an overall pot of performance funding. Currently, the universities are given up to 10 points for performance on each of 10 metrics (e.g., graduating students in 4 years, percentage of students with high entrance-exam scores, employment rates of graduates, etc.). The points are awarded either for meeting certain standards of "excellence" for each metric or for significantly improving performance from the previous year on each metric. The universities are then ranked, and those having at least 55 points get back their share of performance funding, and those in the top of the rankings receive extra funds. See Florida Board of Governors, *Board of Governors Performance Funding Model Overview*, November 2019, https://www.flbog.edu/wp-content/uploads/Overview-Doc-Performance-Funding-10-Metric-Model-Condensed-Version-1.pdf (Retrieved September 1, 2020).

[28] For example, Florida's Governor, Ron DeSantis, has recently informed the state's universities to withhold spending (the same proportion across the board) because of budget shortfalls resulting from the pandemic. See Orlando Sentinel, "DeSantis' Plans to Rework State's $93.2B Budget Could Violate Constitution," June 17, 2020, https://www.orlandosentinel.com/politics/os-ne-coronavirus-florida-budget-desantis-20200617-uzmnositmjhbnlt3slmt2f5d7q-story.html (Retrieved September 1, 2020).

sponsored research, despite large investments in it.[29] Few universities and few faculty members incur any penalties when their "ventures" fail to yield profits or even when they cost their universities large amounts of money.[30] Much of these expenditures are thus wasted (in terms of the purported goals of generating new revenues), though "waste" is rarely a term that gets used for such kinds of expenditures.

Indeed, a freedom of mind would recognize that such "waste" ultimately may be the point of institutional spending in the first place, at least in the United States. F. King Alexander's findings of almost 20 years ago still ring true to those who are critically minded. He explains that since the 1980s, a new set of market incentives and dynamics accelerated the pressure on universities to acquire greater wealth in order to generate more fiscal capacity.[31] In this environment, the primary objective of many universities is "prestige maximization," in which academic and financial standards are defined by their relative status and ranking with other institutions. The goal is to outspend other institutions, especially for top faculty. This inflates educational expenditures to the highest common denominator, thus creating what Alexander calls an "expenditure cold war" among institutions of higher education, now judged not by any intrinsic worth of any particular goal but only in relation to other institutions.[32] In the United States, prestige maximization means spending money to recruit "high-achieving" students, hire and maintain highly productive research faculty, seek external funding for research, develop fund-raising capacities, pay the salaries of the coaches of lucrative college sports, mine faculty and students for intellectual property, develop fields of study deemed prestigious, and so on. On the issue of prestigious fields of study, for example, a former president of my university, Modesto Maidique, in trying to get faculty support for the creation of an expensive medical school said to my college's assembly in 2006 that for our university not to have a medical school is "like going to a formal party in shorts." Conversely, in October 2011, the Herald-Tribune out of Sarasota, Florida, reported that then Florida Governor Rick Scott said that he wanted to shift money away from some degree programs at the state's universities to increase support for science and technology fields. He is quoted in the paper as saying, "If I'm going to take money from a citizen to put into education then I'm going to take that money to create jobs. So I want that money to go to degrees where people can get jobs in this state. Is it a vital interest of the state to have more anthropologists? I don't think so."[33] Scott's

---

[29] See Eyal Press and Jennifer Washburn, "The Kept University," *Atlantic Monthly* (March 2000): 39–54. Despite being 20 years old, this is still one of the best exposés of this kind of waste.

[30] Gary Rhoades and Sheila Slaughter, "Academic Capitalism, Managed Professionals, and Supply-Side Higher Education," *Social Text*, 15, no. 2 (1997): 9–38, 15.

[31] Alexander does not say, but of the market incentives and dynamics he speaks of we can point to policies associated with the new public management movements that gained authority in the political regimes of Margaret Thatcher in the UK and Ronald Reagan in the United States.

[32] See F. King Alexander, "The Silent Crisis: The Relative Fiscal Capacity of Public Universities to Compete for Faculty," *The Review of Higher Education*, 24, no. 2 (2001): 112–129, 117–18.

[33] Zac Anderson, "Rick Scott Wants to Shift University Funding Away From Some Degrees," *Herald-Tribune* (October 10, 2011). http://politics.heraldtribune.com/2011/10/10/rick-scott-wants-to-shift-university-funding-away-from-some-majors/ (Retrieved April 29, 2018).

beliefs led to the performance-funding model in my state, which has exponentially increased spending by the universities to ensure better performance as defined by the model.

Institutions of higher education in the United States (and likely all over the world) must spend revenues in the hopes of generating *more* revenues than they need for subsistence or even to meet the needs of, say, a particular activity such as teaching. The goal is to outspend others. Prestige maximization is nothing more than competition, which can only be done by spending more money, that is, money that many administrators of these institutions say do not have when economic downturns present the possibility of budget cuts. The most prestigious universities compete very well in this "expenditure cold war," but many other institutions cannot compete effectively—unless, of course, they shift budget priorities in order to accumulate more wealth, which, paradoxically, they then must turn around and spend to be seen as prestigious. To ascend the ladder of prestige and status in any national educational context, institutions of higher education must acquire and expend vast amounts of resources, much of which will be wasted, that is, yield no useful return as defined by conventional economics.[34] There can never be enough accumulation because there can never be enough spending.

I say all this only to expose surplus and excess in higher education, as actual institutional survival (as opposed to the survival of the images to which administrators aspire) does not depend on that kind of spending. Such spending is wasteful, when understood in terms of generating profits, but not so under the axiomatic logic of utility, which is concerned not necessarily with yielding returns on investments but on spending for the sake of acquisition. So, it is logical to spend for the purposes of accumulation, even if there actually is little that is accumulated. The goal of acquisition is what makes such wasteful actions rational.

Yet, all this is masked by a discourse of need, one which wrests time, defining the future in terms of the present. If Raymond Williams' point that in our social analyses we are compelled to relegate the present to the past can be read as constituting an erasure of the present, we can read the focus on the future in debates about higher education as a foreclosure of the present. There is a rarely questioned belief, which is much more than a simple platitude, that higher education represents an investment in an individual's or a nation's future.[35] This belief in such a future suggests that the solution to the problem of investing in higher education requires us to *accumulate* and *save*, not spend wastefully, that is, for purposes other than accumulation. All the while students are paying more and more for higher education with little

---

[34] Shelia Slaughter and Gary Rhoades have pointed out better than anyone else, in my opinion, the vast amount of wasted resources institutions spend on technology transfer and academic capitalism; see *Academic Capitalism and the New Economy*.

[35] See, for example, Michelle Asha Cooper, "Investing in Education and Equity: Our Nation's Best Future," *Diversity & Democracy*, Vol. 13, no. 3 (Fall 2010), https://www.aacu.org/publications-research/periodicals/investing-education-and-equity-our-nations-best-future-0 (Retrieved April 26, 2020).

guarantees of employment, and some are denied entry altogether, thus relegating them to a life of economic inequality (if we are to believe the conventional logic of the value of higher education).

This future-oriented view thus assumes a higher education that can only be *necessary* as defined by the discourse of utility, which assumes—inappropriately, as we will see—that the entire point of human existence is to accumulate resources rather than to spend them (even when, paradoxically, one is spending more than one has in order to accumulate). The future-oriented spending on higher education for the sake of accumulation does have a destructive effect in the present, rising global poverty, being just one of them. It may be, then, that perhaps Lee Edelman is correct, that "political self-destruction inheres in the only act that counts as one: the act of resisting enslavement to the future in the name of having a life."[36] Perhaps. What I can say more confidently is that we must see the future as a discursive effect of capitalism. Freedom from the discourse of utility entails rejecting the idea of the future, and to situate the practices justified in its name as squarely and oppressively in the living present.

The Politics of Needs: A Wasteful Higher Education

In order to understand what I mean by "rejecting the future," one must see political economy, as Bataille explains, not in terms of production, as conventional economics would have it, but in terms of consumption (i.e., the expenditure of wealth). From the viewpoint of general economy, Bataille argues, we can only spend wealth, only squander our profits. If part of wealth is to be wasted anyway, it is possible, even logical, Bataille suggests, to surrender commodities without return.[37] But everything in capitalist societies works to hide this fact: That the point of wealth is to give it away. At some point, the acquisition of wealth leads to surplus, and we will reach a point where what matters is not to produce and accumulate but to spend. There can be anguish about this only from the viewpoint of the particular, or from a restricted economy, one which is opposed to the general viewpoint based on the exuberance of life. The understanding and use of wealth, which is always in surplus, are the determining elements of a society. Wealth changes meanings according to the advantages expected from its possession. In a capitalist society the advantage that matters most is the possibility of investing. This society prefers an increase of wealth to its immediate use.[38]

Again, from the viewpoint of general economy, we can only spend wealth, only squander our profits. To allow us to see the inevitability of squandering wealth,

---

[36] Lee Edelman, *No Future: Queer Theory and the Death Drive* (Durham: Duke University Press, 2004), 30.

[37] Bataille, *The Accursed Share, Vol. I*, 25.

[38] Ibid., 118–19.

3 Higher Education and the Politics of Need

Bataille argues, the loss of wealth from nonproductive expenditure must be as great as possible for it to take on its true meaning.[39] Loss of energy, political and otherwise, is a fact of existence. We can either spend luxuriously (e.g., on the arts or any activity directed to intimate feeling) or violently (e.g., war), and this expenditure, or, rather, this choice, is what Bataille calls the "accursed share." Poverty, for example, has never had a strong enough moral hold to subordinate conservation to expenditure, that is, to require that the choice be made to spend profusely to alleviate poverty as opposed to conserving wealth (even when it can be proven that spending to fix poverty raises the standard of living for everyone, thus promoting economic stability). So, the poorer classes have been excluded from much of the wealth accumulated by those with financial resources and thus from the political processes that might change this. This means that the poor classes can have no other form of power than the revolutionary destruction of the classes.[40]

War and political violence—of the kind, for example, that the increasingly global Black Lives Matter movements protest against—are the dangers born of unfettered production of capital; they are the most violent expenditure of surplus wealth.[41] In capitalist societies, Bataille argues, energy is always at its boiling point. He argues, for example, that the immense wealth of the United States, its excessive production and unfettered accumulation, leads to war, unless that excess is redirected and spent otherwise. Given all the wars engaged in by the United States since World War II, and also given the vast amount of resources spent on, and the violence generated by, its countless faceless-enemy wars, such as that on terrorism, drugs, and crime (but no resources, ironically, on, say, eliminating gun violence), Bataille's arguments seem rather prophetic. The United States' commitment of excess wealth to military maneuvers, within its borders and abroad, will not lead to peace (or safety), as its political leaders argue, but will only make war, and political violence against its own citizens, inevitable. It will move toward peace only, Bataille argues, if it assigns a large share of its wealth to raising the global standard of living, to economic and political activity, to giving its surplus wealth an outlet other than war.[42]

Spending lavishly on higher education, without concern for utility, could provide such an outlet. Globally, however, higher education is characterized by a crisis/scarcity discourse reflecting anxiety over problems created after our political institutions, and their individuals, have satisfied the needs they require for subsistence. The need to expend energy (including money) in higher education to promote economic growth, democratic dispositions, and so forth arises from the fact of luxury; the problems these needs create are ones of surplus wealth.

The promotion of any nation's dominance in the "global marketplace" through education, a discourse particularly prevalent in the United States, is not actually

---

[39] Bataille, *Visions of Excess*, 118.

[40] Ibid., 120–1.

[41] The militarization of police forces provides an example of how much surplus wealth goes into ensuring political violence.

[42] Bataille, *The Accursed Share Vol. I*, 187.

something without which one would die; it is a discourse which masks the fact that it promotes capitalist interests and justifies their consequences. Expansion of higher education is a luxury for rapidly growing economies, or those that want to appear that way, which provide resources for it to ensure technological dominance in an increasingly, we are told repeatedly, competitive global information economy. The fallacy of this view of higher education is well accepted by critical theorists. But any purpose attributed to higher education, even by critical theorists, similarly masks what is at stake. The "need" to spend resources on higher education to "solve social problems," "promote economic growth," "teach critical thinking," "ensure democracy," or whatever, arises from the very fact of luxury; any problems it generates are ones resulting from the expenditure of surplus wealth.

Yet, the rhetoric of crisis, I fear, will predominant once the current pandemic is deemed to be over by health and political experts. Let me be clear here: The fear I have is not that we will be told a bunch of lies about economic suffering—indeed, as I have been arguing, we should not privilege a framework of truth/lies—but that the rhetoric of crisis will justify more acquisition and conservation of wealth for the already rich and austerity and cutbacks for everyone else. Higher education will be posited as necessary for future economic stability over and perhaps against other needs, such as public health and better wages. The rhetorical positioning of higher education as a need, however, will foreclose questions about exuberance. My argument here, I must stress, is intended neither as being against the funding of higher education to allow students to enter the workplace, nor that saving is illogical. Helping students matters, of course, and not all surplus should be spent; some surplus must be reserved for growth. But such goals can only be pragmatic and thus only lead to provisional solutions in a restricted economy. In the end, in a general economy, surplus must be spent, and we can do so only luxuriously or violently.

It is the discourse of need that frames our fundamental problems, and it generates anxiety over solutions because it privileges accumulation and conservation. So, as Nancy Fraser illustrates, political struggles over needs is always political struggle over the power to define the needs.[43] This discourse of need can serve both right and left politics, even though each kind of politics promotes policies and practices that have different effects on people's lives, and each furthers (or counters) the aims of capitalism in different ways. For example, some right-leaning political projects use the discourse of needs to promote austerity practices that entrench social stratification in societies and across societies, all in the name of accumulation and conservation; the left-leaning projects counter such right-leaning ones by advocating for more welfare policies and social justice. But each must be questioned for how it positions need and what such positioning allows and forecloses in the ways we feel about the expenditure of wealth.

When we succumb to the logic of utility, to repeat this important point, we fail to see the fact that higher education is only really an expenditure of surplus wealth and, as all surplus, must be spent wastefully. It is, Bataille argues, only to the

---

[43] Nancy Fraser, "Talking About Needs," *Ethics*, 99 (1989): 291–313, 292–6.

particular living being that the problem of necessity presents itself. Thought about in this way, higher education, when seen from the viewpoint of particular living beings—for example, those who attend college, those who fund higher education—appears necessary, and the thinking about expenditures seems always at a crisis point.

Seen from the viewpoint of general economy, however, education (higher or otherwise) can only be the result of luxury and too much wealth, one that ultimately must be squandered and for no purpose. Our only recourse is to attempt to prevent that squandering from becoming violent. In other words, the energy we spend on education must be lost without purpose, and this inevitability prevents educational expenditures, in the end, from being "useful." But this loss should not be understood in terms of utility; it should be understood only as more or less *acceptable*. That is, loss is inevitable; we can only deem it a matter of "acceptable loss," preferable to another that we regard as unacceptable. The real problem for us with regard to educational expenditures, then, is one of acceptability, not utility.[44]

The only solution to educational problems, Bataille would propose, I think, is to spend lavishly and wastefully on education in order to bring down political pressure to below the boiling point. This is not an argument for the wasteful spending related to, say, prestige maximization, since that spending is paradoxically at its root *useful*, that is, for the purposes of acquiring more wealth. And arguments by scholars like Slaughter and Rhoades pointing to such waste are also embedded in a logic of utility, for these arguments also put forth a better use for those resources. The solution to the problems of higher education is not to spend so as to be useful but to spend luxuriously and without return.

The idea of useless expenditure, however, can only appear *impossible* to us. The discourse of utility prevents us from seeing an excess of resources over needs (i.e., real needs, such that society would perish without satisfying them). Utility, however, has become the historical, political, and economic basis for social reality, conditioning almost all knowledge and truth claims.[45] It is hard to think in terms of noneconomic logic, given the extent to which economics has colonized the social sciences.[46] We cannot see political problems as resulting from surplus wealth, Bataille argues, because this is masked by a misconception that *humanity* means working and living without enjoying the fruits of one's labor.[47] Conventional

---

[44] Bataille, *The Accursed Share Vol. I*, 31.

[45] See William Pawlett, "Utility and Excess: The Radical Sociology of Bataille and Baudrillard," *Economy and Society*, Vol, 26, no. 1 (1997): 92–125, 95.

[46] See Ben Fine, "A Question of Economics: Is It Colonizing the Social Sciences?" *Economy and Society*, Vol. 28, no. 3 (1999): 403–425, 404. See also Introduction to *The Philosophy of Economics: An Anthology, third ed.*, ed. Daniel Hausman (Cambridge, UK: Cambridge University Press, 2008), 2–3. For my argument about how higher education produces the very economists who "economize" the social world, see Benjamin Baez, "An Economy of Higher Education," in Joseph Devitis, ed., *Contemporary Colleges and Universities: A Reader* (New York: Peter Lang, 2013), pp. 307–321.

[47] According to Pawlett, even Marx presupposed such a theory. See Pawlett, "Utility and Excess," 93–4.

economics enforces the logic that the true measure of human productivity is to increase the economy of labor and that there can be no growth or progress without doing this.[48]

This much Marx saw in capitalism. He explained that labor entails for the one who labors two kinds of consumption: one required of the means of production, which the capitalist consumes (productive consumption), and one that occurs when laborers use wages to satisfy their needs (individual consumption). In the former, the laborers belong to the capitalist, but in the latter, they belong to themselves.[49] To the extent, however, that both kinds of consumption for Marx are related to production, as consumed labor by capitalists and as what labor allows one to consume via wages, capitalism reduces everything to a *thing*, a commodity; it requires in essence a surrendering to *things*.[50] As Bataille stated, the efficacious activity of the human being makes him or her a tool, which only produces; the human being becomes a *thing* like a tool, and so he or she becomes a product. The tool's meaning is giving by the future, by what the tool will produce, that is, by the future utilization of the product.[51] And acquisition is the point of it all.

The modern state for Bataille is a society of acquisition, not a society of consumption (i.e., the expenditure of wealth). Education writ large, therefore, represents acquisition—of knowledge, of skills, of wealth, of things, and of people even, as the World Bank report I quoted earlier suggests. And when education furthers utility like this, it teaches us that we need to acquire *things*, things to which we then surrender, and so useful education can only credential us as *things*. In a society of acquisition, education can only be *useful* if it leads to acquisition. Education is thus not an end in itself but only a means to acquisition. Its purpose, therefore, is to ensure servility to utility. In this world of servility, higher education must teach us that to be fully human we must be useful, that is, we must produce.

Bataille proposes, conversely, that *sovereignty* is the freedom from usefulness and necessity.[52] We have to make consumption, he argues, the sovereign principle of activity. Sovereignty, for Bataille, is not to be confused with political entities or individual supremacy. It is the principle of "life beyond utility;" it begins when "necessities ensured, the possibility of life opens up without limit."[53] The "sovereign moment" thus arrives when nothing matters but that moment, when we can enjoy present time with nothing else in view but present time.[54] We may not be able

---

[48] See Lyndon H. LaRouche, Jr., *So, You Wish to Learn All About Economics? A Text on Elementary Mathematical Economics* (New York: New Benjamin Franklin House, 1984), 23. See also, Louis O. Kelso and Mortimer J. Adler, *The New Capitalists: A Proposal to Free Economic Growth from the Slavery of Savings* (New York: Random House, 1961), 2–3.

[49] Marx, *Capital*, 571.

[50] Bataille, *The Accursed Share, Vol. I*, 57.

[51] Georges Bataille, *The Accursed Share: An Essay on General Economy, Volumes II & III*, trans. Robert Hurley (New York: Zone Books, 1991), 218.

[52] Ibid., 197.

[53] Ibid., 198.

[54] Ibid., 199.

3 Higher Education and the Politics of Need

to eliminate useful work, but we cannot be reduced to it without eliminating ourselves. The only happiness is spending luxuriously and selfishly. The reader may quip here that selfishness is what capitalism requires and that it is selfishness that had led to, say, environmental degradation. Yet, that kind of capitalist selfishness is driven by the unfettered accumulation of wealth, and it only proves the senseless destructive effects of too much wealth.

It is the most profitless, nonproductive expenditures about which I am referring, the ones about which we are the most passionate, and political stability may require that we channel resources toward these expenditures.[55] The anxiety generated by a concern for others—the nation, even our children—draws us into servitude, because it forces us to acquire things to save for the future, and thus it reduces us to *things*. We cannot attain sovereignty, Bataille suggests, if we plan for the future. We experience freedom only when we live for the sovereign moment. The discourse of utility prevents us from knowing this about ourselves: that giving in to freedom is to be placed under the sign of the sovereign moment. Thus, only those aspects of educational institutions which serve no useful purpose, which can come only from a sudden expenditure of energy, may move us toward sovereignty: thought, play, laughter, tears, gossiping, dance, affection, arguing, fighting, unrest, and so on.

Yet, again, our very language gets in the way of appreciating the kind of sovereignty to which Bataille refers, since it is a language of utility.[56] Indeed, even in making my argument about freedom, our language forces me to position it as some kind of need, though I am trying not to do so. The language of necessity, of crisis, of usefulness, and of the future, in both conservative and progressive discourses on the value of education, can only be a barrier to rethinking higher education. Our language implies the necessity of ends, in relation to which it defines the means, but it cannot isolate an end and say of it, positively, that it is of no use.[57] The sovereign moment is foreign to the language of utility; we are constantly drawn back to usefulness, to necessity.

It is the idea of *need*, therefore, that may be the most significant hegemonic concept for capitalism. The definition of products and individuals as *useful* and as responding to individual or social *needs* is

> the most accomplished, most internalized expression of abstract economic exchange; it is its subjective closure.... . [The] truth of capital culminates in this 'evidence' of man as a producer of value. Such is the twist by which exchange value retrospectively originates and logically terminates in use value.[58]

All this is to say that understandings of higher education should, at least at some point, eschew concerns with the materiality of something that can be called a "need" and instead attend to the ways any educational need is framed, what imperatives are privileged, how individuals made are governable, and how all this is countered (or

---

[55] Pawlett, "Utility and Excess," 101–2.
[56] Bataille, *The Accursed Share Vol. II & III*, 294–295.
[57] Ibid., 315.
[58] Jean Baudrillard, *The Mirror of Production*, trans. Mark Poster (New York: Telos Press, 1975), 25.

might be, if one releases oneself from abstract exchanges). When one claims an imperative need to a solve a problem in higher education, one should reflect on whether the anxiety generated by such imperative prevents one from understanding that the problem might be one of excess wealth, which has to be spent, hopefully not violently but certainly purposelessly.

So, hopefully, I can reposit more clearly the structure of feeling with which I began. Something is happening that the contestations over higher education, as well as what appears to be increasing social unrest, are suggesting. We are perhaps now seeing neoliberal's logic demise. Globally, we are seeing clearly and thus contesting the brutal practices justified by such logic. And, therefore, arguments about the necessity of higher education, when framed in a logic of need, might actually be providing the hegemonic basis for such practices. The time may be right to question the need for higher education, or anything actually.

Sovereignty in Higher Education: A Conclusion of Sorts

In all honesty, I am not sure if Bataille is correct in his central assessment of modern societies, but I am intrigued by the avenues of thought his work presents for me and, I hope, for the reader. I believe that all you can ask of a text, and thus even of higher education writ large, is that it opens up new lines of (unproductive) thought. Bataille avoids what conventional economists do, which, ironically, would make his work useless to them. But because economists play a dominant (hopefully waning) role in how we can think about higher education, I too want to avoid what they say in order to see what they actually do in saying what they say. Economists force us to understand education as a necessity, and even when they argue it is not necessary, they prevent us from seeing it as a luxury that we are compelled to spend without return.

As we experience the present of the pandemic, we must attend to possible structures of feeling, or to "social experiences in solution."[59] Prior to the pandemic, there seemed already a sense that our lives and our worldviews were amiss, manifesting itself in unrests of all sorts, of which the competing debates over the value of higher education are but very small examples. Among other phenomena, we are experiencing anger over growing economic inequality, concerns over the rise (or re-rise) of right-wing political movements—and the mini-fascisms they engender—within nation-states, challenges to the increasingly exclusionary nature of higher education as politicians promoted ideas about universal access, anxieties over the rapidly rising costs of higher education, and all the anti-capitalist protests throughout the world that are associated with all these phenomena. All of this reflects more or less explicit misgivings, fears, and antagonisms over what I think is "capitalism's axiomatic," as Gilles Deleuze and Felix Guattari call it. The capitalist axiomatic erases

---

[59] Williams, *Marxism and Literature*, 133–4.

every other logic (e.g., that of the nation-state, of familial and other social identities, etc.) and converts everything that it can into what is calculable (mostly in terms of money). While capitalism attempts always to repel its own limits, it nevertheless unleashes resistances that it cannot capture, that is, those it cannot subject to its axiomatic or does not see as dangerous enough to try until it is too late (e.g., antisocial affective engagements that are initially seen as mental illnesses).[60]

Bataille's ideas might allow us a moment of freedom from capture by this axiomatic, I think—a sovereign moment. What might this look like? Bataille's ideas of political economy might allow us, following Doreen Massey, to *spatialize* the economy, higher education, or even needs, in order to see them as a product of historically verifiable interrelations, ones with winners and losers, ones with oppressions, for sure, but also ones with plural exchanges, ruptures, and excesses.[61] Spatializing higher education, for example, might allow us to attend to those affective and intimate experiences, those micro-operations and interrelations, that expose the existences of walls (physical and metaphorical) and other discursive barriers that require us to think of utility as inevitable. Bataille would propose, if perhaps not a spatializing, a "heterology," or thought that is opposed to any homogenous representation of the world—any axiomatic, I would add.[62] This is akin, I think, to Deleuze and Guattari's moment of "becoming imperceptible," or when we can perceive something at a "molecular level," that is, as made up of numerous micro-operations and interconnections, with no imposition of a unifying framework to impede such perception.[63]

Such spatializing, heterology, or becoming imperceptible would allow us to reevaluate critiques leveled at institutions of higher education in the debates over financing. We would see as an example of capitalism's axiomatic any critique that asserts that higher education spending is inefficient, wasteful, and so forth. Any such claim should be critiqued for its promotion of capitalist interests, but waste should not be viewed under a logic of utility and necessity. Spending wastefully is what must happen. Such spending can only be deemed acceptable or unacceptable in a general economy attending to the abundance of wealth. We might thus defend wasteful spending because it is wasteful. Such a defense "destroys utility" and exposes capitalism's fissures. Bataille informs us that only wasteful spending—expenditure without return—permits the introduction of disruption in a world governed by utility.

But, what other spatializing, heterology, or becoming imperceptible can allow us to do more than just critique capitalism and expose its fault lines? What does it mean to live and work in higher education once we accept it as really only an

---

[60] See, generally, Gilles Deleuze and Felix Guattari, *Anti-Oedipus: Capitalism and Schizophrenia*, trans. Robert Hurley, Mark Seem, and Helen R, Lane (London: Penguin Books, 2009, c. 1972), 247–50; Gilles Deleuze and Felix Guattari, *A Thousand Plateaus: Capitalism and Schizophrenia*, trans. Brian Massumi (Minneapolis: University of Minnesota Press, 1987, c. 1980), 461–73.

[61] Doreen Massey, *For Space* (Los Angeles: SAGE, 2005), 9.

[62] See Bataille, *Visions of Excess*, 97.

[63] Deleuze and Guattari, *A Thousand Plateaus*, 279–83.

exuberance and ourselves as professors as only effects of such excess? Bill Readings would say that working in higher education would relate to *Thought*, "which belongs to an economy of waste than to a restricted economy of calculation."[64] He posits Thought against the university of excellence. Following Readings, Gary Rolfe seems to justify our existence by arguing that Thought would be invisible, subversive, and virtual, neither inside nor outside, but alongside the university of excellence.[65] Perhaps.

What seems more certain to me are the possibilities permitted by having any "visions of excess," as Bataille might say, whatever they may be, that seek to get us beyond utility, that get us to sovereign moments. We need not justify ourselves then, for the expenditure of wealth in nonproductive activities is necessary to bring pressure down below the boiling point. These visions in themselves would be luxurious expenditures, utterly without meaning under a capitalist axiomatic. They are useless for the university of excellence or to a restricted economy of education. But that uselessness may, at the limits of possibility, destroy utility and allow us a sovereign moment, qualifying in capitalist time as a moment, which may be all we really have to experience something like freedom.

References

Alexander, F. K. (2001). The silent crisis: The relative fiscal capacity of public universities to compete for faculty. *The Review of Higher Education, 24*(2), 112–129.
Althusser, L., & Balibar, É. (2006). *Reading capital* (B. Brewster, Trans.). London: Verso.
Anderson, Z. (2011). Rick Scott wants to shift university funding away from some degrees. *Herald-Tribune*. http://politics.heraldtribune.com/2011/10/10/rick-scott-wants-to-shift-university-funding-away-from-some-majors/. Retrieved April 29, 2018.
Baez, B. (2013). An economy of higher education. In J. Devitis (Ed.), *Contemporary colleges and universities: A reader* (pp. 307–321). New York: Peter Lang.
Barnett, R. (2017). *The ecological university: A feasible utopia*. London: Routledge.
Bataille, G. (1985). *Visions of Excess: Selected Writings, 1927–1939* (A. Stoekl, Ed & Trans.). Minneapolis: University of Minnesota Press.
Bataille, G. (1988). *The accursed share: An essay on general economy, Volume I* (R. Hurley, Trans.). New York: Zone Books.
Bataille, G. (1991). *The accursed share: An essay on general economy, Volumes II & III* (R. Hurley, Trans.). New York: Zone Books.
Baudrillard, J. (1975). *The mirror of production* (M. Poster, Trans.). New York: Telos Press.
Becker, G. (1993). *Human capital: A theoretical and empirical analysis with special reference to education* (3rd ed.). Chicago: The University of Chicago Press.
Caplan, B. (2018). *The case against education: Why the education system is a waste of time and money*. Princeton: Princeton University Press.

---

[64] Bill Readings, *The University in Ruins* (Cambridge, U.S: Harvard University Press, 1996), 175.
[65] Gary Rolfe, *The University in Dissent: Scholarship in the Corporate University* (London: Routledge, 2013), 36.

Cooper, M. A. (2010). Investing in education and equity: Our nation's best future. *Diversity & Democracy, 13*(3). https://www.aacu.org/publications-research/periodicals/investing-education-and-equity-our-nations-best-future-0. Retrieved April 26, 2020.

Deleuze, G., & Guattari, F. (1987). *A thousand plateaus: Capitalism and schizophrenia* (B. Massumi, Trans.). Minneapolis: University of Minnesota Press.

Deleuze, G., & Guattari, F. (2009). *Anti-oedipus: Capitalism and schizophrenia* (R. Hurley, M. Seem, & H. R. Lane, Trans.). London: Penguin Books.

Edelman, L. (2004). *No future: queer theory and the death drive*. Durham: Duke University Press.

Fine, B. (1999). A question of economics: Is it colonizing the social sciences? *Economy and Society, 28*(3), 403–425.

Florida Board of Governors. (2019). *Board of Governors performance funding model overview*. https://www.flbog.edu/wp-content/uploads/Overview-Doc-Performance-Funding-10-Metric-Model-Condensed-Version-1.pdf. Retrieved September 1, 2020.

Fraser, N. (1989). Talking about needs. *Ethics, 99*, 291–313.

Hausman, D. (Ed.). (2008). *The philosophy of economics: An anthology* (3rd ed.). Cambridge: Cambridge University Press.

Hunt, E. K., & Sherman, H. J. (1981). *Economics: And introduction to traditional and radical views* (4th ed.). New York: Harper & Row.

Hutchins, R. M. (1995). *The higher learning in America*. London: Routledge.

Kant, I. (1979). *The conflict of the faculties* (M. J. Gregor, Trans.). Lincoln: University of Nebraska Press.

Kelso, L. O., & Adler, M. J. (1961). *The new capitalists: A proposal to free economic growth from the slavery of savings*. New York: Random House.

Keynes, J. M. (1997). *The general theory of employment, interest, and money*. New York: Prometheus Books.

KGUN 9 On Your Side. (2020). *UArizona announces pay cuts, furloughs for all faculty, staff*. https://www.kgun9.com/news/coronavirus/uarizona-announces-pay-cuts-furloughs-for-all-faculty-staff. Retrieved April 26, 2020.

LaRouche, J., & Lyndon, H. (1984). *So, you wish to learn all about economics? A text on elementary mathematical economics* (p. 1984). New York: New Benjamin Franklin House.

Marginson, S., & Considine, M. (2000). *The Enterprise University: Power, governance, and reinvention in Australia*. Cambridge: Cambridge University Press.

Marsh, J. (2011). *Class dismissed: Why we cannot teach or learn out of inequality*. New York: Monthly Review Press.

Marx, K. (1967). *Capital, Volume 1: A critical analysis of capitalist production* (F. Engels, Ed., S. Moore & E. Aveling, Trans.). New York: International Publishers.

Maslow, A. H. (1943). A theory of human motivation. *Psychology Review, 50*(4), 370–396.

Massey, D. (2005). *For space*. Los Angeles: SAGE.

Newman, J. H. (1982). *The idea of the university*. Notre Dame: University of Notre Dame Press.

Nisbet, R. A. (1971). *The degradation of the academic dogma: The University in America, 1945–1970*. New York: Basic Books.

Orlando Sentinel. (2020). DeSantis' plans to rework state's $93.2B budget could violate constitution. https://www.orlandosentinel.com/politics/os-ne-coronavirus-florida-budget-desantis-20200617-uzmnositmjhbnlt3slmt2f5d7q-story.html. Retrieved September 1, 2020.

Pawlett, W. (1997). Utility and excess: The radical sociology of Bataille and Baudrillard. *Economy and Society, 26*(1), 92–125.

Press, E., & Washburn, J. (2000, March). The kept university. *Atlantic Monthly*, 39–54.

Readings, B. (1996). *The university in ruins*. Cambridge: Harvard University Press.

Reiff, M. R. (2014). How to pay for public education. *Theory and Research in Education, 12*(1), 4–52.

Rhoades, G., & Slaughter, S. (1997). Academic capitalism, managed professionals, and supply-side higher education. *Social Text, 15*(2), 9–38.

Rolfe, G. (2013). *The university in dissent: Scholarship in the corporate university.* London: Routledge.
Slaughter, S., & Rhoades, G. (2004). *Academic capitalism and the new economy: Markets, state, and higher education.* Baltimore: The Johns Hopkins University Press.
Thompson, G. F. (1997). Where Goes economics and economies? *Economy and Society, 26*(4), 599–610.
Veblen, T. (1996). *The higher learning in America.* New Brunswick: Transaction Publishers.
Washburn, J. (2005). *University, Inc.: The corporate corruption of American higher education.* New York: Basic Books.
Williams, R. (1977). *Marxism and literature.* Oxford: Oxford University Press.
World Bank. (2017). *Higher education.* https://www.worldbank.org/en/topic/tertiaryeducation. Retrieved April 26, 2020.
Zafirovski, M. (2008). Classical and neoclassical conceptions of rationality: Findings of an exploratory study. *The Journal of Socio-Economics, 37*(2), 789–820.

Benjamin Baez is a professor of higher education and chair of the Department of Educational Policy Studies at Florida International University. He received his law degree in 1988 and his doctorate in higher education in 1997, both from Syracuse University. Among other books, he is the author of *Technologies of Government: Politics and Power in the "Information Age"* (Information Age Publishing) and *The Politics of Inquiry: Education Research and the "Culture of Science"* (with Deron Boyles) [Winner of a 2009 CHOICE Award for Outstanding Title and 2010 American Educational Studies Association Critics Choice Selection] (SUNY Press). His articles have also appeared in a number of journals, including *Discourse: Studies in the Cultural Politics of Education, Educational Policy, Educational Theory, JCT: Journal of Curriculum Theorizing, The Journal of Higher Education, The Review of Higher Education, Studies in the Philosophy of Education,* and *Teachers College Record.* His teaching and research interests include the economics of education, the sociology and philosophy of knowledge and teaching, and diversity in higher education.

Chapter 4
Education as Promise: Learning from Hannah Arendt

Jon Nixon

Introduction

The 'university becoming' will need to question not only the increasingly undemocratic and illiberal societies within which it operates but also its own sense of purposefulness. The literature within the field of higher education has been good at challenging neoliberalism: its anti-public sector and pro-private sector policies and the impact of that policy orientation – coupled with post 2008 economic austerity measures leading to escalating levels of inequality – on higher education and society at large.[1] But it has been less good at catching up with analysing and critiquing the post-neoliberal, nationalist and protectionist policies associated with the new authoritarianism establishing itself within old and aspiring democracies across Europe. This new authoritarianism plays fast and loose with the truth, relies on spectacle and nostalgic rhetoric, manipulates the supposed 'free' press and is fronted by charismatic (and often hopelessly ineffectual) leadership.

This is a murky swamp. So what is the role of the university in cleansing it? I argue that the liberal university has a vital role to play in ensuring belief in the truth. As Timothy Snyder– a contemporary historian who writes in the spirit of Arendt – puts it: 'To abandon facts is to abandon freedom. If nothing is true, then no one can criticize power, because there is no basis upon which to do so. If nothing is true, then all is spectacle' (Snyder 2017, 65). But, of course, all is *not* spectacle (which is Snyder's point), and the university is one of the institutions that is dedicated to

---

[1] In my 2017 *Higher Education in Austerity Europe*, I tried to capture this moment of critical reflection by bringing together leading scholars across Europe to reflect upon their experience of 'austerity Europe' (See Nixon 2017).

J. Nixon (✉)
Middlesex University, London, UK

© The Author(s), under exclusive license to Springer Nature
Switzerland AG 2021
S. S. E. Bengtsen et al. (eds.), *The University Becoming*, Debating Higher Education: Philosophical Perspectives 6,
https://doi.org/10.1007/978-3-030-69628-3_4

getting behind the scenes. There may (to shift metaphors) be no clearly defined road map, but there is a promise of handing on from one generation to another the resources of hope and imagination, of truth and honesty and of magnanimity and outreach. That is what the liberal university stands for: the constant reminder, particularly in dark and precarious times, of the need to *stop and think*.

I choose Hannah Arendt as my guide and mentor through this swamp: not some contemporised Arendt drawn kicking and squealing into the twenty-first century but Arendt as an historically located public intellectual and educator who speaks to us from her own place and time. It is the responsibility of contemporary readers to judge the relevance – if any – of Arendt's thoughts for their own individual, professional and institutional situations. For me, she speaks to the moral purposefulness of education, its relevance to our ethical well-being as expressed through our everyday actions and choices and its focus on an educated citizenry at home in the world.

Arendt: The Thinker

Thinking, argued Arendt, is an innate human capacity. It enables us to have present in our minds a multiplicity of standpoints in a process she called 'representative thinking': '[t]he more people's standpoints I have present in my mind while I am pondering a given issue … the stronger will be my capacity for representative thinking'. This innate and defining feature of humanity means that our mental horizons are not static and fixed but constantly shifting and expanding. 'It is', she maintained, 'this capacity for an "enlarged mentality" that enables men[2] to judge' (Arendt [1961] 1977, 241); and it is this ability to form judgements that opens up the possibility of what Arendt understands by human action, as opposed to routinised behaviour or mindless activity. If thinking involves a withdrawal from the public realm of human action, judgement marks the specific point of re-entry: the point at which purposeful, considered action becomes a possibility and a hope.[3] The need to *stop and think* as a prelude to judgement and action was a recurring theme throughout the first volume of her final work (Arendt 1978).

Arendt was one of an illustrious circle of Jewish artists and intellectuals who fled Nazi Germany during the 1930s. Together they formed what the historian Tony Judt described as 'a very special and transient community, that twentieth-century republic of letters formed against their will by the survivors of the great upheavals of the century' (Judt 2009, 88–89). Many, of course, never made it, among them Walter

---

[2] Writing in English Arendt typically wrote 'men' when she wanted to emphasise not the difference between the sexes but their common humanity. In German she wrote *Menschen*, without gender specificity, not *Manner*.

[3] For an elaboration of the notion of 'the thinking university', see Bergsten and Barnett's (2018) edited collection of papers that examine – from various philosophical perspectives – the place of thought in higher education; for a discussion of the pedagogical implications of the relation between thoughtfulness and hopefulness, see Hyvönen 2019.

Benjamin who died attempting to cross from occupied France into Spain. Among those who did escape were Theodor Adorno, Erich Auerbach, Bertolt Brecht as well as Arendt herself. Each of them shared a similar intellectual and cultural background having studied or worked if not together then in many of the same institutions. Although differing in age, each had also experienced the rigours of WWI, the brief and abortive German Revolution that followed and the years of deep economic deprivation that were a consequence of the punitive terms set by the Treaty of Versailles. Working in different fields, on different topics and in different locations, each went on to produce work that was to have a huge impact on the arts and humanities and on the social and political sciences for generations to come.

Arendt's unique contribution to this collective endeavour was as a political thinker who insisted on working outside the frame of any particular discipline and on matters of worldwide concern. She was an uncompromisingly independent thinker who was always attempting to reconcile her republican values – her belief in the public realm as the space of democratic politics – with the pragmatic complexities of *realpolitik*: how are those values being eroded, denigrated or simply abolished within our current systems of governance? How are they being pushed forward, given a voice, a presence? Crucially, how might we develop a citizenry with the resources necessary to find that voice and insist on that presence? Unforgiving of the atrocities of fascism, as it manifested itself in Nazism, and appalled by Stalin's perversion of Marxism, she sought to articulate a notion of politics that was radically different from both these ideologies – and, indeed, radically different from any political regime based upon the adherence to a particular ideology.

A defining feature of much of her work is its focus on specific contemporary events that she saw as having significant social and political implications. In all such cases she framed her analysis within a broad historical perspective and highlighted points of general philosophical and political import: in her intervention in the debate on integrated schooling, she reflected on the relation between the state and the individual (Arendt 2003, 193–226); her report on the Eichmann trial provided an opportunity to reflect on the nature of evil (Arendt [1963] 2006a, b); while her commentary on *The Pentagon Papers* is, among other things, a discourse on the relation between truth, politics and deceit (Arendt 1972, 1–47). She was rightly seen as a public intellectual – and public educator – not just because she focused on particular public concerns in the here and now but because she highlighted the universal and historic significance of those concerns in such a way that they continue to speak to us decades after her death.

Her work is also characterised by the way in which it is informed by her own experience. Of course, that experience was filtered and refined by means of an intense process of reflection – the 'two-in-one' of solitary thinking (Arendt 1978, 179–193), the exercise of close and critical reading (Arendt 2007a) and the continuing dialogue with colleagues and friends (Nixon 2015) – but Arendt never loses touch with the experience itself: her first-hand experience of totalitarianism, of exile and statelessness[4] and of being a Jew in an anti-Semitic society (see, e.g. Arendt [1951] 1973, [1957] 1997, 2007b). These are the themes that drive her work forward and give it a sense of overall coherence (notwithstanding the immense range and variety of her writing).

Her essays and articles, no less than her major works of conceptual and historical analysis, are all attempts to think through the unthinkable in her own personal history and that of those who were caught up in the events she witnessed. For Arendt, explanatory frameworks are not pregiven. Rather, they are the hard-won outcomes of a long, involved and deliberative process of critical and self-critical thinking. To think, she declared, is to think without banisters:

> Even though we have lost yardsticks by which to measure, and rules under which to subsume the particular, a being whose essence is beginning may have enough of origin within himself to understand without preconceived categories and to judge without the customary rules which is morality. (Arendt 1994, 321)

New Beginnings

The notion of natality – of human life as a unique beginning – is central to Arendt's thinking. It is a core element within an intricate network of concepts that spans her entire corpus: a network that includes action, appearance, freedom, judgement, labour, natality, plurality, persuasion, power, public space, violence and work. Her lifelong preoccupation with these concepts – their interrelations and the distinctions between them – is a further distinguishing feature of all her work. The pattern changes with each new shift of the kaleidoscope – each new twist of the argument – but the core conceptual elements remain constant.

To understand Arendt's mode of thought, we need to pay close attention to her distinctive use of these concepts. The distinction, as elaborated in *On Violence*, between power as empowerment through collective action and violence which seeks to destroy collective power is crucial to an understanding of her thinking as it develops across the full range of her political writing (Arendt 1970a, 44–46). Similarly, her distinction between labour as the type of human activity that is required for human survival and work as the type of activity involved in creating an artificial world where life has some durability and permanence is not only central to the argument developed in *The Human Condition* but underpins all her thinking on the development of human society and the rise of post-WWII consumer society (Arendt [1958] 1998, 79–93).

Natality – the incontrovertible fact of human birth – is vitally connected to Arendt's notion of action: 'the new beginning inherent in birth can make itself felt in the world only because the newcomer possesses the capacity of beginning something anew, that is, of acting'. The initial new beginning heralds a unique entry into

---

[4] Arendt's work has important implications for work in the area of education and the refugee crisis. See, for example, Hayden and Saunders 2019; Veck 2020.

the human world, but this first birth opens up the possibility of further new beginnings in which the individual enters the world of human action: 'In this sense of initiative, an element of action, and therefore of natality, is inherent in all human activities' (Arendt [1958] 1998, 9). Although she stresses the human capacity to begin, to initiate, we do not act in isolation. To act is to assert both one's common humanity and one's unique human agency. Through our actions we insert our own distinctive selves into our shared world of human affairs.

Education was for Arendt one of the doorways into that world. However, she made a sharp distinction between the education of children and the education of young adults. Her two essays on the former – 'Reflections on Little Rock' and 'The Crisis in Education' – are premised on the assumption that children are as yet unformed and that adults have a responsibility to guide them into the world of human affairs while protecting them from the full blast and turmoil of that world (Arendt 2003, 193–226, [1961] 1977, 173–196). This assumption lay behind her highly questionable attack on the federal imposition of integrated schooling, as advanced in 'Reflections on Little Rock', and her reflections, in 'The Crisis of Education', on 'the dangers of a constantly progressing decline of elementary standards throughout the entire school system' (Arendt [1961] 1977, 173). Arendt seems to have been acutely aware of the vulnerability of the child in an adult world.

Her views on the education of young adults – and of the role of the university in that process – were markedly different. What few reports we have of her own teaching style within the university context suggests that she was centrally concerned with enabling her students to think for themselves, express their own opinions and argue and deliberate with one another. Jerome Kohn, now the pre-eminent Arendtian scholar, studied under Arendt in the late 1960s. In an exchange of letters with Elisabeth Young-Bruehl, another erstwhile student of Arendt who went on to become her biographer, Kohn recalls the experience of being taught by Arendt during that period of student unrest and violent demonstrations against the war in Vietnam:

> For this theorist of action, teaching itself was an unrehearsed performance, especially in the give-and-take, what she called the 'free-for-all' of the seminar, where she asked her students real rather than rhetorical questions and responded, usually in entirely unexpected ways, to theirs … In her seminar, every participant was a 'citizen', called upon to give her or his opinion, to insert him or herself into that miniature polis in order to make it, as she said, 'a little better'. (Young-Bruehl and Kohn 2001, 254–255)

In *On Violence* Arendt inveighed against what she saw as 'this new shift toward violence in the thinking of revolutionaries' (Arendt 1970a, 15). What she found particularly shocking was the blurring of the distinction between power and violence (concepts which, as we have seen, she held to be antithetical). She reserved some of her sharpest criticism for Jean-Paul Sartre, whom she saw as falsely glorifying violence in the name of empowerment, and had little time for – and little contact with – any of the fashionable Left Bank intellectuals of the day, the exception being Albert Camus whose moral integrity and honesty she greatly admired. In a letter to Blücher posted from Paris on 1 May 1952, she wrote: 'Yesterday I was with Camus; he is without doubt the best man they have in France. All the other intellectuals are at most bearable' (Kohler 2000, 164).[5]

Her attitude towards *non-violent* civil disobedience was very different. On 19 February 1965, she wrote to her friend and early mentor Karl Jaspers regarding the student protests at the University of California, Berkeley, where students were demonstrating for the right to be politically active on campus, to have a voice in university decisions and to end discrimination against minority students: 'Their organization is superb. In Berkeley they've achieved everything they set out to achieve, and now they can't and don't want to stop'. She added that the students involved in the protests now 'know what it's like to act effectively' (Kohler and Saner 1992, 583). The campus had become an extension of the 'free-for-all' of the seminar room: an *organised* 'free-for-all' in which 'every participant was a "citizen", called upon to give her or his opinion, to insert him or herself into that miniature polis in order to make it ... "a little better"' (Young-Bruehl and Kohn 2001, 255).

Arendt was not suggesting a headlong rush from thought to action. She was adamant that thought and action are distinct and that judgement is something different again. Nevertheless, these concepts are vitally connected. Her notions of 'representative thinking' and 'enlargement of mind', writes Dana Villa (1999, 88), 'point to the faculty of judgement as a kind of bridge between thought and action'. Only when thinking has done its work and judgements have been formed does the action begin; but, conversely, '[o]nly when action has ceased and words such as courage, justice, and virtue become genuinely perplexing does thinking actually begin' (Villa 2001, 19).

What binds together thought, action and judgement is the notion of plurality: '[W]e know from experience', writes Arendt in her 'Introduction *into* Politics' (which formed the basis of a course she gave at the University of Chicago in 1963), 'that no one can adequately grasp the objective world in its full reality all on his own'. She continues:

> If someone wants to see and experience the world as it 'really' is, he can do so only by understanding it as something that is shared by many people, lies between them, showing itself differently to each and comprehensible only to the extent that many people can talk *about* it and exchange their opinions and perspectives with one another, over against one another. (Arendt 2005, 128, original emphasis)

To understand the world is to comprehend it in all its plurality. Only through a process of shared comprehension can we begin to form judgements which position and define us within that world. When these judgements coalesce around common interests, individuals achieve the collective agency necessary for concerted action.

---

[5] Arendt's views on revolution should be read with reference to her 1958 essay, 'The Hungarian Revolution and Totalitarian Imperialism' (Arendt 2018, 105–156). There is not the space in my contribution to this volume to deal with this issue, but interested readers might turn to Chapter 9 of my *Hannah Arendt and the Politics of Friendship* for a discussion of the continuing relevance of Arendt's views on social change within a revolutionary context (Nixon 2015, 175–190) and to my discussion in *Rosa Luxemburg and the Struggle for Democratic Renewal* of Arendt's indebtedness to Rosa Luxemburg in her thinking on the decentralisation of power (Nixon 2018b, 50–53).

This dialectic of thinking, judgement and action lies at the heart of Arendt's political thought as it developed in the wake of her pioneering *The Origins of Totalitarianism* (Arendt [1951] 1973). It suggests the need for an in-between space in which thinking, judgement and action are allowed free play: a safe space between the private world of solitary thought and the public world of human action – a space in which opinions can be aired and judgements tested. Friendship, as I have argued elsewhere, constituted for Arendt one such in-between space (Nixon 2015, 2018a). At best, education provides a similar space: a space in which to venture out, test the water and 'think with enlarged mentality – that means you train your imagination to go visiting' (Arendt 1978, II, 257).

The Power of Promise

The stories we tell ourselves about ourselves reveal an agent, but, writes Arendt, 'this agent is not an author or producer'. Embroiled as we are in 'innumerable, conflicting wills and intentions', the outcomes of our actions collide and coalesce in wholly unpredictable ways. Such is that unpredictability, claims Arendt, 'that action almost never achieves its purpose' (Arendt [1958] 1998, 184). This unpredictability, she maintains, is the price we pay for the irreducible plurality of the human condition: a condition which results from our freedom of will and results in the tangle of unforeseen – and unforeseeable – consequences. We are equal in our shared capacity for action, new beginnings, but distinct in the particular actions that define our unique trajectories.

Human beings can minimise the impact of the unpredictable by acting in concert and thereby reducing the clash of conflicting wills and intentions. When we act in this way, we generate what Arendt understands by power, the 'only limitation [of which] is the existence of other people … [H]uman power corresponds to the condition of plurality to begin with'. Nevertheless, power is 'dependent upon the unreliable and only temporary agreement of many wills and intentions' unless provided with the durability and potential permanence of binding agreements that stand as a bulwark against the uncertainty of the world (Arendt [1958] 1998, 201). Arendt wrote of such agreements with reference to 'the power of promise', the effect of which is 'the enormous and truly miraculous enlargement of the very dimension in which power can be effective' (Arendt [1958] 1998, 245). We cannot predict or control the future by virtue of our binding promises, but we can begin to shape and work towards a common future. It is that dimension of temporal enlargement – 'the enormous and truly miraculous enlargement' – that gives validity to the promise.

Public institutions are the embodiment of the kinds of promises to which Arendt is here referring: promises regarding, for example, our health and well-being, our access to justice and the right of every child and young person to a basic education. Without our hospitals, law courts, schools and universities, the practices we associate with these institutions would lack the wherewithal for development over time. We may criticise our institutions, but, without them, the promises they embody would be baseless. Their existence as the cornerstones of liberal, democratic society vindicates Edmund Burke's famous definition of society as a partnership 'not only between those who are living, but between those who are living, those who are dead, and those who are to be born' (Burke [1790] 1961, 110).

Although Arendt herself did not make the connection, we might view universities as the embodiment of a promise given by one generation to succeeding generations to pass on whatever truths – albeit partial and provisional (but always hard-won) – have been gathered from the ongoing practice of research, scholarship and teaching. Of course, such truths are constantly revised, challenged and refined by the coming of the new and the young. Indeed, without those new beginnings, truth would wither into irrelevance and, over time, become an untruth – or, even worse, one of the old lies used to justify the unjustifiable. Nevertheless, the responsibility of each generation to pass on the goods of its collective learning, and, in so doing, expose them to the scrutiny of future generations, remains of paramount importance.

In her essay on 'Truth and Politics', Arendt drew a distinction between 'rational truth' and 'factual truth'. 'Facts and events', she argued, 'are infinitely more fragile things than axioms, discoveries, theories – even the most wildly speculative ones – produced by the human mind'. Moreover, she insisted, once a 'factual truth' –as opposed to a 'rational truth' – is lost, no rational effort will ever bring it back:

> Perhaps the chances that Euclidian mathematics or Einstein's theory of relativity – let alone Plato's philosophy – would have been reproduced in time if their authors had been prevented from handing them down to posterity are not very good either, yet they are infinitely better than the chances that a fact of importance, forgotten or, more likely, lied away, will one day be rediscovered. (Arendt [1961] 1977, 231–232)

In highlighting both the vulnerability and significance of 'factual truth', Arendt anticipates Edward W. Said's insistence that the prime task of the intellectual is 'to protect against and forestall the disappearance of the past' and, through the practice of research, scholarship and teaching, to stand against 'the invidious disfiguring, dismembering, and disremembering of significant historical experiences that do not have powerful enough lobbies in the present and therefore merit dismissal or belittlement' (Said 2004, 141).

The urgency of that task is highlighted in Richard J. Bernstein's stark reminder of what can happen to societies that blur the distinction between truth and untruth:

> What happened so blatantly in totalitarian societies is being practiced today by leading politicians. In short, there is the constant danger that powerful persuasive techniques are being used to deny factual truth, to transform fact into just another opinion, and to create a world of 'alternative facts'. (Bernstein 2018, 74)

But truth can only be valued by those who have a disposition towards truthfulness.[6] We may differ as to what personal qualities constitute such a disposition and how they are acquired, but without them – and the possibility of them being acquired

---

[6] For a fuller working out of my claim regarding the relation between trust and truth, see Nixon 2019.

and reacquired by successive generations – it would not be possible 'to protect against and forestall the disappearance of the past'.

Arendt herself placed great emphasis on what she saw as the *existential* nature of truth: its manifestation in the human dispositions and qualities that are unique to a particular individual. In accepting the Lessing Prize of the Free City of Hamburg in 1959, she spoke of Lessing's philosophical legacy not only in terms of his ideas but in terms of his unique personal qualities, chief among which she identified his openness to 'incessant and continual discourse':

> He was never eager really to fall out with someone with whom he had entered into a dispute; he was concerned solely with humanizing the world by incessant and continual discourse about its affairs and the things in it. He wanted to be a friend of many men, but no man's brother. (Arendt 1970b, 30)

Similarly, in her 1957 piece honouring the life and work of Karl Jaspers, she wrote of her friend and former mentor as a uniquely generous individual who in his limitless communicability embodied the core principle around which his work cohered:

> The principle itself is communication; truth, which can never be grasped as dogmatic content, emerges as 'existential' substance clarified and articulated by reason, communicating itself and appealing to the reasonable existing of the other, comprehensible and capable of comprehending everything else ... Truth itself is communicative, it disappears and cannot be conceived outside communication. (Arendt 1970b, 85)

Without the active engagement and interaction of human minds, facts, axioms and theories are reduced to mere 'dogmatic content'. Truth requires an ethos – a culture of curiosity and inquiry and of critical discourse and argumentation – if it is to speak to the future and allow the future to speak back.

One of Arendt's great achievements as a public intellectual – and public educator – was to open up the institutional spaces within which such a culture might develop and flourish. Her own New York apartment – shared with Heinrich Blücher – became a hub of intellectual dialogue and conviviality; Schocken, the New York publishing house where she worked as editor in the late 1940s, became a major focus for new ideas and cultural exchange; and, of course, the seminar room and lecture theatre became – under her tutelage – a place of dialogue in which ideas were developed and challenged, questions asked and explored and students encouraged to think for themselves.

Arendt, like so many of her generation, witnessed the world descend into the bleakest inhumanity. The emergence of totalitarianism was, she argued, an event without precedent and fell outside all the existing moral and political categories, outside any existing conception of criminality. The task for her generation was, she believed, to reclaim our shared humanity – our capacity for new beginnings – and restore it for future generations. That task is as urgent now as it was then. Now, as then, authoritarianism is on the rise, anti-pluralist rhetoric grows ever more strident and the anti-politics of majoritarian populism erects ever more boundaries (Galston 2018; Graziano 2018; Müller 2017). Education offers no panaceas, no easy solutions and no certain certainties. Nevertheless, Arendt was adamant that education is where each generation must start if it is to set about the task of reclamation and, in so doing, fulfil its promise to succeeding generations.

'Education', she wrote (and here she was referring to the education of both children and young adults):

> is the point at which we decide whether we love the world enough to assume responsibility for it and by the same token save it from that ruin which, except for renewal, except for the coming of the new and the young, would be inevitable. (Arendt [1961] 1977, 196)

Truth and Deliberation

Arendt insisted on the public sphere as a 'guarantee against the futility of individual life, the space protected against this and reserved for the relative permanence, if not immortality, of mortals' (Arendt [1958] 1998, 56). Within the public sphere – what for the Greeks was the *polis* and for the Romans the *res publica* – 'the people' constitute not a single voice but a buzzing plurality for which critical thought and the exercise of free will are of paramount importance. She firmly rejected the notion of a 'general will': a generalised will abstracted from the will of individualised agents. Indeed, she argued that it was precisely this notion of a 'general will' that had led to the tragic failure of the French Revolution. By dissolving individual free will into an undifferentiated generality, it denied its own libertarian precepts (Arendt [1963] 2006a, b, 50). For Arendt, the prime purpose of education was to enable each individual to develop the capabilities and dispositions necessary to enter the public sphere as independent-minded citizens.

In affirming the plurality of the public sphere, Arendt was acknowledging both the individuality of the individual and the equal worth of each individual within that sphere. To acknowledge this plurality is to reject the claim that 'the people' can be reduced to a single voice ('the voice of the people') or a generalised will ('the will of the people') as evoked in the ever-increasing hubbub of populist rhetoric. It is also to reject the claim – implicit in that populist rhetoric – that all those who are not in tune with this single voice or generalised will are an entirely negative or deficit element within the body politic.

The *polis* as conceived by Arendt comprises neither a homogeneous mass in which all voices speak as one nor an exclusionary zone from which any voice deemed to be out of tune is automatically excluded. It is, rather, a civic space in which all individuals are deemed equal by virtue of their citizenship and each is acknowledged to be different by virtue of her or his freedom of will: a space dependent upon the free interchange of opinion and reliant on the respect of all parties for a distinction to be drawn and maintained between truth and untruth in the expression of their opinions. When that distinction is lost, deliberately blurred or flouted, the *polis* is put at incalculable risk – as it clearly is with the rise of Donald Trump in the USA, Nigel Farage in Britain, Marine Le Pen in France, Jaroslaw Kaczyński in Poland and Victor Orbán in Hungary.[7]

To acknowledge the plurality of the public sphere is to reject the claim that any one group has a monopoly on the truth. Truth is what we arrive at through a process of deliberation involving the ongoing testing and challenging of contrasting and sometimes conflicting judgements. Truth does not fall outside the world of human affairs but is constituted within it as an ongoing process of agreement-making that is forever being reworked and refashioned. To seek to derail this process through the twisting or distortion of the truth for political gain is not only undemocratic but, in Arendt's terms, anti-political in that it renders inoperable the deliberative infrastructure upon which politics is founded.

Truth, argued Arendt in her analysis of the Pentagon Papers (leaked to the *New York Times* in 1971 and revealing the extent of the state cover-up of the death and casualty toll resulting from the Vietnam War), is one of the foundation stones of democratic politics. It is 'the chief stabilizing factor in the affairs of men', without which the *polis* is – as history shows – at risk of descending into totalitarianism:

> This is one of the lessons that could be learned from the totalitarian experiments and the totalitarian rulers' frightening confidence in the power of lying – in their ability, for instance, to rewrite history again and again to adapt the past to the 'political line' of the present moment or to eliminate data that did not fit their ideology. (Arendt 1972, 7)

Untruth disempowers and ultimately disenfranchises the recipients of untruth; it discredits and ultimately corrupts the purveyors of untruth. Truth alone empowers.

Truth does not appear unbidden. The sifting of truth from untruth – from wishful thinking, wrong-headed belief, deliberate evasions, downright lies, etc. – presupposes the human capacity for what Arendt understood as thoughtfulness: a capacity which she saw as deeply dialogical (the 'two-in-one' of thinking, as she put it), as inclusive of divergent views and opinions (what she termed 'representative thinking') and as fundamental to human flourishing (as elaborated in her notion of 'enlargement of mind') (Arendt 1978, I, 179–193, [1961] 1977, 241, 1978, II, 257). To be thoughtful, argued Arendt, is to engage in the world of human affairs and thereby become worldly. To be unworldly is to be thoughtless and thereby disengaged from the world. Without the thinking person, the *polis* is unthinkable.

But not all ways of thinking route us through from the 'two-in-one' of solitary thought to the dialogical process of thinking, whereby we are able to engage with the world. Throughout her life and work, Arendt struggled to develop and practice a way of thinking that was in her terms 'worldly': a way of thinking that, while confronting the banality of thoughtlessness (and its all-too-easy collusion with evil), rejected the allurements (very real for a person of Arendt's intellectual disposition) of purely abstract thought. In order to understand the moral and ethical premium

---

[7] On the general threat to democracy and the rise of the new authoritarianism, see Applebaum 2020; Gessen 2020; Levitsky and Ziblatt 2018; Snyder 2017; Tucker 2020. On Brexit and Trump, see, for example, Barnett 2017; Harding 2017; Schier and Eberly, 2018. On the re-entry of the far right, see Fekete 2018; Neiwert 2017.

Arendt placed on thoughtfulness, it is necessary to understand how and why she distinguished it from the unworldliness of, on the one hand, *thoughtlessness* (as exemplified in the person of the Nazi operative Eichmann) and, on the other hand, *pure thought* (as expressed in the life and work of the Nazi apologist Heidegger).

Education is about understanding ourselves well enough to steer clear of either of these two polarities. Worldliness – the knowledge of how the world works in all its complex diversity – was Arendt's grounding principle. Without worldliness, there can be no informed citizenry; without an informed citizenry, there can be no *polity*; and without a *polity*, there can be no democracy – and, crucially, no hope of a continuing democracy for future generations. To become educated is to become a distinct part of an informed citizenry, with all the responsibilities that entails.

Arendt believed in the power of collective endeavour. Indeed, she insisted that power, as opposed to force, is generated when – and only when – people act together in the spirit of shared understanding based on contestable and contested opinion. She provides us with no blueprint of what the liberal university might look like, but she does provide us with a dire warning that the institutions of civil society – of which the liberal university is a cornerstone – are a crucial bulwark against the authoritarian populist movements that are once again gaining ascendancy across Europe.

But – and it is a big *but* – while maintaining the values of the university, we need to acknowledge the unending struggle for the recognition of those values and their working through into practice. Anne Applebaum – who, as a historian of the twentieth century totalitarianism and of the threat to liberal democracy, writes in the spirit if not the letter of Arendt – concludes her 2020 *Twilight of Democracy* with a dire warning of the need for vigilance: 'There is no final solution, no theory that will explain everything. There is no road map to a better society, no didactic ideology, no rule book'. The liberal university, she reminds us, exists to uphold the primacy of 'participation, argument, effort, struggle' in the sustainability of liberal democracy (Applebaum 2020, 188–189). The university may, on occasion, provide some provisional answers to some questions, but its prime purpose is to help frame the questions, to broaden their parameters while sharpening their focus, to prioritise fact above the power of spectacle and, when necessary, to spell out the complexities of truthfulness to the simplistic assumptions of power.

***

To *stop and think* is to step back with a view to the possibility of action – action based on the informed judgements that stopping and thinking allow for and that universities exist for. This was the kind of stopping and thinking that gave rise to the great civil rights movements of the mid-twentieth century. The people who walked onto the streets of Alabama had deliberated and thought long and hard together – and when the hour came, they acted together. But, crucially, they were focused on what Martin Luther King defined as 'two important facts': that 'the line of progress is never straight' and that 'final victory is an accumulation of many short-term encounters' (King 1969, 21). Radical change is grounded in the little things.

And those little things concern not only the higher education sector but the wider education policy agenda – or, rather, they involve higher education in addressing these wider issues. If we really want higher education to fulfil its promise to society *as a whole*, then, as Stefan Collini, writing with specific reference to the dire situation in England (but with wider relevance) argues, higher education needs to extend its field of vision:

> [t]he truth is that if you say you want more children from deprived areas to be able to go to university, then don't faff around with entry tariffs: invest in Sure Start centres, preschool groups, subsidised childcare and properly resources primary schools. Make benefits genuinely accessible and life-supporting. (Collini 2020, 1)

Those working in higher education need to work across sectors and with creative and educational thinkers in the arts, business and science communities across society to begin to establish a holistic vision of the *promise* of education for all.

References

Applebaum, A. (2020). *Twilight of democracy: The failure of politics and the parting of friends.* London: Allen Lane.

Arendt, H. ([1951] 1973). *The origins of totalitarianism* (New edition with added prefaces). San Diego/New York/London: Harcourt Brace and Company.

Arendt, H. ([1957] 1997). *Rahel Varnhagen: The life of a Jewess*, edited by L. Weissberg; translated by R. and C. Winston. Baltimore/London: John Hopkins University Press in cooperation with the Leo Black Institute. (first published by Leo Black Institute in 1957).

Arendt, H. ([1958] 1998). *The human condition* (2nd ed.). Chicago/London: The University of Chicago Press.

Arendt, H. ([1961] 1977). *Between past and future: Eight exercises in political thought.* New York: Penguin Books (first published by Faber & Faber, 1961, and with additional material by Viking Press, 1968).

Arendt, H. ([1963] 2006a). *On revolution.* London: Penguin (first published in the USA by the Viking Press, 1963).

Arendt, H. ([1963] 2006b).. *Eichmann in Jerusalem: A Report on the Banality of Evil*, London: Penguin Books (first published in the USA by The Viking Press).

Arendt, H. (1970a). *On violence.* Orlando/Austin/New York/San Diego/London: A Harvest Book, Harcourt.

Arendt, H. (1970b). *Men in dark times.* London: Jonathan Cape.

Arendt, H. (1972). *Crises of the republic.* San Diego/New York/London: Harcourt Brace and Company.

Arendt, H. (1978). *The life of the mind* (one-volume edition). San Diego/New York/London: Harcourt.

Arendt, H. (1994). *Essays in understanding 1930–1954: formation, exile, and totalitarianism* (J. Kohn, Ed.). New York: Schocken Books.

Arendt, H. (2003). *Responsibility and judgment* (J. Kohn, Ed.). New York: Schocken Books.

Arendt, H. (2005). *The promise of politics* (J. Kohn, Ed.). New York: Schoken Books.

Arendt, H. (2007a). *Reflections on literature and culture* (S. Y-AH. Gottlieb, Ed.). Stanford: Stanford University Press.

Arendt, H. (2007b). *The Jewish writings* (J. Kohn, & R. R. Feldman, Eds.). New York: Schocken Books.

Arendt, H. (2018). *Thinking without a banister* (J. Kohn, Ed.). New York: Schocken Books.

Barnett, A. (2017). *The lure of greatness: England's Brexit and America's Trump*. Unbound: Unbound.com.

Bergsten, S. S. E., & Barnett, R. (Eds.). (2018). *The thinking university: A philosophical examination of thought in higher education*. Cham: Springer.

Bernstein, R. J. (2018). *Why read Hannah Arendt now*. Cambridge/Medford: Polity Press.

Burke, E. ([1790] 1961). *Reflections on the revolution in France*, Garden City: Doubleday.

Collini, S. (2020). Universities are in chaos. Yet still we're told it's 'success' *Guardian Journal*, 1–2(1 September).

Fekete, E. (2018). *Europe's fault lines: Racism and the rise of the right*. London/New York: Verso.

Galston, W. A. (2018). *Anti-pluralism: The populist threat to Liberal democracy*. New Haven/London: Yale University Press.

Gessen, M. (2020). *Surviving autocracy*. London: Granta.

Graziano, M. (2018). *What is a border?* (M. Korobko, Trans.). Stanford: Stanford University Press.

Harding, L. (2017). *Collusion: How Russia helped trump win the white house*. London: Guardian/Faber and Faber.

Hayden, P., & Saunders, N. (2019). Solidarity at the margins: Arendt, refugees, and the inclusive politics of world-making. In K. Hiruta (Ed.), *Arendt on freedom, liberation, and revolution. Philosophers in depth*. Cham: Palgrave Macmillan.

Hyvönen, A.-E. (2019). Pedagogies of hopefulness and thoughtfulness: The social-political role of higher education in contemporary societies. In P. Gibbs & A. Peterson (Eds.), *Higher education and Hope: Institutional, pedagogical and personal possibilities* (pp. 21–48). Cham: Palgrave Macmillan.

Judt, T. (2009). *Reappraisals: Reflections on the forgotten twentieth century*. London: Vintage Books.

King, M. L. (1969). *Chaos or community*. Harmondsworth/Ringwood: Penguin.

Kohler, L. (Ed.). (2000). *Within Four Walls: The Correspondence between Hannah Arendt and Heinrich Blucher 1936–1968* (P. Constantine, Trans.). New York/San Diego/London: Harcourt.

Kohler, L., & Saner, H. (Eds.). (1992). *Hannah Arendt Karl Jaspers correspondence 1926–1969* (R. Kimber, Trans.). New York/San Diego/London: Harcourt Jovanovich, Publishers.

Levitsky, S., & Ziblatt, D. (2018). *How democracies die: What history reveals about our future*. London: Penguin Books.

Müller, J.-W. (2017). *What is populism?* London: Penguin Books.

Neiwert, D. (2017). *Alt-America: The rise of the radical right in the age of trump*. London/New York: Verso.

Nixon, J. (2015). *Hannah Arendt and the politics of friendship*. London/New York: Bloomsbury.

Nixon, J. (Ed.). (2017). *Higher education in austerity Europe*. London/New York: Bloomsbury.

Nixon, J. (2018a). Universities as civic spaces: In the footsteps of Arendt and jaspers. In R. Barnett & M. A. Peters (Eds.), *The idea of the university: Contemporary perspectives volume 2* (pp. 447–460). New York/Bern/Berlin/Brussels/Vienna/Oxford/Warsaw: Peter Lang.

Nixon, J. (2018b). *Rosa Luxemburg and the struggle for democratic renewal*. London: Pluto Press.

Nixon, J. (2019). Taking responsibility: Truth, trust, and justice. In P. Gibbs, J. Jameson, & A. Elwick (Eds.), *Values of the University in a Time of uncertainty* (pp. 185–197). Cham: Springer.

Said, E. W. (2004). *Humanism and democratic criticism*. New York: Columbia University Press.

Schier, S. E., & Eberly, T. E. (2018). *The trump presidency: Outsider in the oval office*. Lanham/London: Rowman and Littlefield.

Snyder, T. (2017). *On tyranny: Twenty lessons from the twentieth century*. London: Bodley Head.

Tucker, A. (2020). *Democracy against liberalism: Its rise and fall*. Cambridge/Medford: Polity Press.

Veck, W. (2020). Hannah Arendt, education and the refugee crisis: Natality, compensatory education and assimilation. In W. Veck & H. Gunter (Eds.), *Hannah Arendt on educational thinking and practice in dark times: Education for a world in crisis*. Bloomsbury: London/New York.

Villa, D. (1999). *Politics, philosophy, terror: Essays on the thought of Hannah Arendt*. Princeton: Princeton University Press.
Villa, D. (2001). *Socratic citizenship*. Princeton/Oxford: Princeton University Press.
Young-Bruehl, E., & Kohn, J. (2001). What and how we learned from Hannah Arendt: An exchange of letters. In M. Gordon (Ed.), *Hannah Arendt and education: Renewing our common world* (pp. 225–256). Boulder/Oxford: Westview Press pp.

Jon Nixon is a visiting professor at Middlesex University, UK, and writes within the field of intellectual history and cultural theory. His authored books include *Hannah Arendt: The Promise of Education (Springer, 2020), Rosa Luxemburg and the Struggle for Democratic Renewal (Pluto Press*, 2018), *Gadamer: The Hermeneutical Imagination* (Springer, 2017) and *Hannah Arendt and the Politics of Friendship* (Bloomsbury, 2015). He has recently edited *Higher Education in Austerity Europe* (Bloomsbury, 2017), which includes contributions from leading educationists across Europe. His trio of authored books on higher education policy and practice were published between 2008 and 2012: *Interpretive Pedagogies for Higher Education* (Bloomsbury, 2012), *Higher Education and the Public Good* (Bloomsbury, 2011) and *Towards the Virtuous University* (Routledge, 2008). He is currently completing a book – to be published by Routledge – entitled *Erich Auerbach and the Secular World: Literary Criticism, Historiography and Post-Colonial Theory*.

Chapter 5
Can Academics Be Trusted to Be Truth-Tellers More Than the Rest of Society?

Paul Gibbs

Introduction

This chapter advocates that a university education and the community that supplies it have, at its core, a mission to enable its communities of scholars (staff and students) to make judgements on what can be trusted and that they, themselves, should have a special duty to seek to be truth-tellers. This is a duty upon which society can rely when formulated in academic statements, being able to trust that academics' rhetoric avoids deliberate falsehoods. It is predicated on a notion of trust built on the reliability of concepts and actions which, when tested, produce evidence in correspondence[1] with what is proposed as the outcomes. In this sense, truth is both an epistemic reality and of moral concern and the desire to 'think freely entails that one also desires to think rightly, not for conceptual or psychological reasons, but for moral ones' (Rider 2018: 39): the former in predicting our realities and the latter in value associated with the intention of the action. In building societally reasoned networks of preference and acceptances of 'truth' in this sense, we reveal ourselves both as self-trusting and as trustworthy people.

This requires trust in oneself as an academic to make those judgements, an obligation to make those judgements (which warrants academic freedom) and the courage to speak out when such judgements might be unpopular, risky and potentially unsafe for oneself. However, especially at a time of complexity as O'Neill (2002: 6)

---

[1] I am aware of the philosophical debate regarding truth and use this definition as a working concepts to help build an argument. I also do not intend correspondence to be limited to only certain form of rationale confirmation.

P. Gibbs (✉)
East European University, Tbilisi, Georgia
e-mail: p.gibbs@mdx.ac.uk

suggests, it might be unrealistic that trusting in others should 'require a watertight guarantee of others' performance'; it might be wrong to expect that certain standards are to be maintained by our credentialled and appointed truth-tellers. I would rather assert that, in a time of complexity, we can expect the intent of truth-telling and that this should be a duty placed on academics. Academics as experts, like other professionals, have a duty to speak.

This is not to expect academics to be 'good' in some divine idealistic and medieval sense but to offer evidence, justification and interpretation in knowledge areas where they have recognised expertise. Their audiences should be sceptical where academics, or representation of them, offer advice in commercial settings (e.g. advertisements, 'technical advisors' to television programmes without veto powers or sponsored research) where the purpose is to exploit rather than inform.

Trust has attracted the attention of higher education scholars in a number of forms and for a number of purposes. Moreover, it is public trust, a trust resulting from a reasoned expectation that involves both confidence and reliance that these educational institutions are 'acting responsibly and for the common good' (Bird 2013: 25). However, when political authority and the media pronounce negatively about vice chancellors' pay and the tuition fee system and threaten government interference in European Studies curricula, how can the university within such a milieu speak out against them when, I suggest, it has become compliant with it in many respects? What advantage does it gain in doing so, and how can it enable students to make informed and reasoned decisions on what to believe?

This is important, for in the current era of marketisation, according to Jameson, there is a 'loss of trust' (2012: 411) in UK universities, manifest in government rhetoric and its agencies of quality control. This is not a new observation. As early as 1992, Bok was seeking ways in which US universities could go about restoring public trust. Ten years later, O'Neill wrote of 'crises of trust' (2002: 45) and, after another decade, Collini (2012) made reference to an 'erosion of trust' (2012: 108) in a context where free speech interacts with social media and all are subjected to the force of the transient present.

One of the consequences of the massive changes in higher education is that of the power relationship between teacher and student, owing to its marketisation and its nesting within society rather than being outside of, but critically commenting upon, society. This has led to an accommodation of the prevailing societal values set by the powerful or as a consequence of their values and not a questioning of them through critical reasoning and speaking out, with authority, against what is morally wrong, dehumanising and self-serving about society. Without addressing such issues, any notion of an educated person as one with freedom to think and act becomes superficial, leaving scholars and students in a place that can lack personal integrity. Moreover, in support of Sockett[2] (1989), this seems counter to liberal, transformative principles and leaves many universities in a state of self-deception,

---

[2] His opening line of that paper is 'I take education to be a moral business' (Sockett 1989: 33).

because they are seemingly espousing policies and procedures that undermine what, broadly, a liberal education might be.

Trustworthiness of the University

Trust has attracted attention in the general field of education (where Tschannen-Moran and Hoy's (2000) study of schools is seminal), but relatively little work has been done in higher education. Ghosh et al. (2001), Shoho and Smith (2004), Author (2007), Macfarlane (2009), Smith and Shoho (2007),[3] Carvalho and de Oliveira Mota (2010) and Gibbs and Dean (2015) have provided reviews of the significance of trust within the university and the building of student institutional relationships. The nature of liberal education and the ideal of emancipation through rational autonomy have led to an evolving, enduring and empathetic delivery. Because of its transformative, rather than economically defined, purpose, neoliberal education is dependent on a truth relationship between the provider of the educational process and the recipient: one does not know what one is expected to receive, as it has to be jointly created. In this sense, having trust in the hegemony of state or market control of education is to believe that it will not be used to exploit and manipulate recipients; it will tell the truth in appropriate discourse styles.

An educative relationship of this nature between student and academic without enduring evidence of the trustworthiness in terms of their authorship, accurate assessment of work, their competence in pedagogical practice and their verifiable command of appropriate knowledge, much like that of authority, may be, and ideally should be, cynically received. This is because it appears to grant power, coercion and control to the party in whom trust has been vested. Such an imbalance of power is accepted because the powerful in the relationship are experts and students are not, but it is more than that. It requires that the lecturers recognise and deliver to their obligation of truth-telling within the academy. Moreover, it requires students to take a stance on what they can trust in themselves, not succumbing to what Furedi (2016) calls the 'infantilisation' of higher education but to make existential judgements and assertions based on what they know is feasible and likely to be the truth and, from that position, not to fear the lies of a post-trust era.

This obligation remains even when students become consumers, imbued with certain sovereignty to question delivery methods, value for money and appropriate assessment mechanisms. When academic institutions accept the performative ideal of their function, the students' views on matters are granted equal authority. The expert is stripped not of inherent but of ascribed expertise by the digitally literate and populistically informed student.

---

[3] In this study, the authors found 'an inverse relationship between trust and academic rank'. To that end, the data suggest that the level of faculty trust tends to diminish with ascending academic rank' (Smith and Shoho 2007: 133).

If higher education institutions, like any institutions in society, are to sustain themselves, then faith in their truth-tellers needs to be continually evaluated and renewed, for faith implies a lowering of the level of scrutiny in the acceptance of what they say. In order to do that, they must confront the notion of self-deception that allows for the seeking of truth to be turned into faith, or believing in, and appeasement towards, others. We must hold ourselves and others to account. As O'Neill proposes, we need ways of distinguishing trustworthy from untrustworthy informants. Moreover, if society trusts what universities say about how they can facilitate choice and opportunities for a student's future, our appointment to the academy should signal that. Carelessly embracing league tables when it suits and critically objecting to them when it does not, arguing for social mobility which is not evident or lending academic authority to populist media programmes does nothing to build confidence in the university as a site of truth-tellers.

Amongst the things that we can do to help students is to tell them the truth of what they have been offered for their futures. This is, I believe, a role that is a duty of academics to transcend their disciplines in preparing students for a world in which their contribution is significant and worthy. Indeed, these duties of truth-telling, as Weil (1953) has advocated in the first line of her book *The Needs for Roots*, 'come before that of rights, which is subordinate and relative to the former' (1953: 3). One of these obligations explored by Weil (ibid, 36–39) is truth and the obligations of the truth-teller. If accepted, this might require us to consider a reorientation of the notion of the rights-based contemporary university (O'Neill 2002). This seems to have roots in the Socratic notion of the harmony of truth-telling and behaviour as revealed in 'Laches' as care for the soul: a caring for the morality of oneself through knowing, trusting and being the stance that one takes for oneself. This requires a sense of courage to grasp freedom to be for oneself amongst others. As universities become more instrumental, extended and digital, they are less conducive to such freedoms and so may act in ways that encourage a fiction of the 'good' future, built upon oppression, super surveillance and a lack of hope. At policy level, for instance, it can be seen in the recent UK duplicitous encouragement of free speech in the government's Counter-Terrorism and Security Act 2015, which reaffirms universities' obligation to protect freedom of speech yet requires them to have 'due regard' for the risk of 'radicalisation' amongst students. Its implementation guidelines have been considered discriminatory, and even racist.

One of the consequences of the massive changes in contemporary higher education is the shift in the power relationship between teachers and students, due to the marketisation of higher education and the changes in role for institutions to reflect, rather than critically to comment upon, society. This has led to the assimilation of market values in their own practices, away from a Socratic questioning of them through critical reasoning and speaking out: but this is not new.

However, a lack of originality is no reason to accept self-serving and self-deceptive, politically motivated directives that are imposed upon educational institutions ostensibly to enable greater transparency and accountability, but whose functions are more to do with controls. In the UK, this can be seen in the confusion and inaccuracies of the excellence framework in research, teaching and knowledge in terms of 'what it does' and 'what is it meant to measure'. Ironically, the salary hikes of those whose have led the implementation of these policies on behalf of the government have had their own rewards questioned: a betrayal of those betraying liberal education.

Self-Deception as an Existential Dilemma

Amongst those who have contributed to the notion of self-deception (and a notion of self-consciousness) are Descartes, Kant, Kierkegaard, Wittgenstein, Heidegger and Sartre. Indeed, Neuber (2016) suggests that many find compelling Jean-Paul Sartre's ontological account of 'bad faith' as intentional self-deception. For Sartre, self-deception is accounted for by assuming that there are intrinsically self-deceptive epistemic states that provide claims of certainty, nevertheless accompanied by an inbuilt and incorruptible awareness of being unwarranted. If one does not care about the thoughts of the masses, then one has no reason to self-deceive. One is morally isolated, hedonistic and prudent. Furthermore, if one is concerned about how others might perceive oneself or if one wants to avoid the painful and harmful consequences of one's actions, then self-deception seems feasible and rational, in the sense of the protection of one's social identity or how one wants to be seen.

In Sartre's view, one is culpable for one's own self-deception; it is always intentional. The same applies to Kierkegaard's willed deception, which extends beyond the immediate and ignores the phenomenological reality of one's agency in favour of a personal interpretation that is counter to the evidence presented by one's behaviour– the game of flirting or waiting.[4] As Lopez has suggested, a 'lie or deception can be almost about anything, but bad faith is always, at its root, a lie to oneself about one's facticity and transcendence' (2016: 23). As a lecturer, I might feel forced to comply with pedagogical practices of a certain type, even though I disagree with their value (e.g. online learning), because that is what is required, rather than building arguments against this approach based on student learning models and a lower quality of engagement. I forgo my options to act as an expert pedagogue, because I deceive myself into believing that I have no option and thus abdicate my responsibilities, both as a pedagogue and as a truth-teller. I deceive myself and become compliant with that to which I object. This remains true of the acts of compliance of senior managers with regard to the multiplying excellence framework, which was designed to control but which is accepted readily, although seen as flawed, as in the public's interest and for its protection.

Indeed, Sartre (1992: 38) compares bad faith with ignorance, claiming that ignorance 'conditions knowledge and is defined by it, that is both as possibility of knowledge and as possibility of remaining in ignorance' (ibid, 28). When we fail to act to verify the truth, we hide behind three forms of ignorance: innocence,

---

[4] See Constanti and Author's (2004) discussion on emotional labour and higher education teaching.

contemplation and abstract knowledge. It is the second of these where truth is already constituted before us by a superior authority, leaving us not to question but to act upon what it ascribes as truth. Confronting this ignorance by making conspicuous that which is intended to be hidden is brave, when academics are contracted employees and notions of academic freedoms are questioned (Fish 2014).

In its extreme, self-deception is the ploy of using a deliberate and irresponsible misreading of situations to avoid facing one's responsibility or the negation of self by others.[5] This is both being with others and observing them for one's benefit. It is using others as a means to an end or giving up to others that which is central to one's autonomy, the responsibility for one's actions. What is more, it can readily lead to alienation or self-estrangement from what one might become, by losing oneself in the dualism of object and subject or in the determinism of others.[6] To avoid commitment through which authenticity can be realised, the competencies of being-for-others may be used as a sham of security for inauthentic relationships and engagements. Deception is irrational, for one remains personally culpable for the consequences of one's actions. These self-deceptive acts are destructive, and, if they are rendered against others, 'the withdrawal of respect is its only fit punishment' (Kant 1992: 91).

Such condemnation makes it imperative that members of the academy are able to recognise in their practice where they are deceiving themselves and, because of it, the contagion where such self-deception affects and influences others. Moreover, the social contagion of self-deception leads to a state of negation of trust in the trustworthy. This is evident in examples of academic and managerial practice in the institution. These may include the following: sticking with favoured theories rather than seeking evidence that might contest them, attributing more effort to one's contribution to a paper than is fair, interrupting government policy in a way that is in one's own self-interest rather than the institution's, allowing unintended grade inflation to increase student satisfaction and allowing one's own ideological perspective to contort the needs of students.

Deception and self-deception may be identified in the policy and practice of higher education. They can be seen in how education has drifted from being an end in itself towards a supply economics imperative or where scholars seek favourable student evaluations rather than stretching their capabilities, fuelled by emotional labour and creating personal brands. Although such practices seem counter to

---

[5] In an interesting passage, MacMurray (1995: 69–70) writes: 'Since mutuality is constitutive for the personal, it follows that "I" need "you" in order to be myself. My primary fear is, therefore, that "you" will not respond to my need, and that in consequence my personal existence will be frustrated.' Clearly, the risk to question others, particularly those in authority, is a risky business for the affirmation of oneself.

[6] Sartre deals with the nature of lying as universal in both 'Being and Nothingness' (1986: 48–49) and in 'Existentialism and the Emotion'. There he writes when confronting the liar, 'what would happen if everyone looked at things that way? There is no escaping this disturbing thought except by a kind of double-dealing. A man who lies and makes excuses for himself by saying "not everyone does that" is someone with an uneasy conscience, because the act of lying implies that a universal value is conferred upon the lie' (1990: 18–19).

principles of liberal, transformative education, they present a dilemma. Should we facilitate students and staff to speak the truth to each other when this might not be in their best interests, in a world that encourages compliance rather than free thinking, a world where we are under constant surveillance and are often herded by the industrial and commercial global powers? How, morally, should we prepare them to help them to flourish?

What Can the Higher Education Institution Do?

Those privileged to work in higher education might consider obligations associated with these privileges and conferred status to confront others, when others' opinions are not worthy of acceptance, since self-deception leads to loss of trust in the trustworthy, and a construction of reality in which sources of authority lose all saliency as a source of truth. They become providers of personal justification, where one's own judgement overrides that of others. These deceptions may be hidden in the pretext of a university education that is value for money, for the majority of students, rather than as a social mechanism to manage an increase in age-group demographics.

Such political interventions, intent on deceiving the public, are typified by the revelation of Arendt (1972). In her paper on the systematic lies, deception and self-deception in the Pentagon during America's involvement in Indochina, she shows clearly how these were used to manipulate public opinion. As Peters suggests, it takes little imagination to understand that the notion of facts and evidence in a post-truth era not only affects politics and science but 'becomes a burning issue for education at all levels' (2017: 565). Moreover, he suggests that, as education has seemingly undergone a digital turn, criticality has been mostly avoided and replaced by narrow conceptions of standards and state-mandated instrumental and utilitarian pedagogies. Further, he suggests that this has led to a limiting of focus on job training, 'rather than a broader critical citizenship agenda for participatory democracy' (ibid.).

A comprehensive discussion of trusting of the truth within the confines of academic teaching practices is provided by Curzon-Hobson (2002). He argues that trust is a fundamental element in the pursuit of higher learning, for it is only through a sense of trust that students embrace an empowering experience of freedom, and the exercise of this freedom requires students and their teachers to take a risk:

> It challenges students to think and act according to their own perceptions without recourse to recitation or transcending ideals. This sense of freedom and the experience of risk is that which underpins students' projections to realise their unique potentiality. It requires a sensation of trust that is different from that which forms the bases of prescriptive accountability mechanisms, and is in fact marginalised by such practices. (Curzon-Hobson 2002: 226)

Reflection, evaluation and monitoring are acts of autonomous thinkers of the type that liberal education, and indeed industry, claim to want. These reflective practices also contribute to self-belief, knowledge and truth, which differentiate the self from others. To trust in one's own ability to make decisions on one's own preference is central to liberal ideals of autonomous, free action. To be able to accept the responsibility that this implies, of constituting a reasoned world reality, facilitates the ontological integration of self. It encourages creativity, confidence and community through the negotiation of shared realities. To reach that position, students must be able to distinguish between their justified confidence in their competence in certain arenas and where they are incompetent. Students are likely to retain their self-trust only while that which they hold as trustworthy maintains its social validity: they are able to argue rationally for what they hold to be true or to assimilate into what their community holds as truth. This revelation process, as we have seen, is interpreted by Tierney (2006) as a 'grammar of trust'.

Higher education should encourage self-trust through reasoned argument and debate. For students to be prepared to risk the socially constructed self to a process of authentic discovery of truth demands mutual and empathetic trust. Students need to trust that, if they stray too far from the commonality of experience, they will not be expelled or vilified as eccentrics or charlatans. This leads to sincerity and empathy and can manifest itself in the *praxis* of critical being (Barnett 1997). The recognition of the existence of the potential for such mutuality is held in the collective goodwill of all stakeholders of the institution and is (or, perhaps, ought to be) the basis of public trust in higher education institutions.

Academics have a dependency relationship with students that requires empathetic trust to avoid the potential for exploitation of the vulnerabilities of both student and academic. In relation to the discipline, academics are trusted by their peers to share common goals that include responsible conduct in research and authorship practices, no form of harassment and the avoidance of conflict of interest. These erode the fabric of trust on which worthwhile social interactions are constructed. A test of a profession's trust may take place when one of its numbers contravenes these principles. Is a sanction dependent on incompetence, assuming moral good intent, or is it based on the competence of deceit being caught?

Teaching in higher education also carries privileges and associated obligations: 'If we can clarify our perception of duty and gain public acceptance of it, we will have fulfilled an important obligation to the society that nurtures us. These obligations constitute the highest institutional form of academic duty' (Kennedy 1997: 22). These are the closing sentences in the first chapter of Kennedy's *Academic Duty*. By placing duty central to the notion of academics in higher education institutions, Kennedy identifies a moral responsibility for academics that offers a way of establishing the trust that was shared between the university sector and the general public. Nixon is more direct, in that the prime principle of the university is not academic freedom but academic duty. This duty is a duty of 'accuracy in one's beliefs, sincerity in respect of proclaiming those beliefs, authenticity in living according to the beliefs that one sincerely holds and recognition of other's right to do likewise' (2008: 28).

Duty itself and in the existential sense is not, however, the Kantian imperative of following given universals (although we might choose to act as if they did) nor the liberal balance of rights but is an accountability to oneself to have the courage and skill to interpret one's individuality within our world as a dialectic between oneself and humanity. In this, it is an ethical exercise and is built through trust as an implicit obligation – voluntarily accepted, in the case of an academic – to pursue worthy activities and not the mechanisms of competencies.

To re-establish such an obligation, if indeed it has really been missing, will not be a quick fix in this environment of managerialism. It might require a fundamental commitment to excellence for the revelation of the potentialities of those who offer themselves to the pursuit of higher education. It requires that academics speak out against falseness and not be complicit, either by commission or omission. To confront post-trust, an academic should not be an apologist for those who speak of their power, rather than to it. In this sense, I am reminded of Foucault's Paris lectures (2010) on *parrhesia*, of speaking to the truth and of Peters' (2003) discussion of truth-telling as an educational practice. To speak out when the consequence may be unfavourable to oneself requires courage and a reconstitution of what higher education has become. This is a return to an ethos of personal growth that better represents what humanity might become, rather than offering a service of blinkered higher skill training. Moreover, it requires the teacher to be trustworthy. It requires a form of self-trust that can avoid the deception of society and of oneself, a deception that was prevalent even before a post-trust era but which is more acute and accepted within it.

Concluding Remarks: Self-Trust at the Foundations of Higher Education

Trust education between student, tutor and institution has, in the main, been considered as a virtue of 'good' higher education. Within it, there are opportunities to question the importance of self and one's contribution to society, and this might well help to settle the purpose of higher education and why it needs to have public trust. Certainly, in an educational framework where the self has to expose its vulnerability to another, anything other than a moral duty of trusting care would make the offer of education potentially loaded and exploitative. Barnacle and Dall'Alba (2017) make this case well when they argue that care is not just for the physical welfare of students but should inform a conception of student engagement that resists, rather than unwittingly reinforces, performativity and neoliberal values (2017: 1328). Indeed, I follow Olafson (1998) in that a failure to respect others is a violation of the trust placed in us, as academics, by those to whom we are responsible.

The most important question for the future of higher education seems to be 'can we trust those who control it to deliver anything other than competencies aimed at securing employment, thus placing education in the hands of the industrialist, or is there a role for the professional educationalist?' To hold someone accountable for their use of state-sponsored education in the sense of value (of money, citizenship and morality) requires a clear statement of the expected responsibility and output. A competence model of education has benefits for those who feel attracted to this economic expediency model. However, the appropriateness of such business comparisons is debatable and, even if valid, changes not only the process of becoming but the very nature of the autonomous individual.

I suggest that a failure to speak out against bad faith in our engagements with students and within the institutions we work and for them, likewise to speak out to policy, can easily result for both students and educators in the objectification of the other. This is achieved by unwarrantedly placing an individual into one of the categories above 'so that his or her independence and responsibility as a human being is denied, and thereby stultifying his or her potential learning gain' (Blenkinsop and Waddington 2014: 10). As the primary aim of higher education, competency of trust replaces moral trust with the pragmatic and short-term notion of uncontextualised competency, which ultimately dilutes the moral dimension of the relationships embedded in what we expect from the university: quite simply, in what and in whom can we trust? Lastly, just how much do we care about truth and trust when we elect politicians whose only consistency is their history of deceit and self-deception?

References

Arendt, H. (1972). Lying in politics. In *The crisis of the republic*. New York: Harvest Books.
Author. (2007). Does advertising pervert higher education? Is there a case for resistance? *Journal of Marketing for Higher Education, 17*(1), 3–11.
Barnacle, R., & Dall'Alba, G. (2017). Committed to learn: Student engagement and care in higher education. *Higher Education Research & Development, 36*(7), 1326–1338.
Barnett, R. A. (1997). *Higher education: A critical business*. Buckingham: SRHE/Open University Press.
Bird, S. J. (2013). *Public trust and institutions of higher learning: Implications for professional responsibility*. London: Portland Press. http://www.portlandpress.com/pp/books/online/wg86/086/0025/0860025.pdf
Blenkinsop, S., & Waddington, T. (2014). Self-deception in the classroom: Educational manifestations of Sartre's concept of bad faith. *Educational Philosophy and Theory, 46*(14), 1–11.
Bok, D. (1992). Reclaiming the public trust. *Change, 24*(4), 12–19.
Carvalho, S., & de Oliveira Mota, M. (2010). The role of trust in creating value and student loyalty in relational exchanges between higher education institutions and their students. *Journal of Marketing for Higher Education, 20*(1), 145–165.
Collini, S. (2012). *What are universities for?* London: Penguin.
Constanti, P., & Author. (2004). Higher education teachers and emotional labour. *International Journal of Educational Management, 18*(4), 243–249.
Curzon-Hobson, A. (2002). A pedagogy of trust in higher learning. *Teaching in Higher Education, 7*(3), 265–276.
Fish, S. (2014). *Versions of academic freedom: From professionalism to revolution*. Chicago: Chicago University Press.
Foucault, P. (2010). *The government of self and others*. Basingstoke: Palgrave Macmillan.
Furedi, F. (2016). *What happened to the university?* London: Routledge.
Ghosh, A., Whipple, T. W., & Bryan, G. A. (2001). Student trust and its antecedents in higher education. *Journal of Higher Education, 72*(3), 322–340.

Gibbs, P., & Dean, A. (2015). Do higher education institutes communicate trust well? *Journal of Marketing Higher Education, 25*(2), 155–170.
Jameson, J. (2012). Leadership values, trust and negative capability: Managing the uncertainties of future English higher education. *Higher Education Quarterly, 66*(4), 391–414.
Kant, I. (1992). *Kant on education* (A. Churton, Trans.). Bristol: Thoemmes Press.
Kennedy, D. (1997). *Academic duty*. Cambridge, MA: Harvard University Press.
Lopez, J. K. (2016). *Self-deception's puzzle and processes*. Lanham: Lexington Books.
Macfarlane, B. (2009). A leap of faith: The role of trust in higher education teaching. *Nagoya Journal of Higher Education, 9*, 221–238.
MacMurray, J. (1995). *Persons in relation*. London: Faber and Faber.
Neuber, S. (2016). Self-awareness and self-deception: A Sartrean perspective. *Continental Philosophy Review, 49*(4), 485–507.
Nixon, J. (2008). *Towards the virtuous university the moral bases of academic practice*. London: Sage.
O'Neill, O. (2002). *A question of trust* (BBC Reith lectures). Cambridge: Cambridge University Press.
Olafson, F. A. (1998). *Heidegger and the ground of ethics*. Cambridge: Cambridge University Press.
Peters, M. (2003). Truth-telling as an educational practice of the self: Foucault, *parreshia* and the ethics of subjectivity. *Oxford Review of Education, 29*, 207–223.
Peters, M. (2017). Education in a post-trust world. *Educational Philosophy and Theory, 49*(6), 563–566.
Plato's Apology, G. M. A. Grube, Trans. in *The complete works* (J. Copper, Ed., pp. 17–36). Cambridge: Hackett Publishing.
Plato's Laches, R. K. Sprague, Trans. in *The complete works* (J. Copper, pp. 708–745). Cambridge: Hackett Publishing.
Rider, S. (2018). On knowing how to tell the truth. In M. A. Peters, S. Rider, M. Hyvonen, & T. Besley (Eds.), *Post-truth, fake new* (pp. 27–42). Singapore: Springer.
Sartre, J.-P. (1992). *Truth and existence*. Chicago: University of Chicago Press.
Shoho, A. R., & Smith, P. A. (2004). An exploratory analysis of faculty trust in higher education. In W. K. Hoy & C. G. Miskel (series eds), *Educational Administration, Policy, and Reform: Research and measurement* (pp. 279–303). Greenwich: Information Age.
Smith, P. A., & Shoho, A. R. (2007). Higher education trust, rank and race: A conceptual and empirical analysis. *Innovation in Higher Education, 32*(3), 125–138.
Sockett, H. (1989). A moral epistemology of practice? *Cambridge Journal of Education, 19*(1), 33–39.
Tierney, W. G. (2006). *Trust and the public good*. New York: Peter Langer.
Tschannen-Moran, M., & Hoy, W. K. (2000). Trust: A multidisciplinary analysis of the nature, meaning, and measurement of trust. *Review of Educational Research, 70*, 547–493.
Weil, C. (1953). *The need for roots: A prelude to a declaration of duties toward mankind*. London: Routledge.

Paul Gibbs is a professor and director of the Doctoral School, East European University. He is an emeritus professor of Middlesex University, founder of the Centre for Education Research and Scholarship, and visiting professor at UTS Sydney and Azerbaijan University. He is a fellow of ATLAS and of the Centre for Higher Education Policy, New College Oxford. He is an educator and researcher, having taught notions of transdisciplinarity alongside social realism and Heideggerian hermeneutics, and has over thirty successful transdisciplinary professional doctorate students. He has published twenty books on topics ranging from the marketing of higher education to vocationalism and higher education and has published more than hundred academic articles. He is also the series editor of *SpringerBriefs on Key Thinkers in Education*.

Part II
Student Being and Becoming

Chapter 6
Higher Education: Learning How to Pay Attention

Sharon Rider

Introduction

About 12 years ago, I found myself elected Vice Dean of the Faculty of Arts at Uppsala University, a commission that I held for 6 years. It was during this period that I came to see philosophical problems as falling roughly into two categories. In the one case, perhaps the most common, they are internal to the discipline. One might call these "intellectual problems." They arise in and out of technical distinctions and the accepted conventions of the conceptual apparatus found in journals and seminar rooms. In these cases, one may look for examples from "real life" to illustrate or buttress a point, but the problems are formulated first and foremost within the prevailing framework, not out of a need for clarity in order to make a decision about what has to be done or about how we should think in order to act. Then there is another kind of philosophical problem, which begins precisely in uncertainty, doubt, or hesitation, or, as Wittgenstein says, not finding your way about. Over the years, such "deep" problems of philosophy tend to become institutionalized and scholasticized, that is, they give rise to the various techniques and concepts that various schools of thought take as their points of departure. It is this second category of problems, ones that are not themselves technical in nature, that were in the forefront of my mind in my capacity as Vice Dean.

Since I was obliged to make decisions that would have direct or indirect consequences for others, I really needed to get clear on questions such as the following: By what means do we determine that what we have produced in our classrooms and journals constitutes "knowledge"? How do we arrive at the criteria for establishing that a phenomenon is "better understood" or that a certain idea has been

---

S. Rider (✉)
Department of Philosophy, Uppsala University, Uppsala, Sweden
e-mail: sharon.rider@filosofi.uu.se

© The Author(s), under exclusive license to Springer Nature Switzerland AG 2021
S. S. E. Bengtsen et al. (eds.), *The University Becoming*, Debating Higher Education: Philosophical Perspectives 6,
https://doi.org/10.1007/978-3-030-69628-3_6

"discredited"? What is the connection between the two? What is the role of method? What are the consequences of institutionalization for conceptualization? Such questions are, after all, implicit when we approve course plans for new disciplines or formulate curricula for PhD programs. At times, I had to render judgments involving fields beyond my own areas of expertise, or even competence, such as when hiring or promoting faculty members in, say, Egyptology or Library Sciences. On what basis could I do that? Only by trusting the expertise of others. And on what grounds did I do that? In short, I was, not merely in theory, but in fact, confronted by a host of serious questions having to do with, inter alia, reliability, normativity, and certainty.

I asked myself: What are we doing here, actually? Why do we do the things we do? Perhaps we ought to do them differently? Should we rethink the whole idea of the Arts—of the university? In this way, committee meetings, interviews with prospective faculty members, written statements in response to inquiries from higher management, reviews of PhD programs and faculty board discussions of course plans, and so forth together formed a kind of off-stage presence in my academic work as a teacher and scholar. As I delved more deeply into questions having to do with the meaning and mission of higher learning, I was heartened to see that they had occupied many of the greatest minds of the twentieth century. There was, in short, plenty of material from which to take my bearings. The following is one trajectory among others that I found helpful for orienting my thinking about the point and purpose of the university.

Still, one might reasonably question whether a recondite academic discipline such as philosophy has become can tell us anything significant regarding real-life issues such as threats to academic freedom, the diminished status of the humanities in society, and so forth. My response is that it all depends upon what idea of having something worth telling ("knowledge") is at stake. Since the 1920s, "philosophical anthropology" has become a term of art for an approach to the so-called problem of knowledge with roots in Immanuel Kant's practical anthropology (Kant 2006) and Ludwig Feuerbach's anthropological theology and associated with names such as Max Scheler (2008), Martin Buber (1945; 1965), Ernst Cassirer (1944), and Paul Ricoeur (2016).[1] An important distinguishing characteristic of this manner of analyzing questions having to do with knowledge, thinking, willing, and judgment is that it does not take empirical psychology as its starting point for understanding mentality. I mean by this that "the mental" is here not understood as brain states or events, hidden happenings in the head, as it were, nor is "the mind" and its actions

---

[1] Immanuel Kant, *Anthropology from a Pragmatic Point of View*, trans. Robert Louden (Cambridge: Cambridge University Press 2006); Max Scheler, *The Human Place in the Cosmos*, övers. Manfred S. Frings (Evanston, Ill: Northwestern University Press, 2008); see also Martin Buber, "The Philosophical Anthropology of Max Scheler," *Philosophy and Phenomenological Research*, vol. 6, no. 2, 1945, pp. 307–321; Martin Buber, *The Knowledge of Man: A Philosophy of the Interhuman* (New York: Harper & Row, 1965); Ernst Cassirer, *An Essay on Man: An Introduction to a Philosophy of Human Culture* (Yale University Press, New Haven, 1944); and Paul Ricoeur, *Philosophical Anthropology*, Johann Michel and Jérôme Porée (eds.), trans. David Pellauer (Cambridge: Polity, 2016)

conceived in terms of broad sociological categories, but rather as something that is always already on display and is expressed and manifested in specific human institutions, practices, and artifacts. Taking the perspective of philosophical anthropology, I think, we might locate the source of a number of problems in contemporary higher education in fundamental misconceptions about the conditions of thought that are based on psychologistic and sociological premises about the nature of thinking, or human mentality, which premises may be more equivocal than we may think.

This is not to say that we cannot or ought not make use of results from inquiries in psychology, for instance. But as helpful as they might be, they cannot in themselves provide an adequate answer to the question that has been on my mind for many years, to wit: Has our way of thinking, our mentality, changed fundamentally without our noticing? If so, in what does this change consist? And what are the ramifications for higher education?

In this paper, I will discuss the idea that the university should provide a training of the mind that is not reducible to techniques for the efficacious screening and shifting of information. That doesn't mean that the latter is unnecessary or undesirable. To the contrary, given how bombarded we are with information from morning to night in the digital age, it is clearly beneficial, essential even, that we learn how to manage it all and to navigate treacherous waters with skill. Nonetheless, there is a risk that we devote so much effort to developing methods and protocols for preparatory and prophylactic information management that we lose sight of the question of why we read, study, teach, and learn. There is especially a risk that a re-orientation in *how* we read and study ultimately implies a transmutation of *why* we read, the aim and function of reading and studying themselves. As our proficiency in scanning and skimming becomes second nature, it can come to supplant our hard-won aptitude for careful analysis, concentration, reflection, and self-correction (Piper 2012; Turkle 2015; Wolf 2018). In short, we should not take our capacity for focused attention for granted. Indeed, one might think that in our era of perpetual distraction, the question of what is required for paying attention is more urgent than ever.

Pedagogical Form and Intellectual Content

In the last few decades, the use of graphs, pictures, and film clips has become de rigueur in higher education, even when the content of the presentation is in no way supported by the accompaniment of images or explicated by summary PowerPoint rubrics. While it is still common in philosophy to lecture without multimedia, it has become a sine qua non of academic professionalism in other fields. A younger colleague of mine from the educational sciences was aghast on one occasion when I gave a keynote without slides. In her field, she said, that would be a sign of disrespect, signaling that I didn't bother to come prepared. I was rather disheartened to hear this. To my mind, the time I might devote to putting together a polished presentation of slides was better spent arranging by thoughts, checking my sources, and reworking my wording. After all, as far back as the days of Socrates, philosophy is, if anything, thinking about thinking, or discourse about discourse, which is to say: talk about talk. Naturally, giving your audience or interlocutors signposts in the form of outlines, illustrations, headings, and key words to remind them of the basic structure of your reasoning is often helpful. Even Socrates would from time to time make use of other media. He might, for instance, draw the lines of a square on the ground to help a slave boy solve a geometric problem, as in the *Meno*. But in the main, he just conversed with people.

At the same time, emphasis on the form of presentation has two drawbacks. The first is that it can give a false impression of rigor, as if the symmetry of the visual model or the numbered headings ensures coherency—i.e., as if the arrangement of the titles and images were the content. On the other hand, one could, of course, present quite intricate and detailed arguments in subheadings and sub-subheadings; but then the whole point of visual representation—transparency and legibility—is lost. You might as well just talk. It is the second disadvantage that I want to stress, since it is actually the topic of my paper. I mean that arranging one's thoughts in neat little packages to facilitate the assimilation of the material means requiring less effort on the part of the audience. I want to propose that having to *listen* to a line of thought, like *looking* rather than merely seeing, taking one's *own* notes on the basis of one's *own* best attempts to understand what is right, wrong, or just indifferent about what is being said, and, at the same time, reflect on the questions and doubts to which they lead, is the very essence of thinking and learning at higher levels. As John Dewey stressed, to the extent that we are thinking at all, we are all always learners. The university is the institutionalization of the insight that thinking requires effort.

Even if we say that the ability to pay close attention is innate in human beings, it is a capacity that needs to be activated and practiced to be realized. Babies see and hear things. They may be intrigued, even riveted, by a color, shape, movement, or sound. But by the same token, they can be diverted by another color or movement. What they cannot do is intentionally bracket out actual or potential distractions in order to pursue a thought from beginning to end. In this strict sense, they cannot be said to be "paying attention" when they stare at the rolling red ball. But what is it that we adults do when we look, listen, take notice, or concentrate on something? One might characterize the history of philosophical and scientific thinking in the West as the attempt to discover or formulate an answer to that question, which would mean to capture more precisely what we do when we are *thinking*, properly speaking. What has been sought, one could say, is a method that would keep thinking in line and on track when we so desire or when circumstances require.

Think, for instance, of *diaeresis*, the principle of analysis that is so central to Plato's later dialogues,[2] by which means the interlocutors are meant to arrive at an adequate definition for something by repeating the procedure of dividing it into two parts and eliminating one alternative. One might also consider Descartes' methodological doubt, that is, the concentrated effort to doubt all that is in principle

---

[2] I'm thinking here of Plato's *Phaedrus*, the *Sophist*, the *Statesman* and the *Philebus*, but also the *Laws* and the *Timaeus*.

dubitable to see if it were possible to moor thinking on epistemic terra firma. David Hume's experimental method, Immanuel Kant's critical philosophy, G.W.F. Hegel's dialectical argumentation, Karl Popper's critical rationalism, or Hermann Weyl's *Besinnung* (Weyl 1955) can all be viewed in this light.[3] But perhaps the most ambitious contribution to philosophy in terms of "attention" is Edmund Husserl's attempt to build an entire philosophical system on the connection between attention and intention. This entailed focusing on how the act of intending or taking notice constitutes its object, the content of thought. As this essay is not concerned with the idea of reduction or Husserl's phenomenological project as a whole, I will not attempt to argue one way or another about how to interpret either. Here, I simply want to remind the reader that "attention" has in one way or another been a central question for philosophy and suggest that this question is intimately bound up with fundamental problems in teaching, learning, and education. My specific aim in what follows is to offer a partial answer to the question of what makes higher education "higher" in light of what I have said thus far about "attention." In particular, I will discuss the conditions of possibility for paying attention in terms of time, place, and the embodiment or situatedness of thinking.

Conceptual Form and Academic Content

Let us revisit Kant for a moment. *The Critique of Judgment* was long overshadowed by the first two critiques, *The Critique of Pure Reason* and *The Critique of Practical Reason*. But since the middle of the twentieth century, Kant's ideas about judgment have had a significant influence not only on aesthetics but also on political and cultural theory (Arendt 1981; Gadamer 1989)[4]. There is also much to be gained from paying attention to certain crucial passages to be found there when we contemplate higher education and intellectual character formation. We might first of all notice what Kant has to say about what is required for the development of an "enlightened" or "cosmopolitan" mentality or way of thinking. He argues that the free exchange of ideas and evaluations is both a consequence of and a precondition for the mature exercise of judgment. In the famous paragraph §40, Kant discusses different senses in which one can speak of a common human understanding, which can be expressed as three "maxims" of enlightened thinking. These all have the character of exhortations to the individual to (1) think for himself; (2) put himself in the place of everyone else; and (3) order his thoughts so that they are consistent. These three maxims are, respectively, the maxim of unprejudiced thought, the maxim of enlarged thought, and the maxim of consecutive thought.

---

[3] See especially "Insight and Reflection," T. L. Saaty & F. J. Weyl (eds.), *The Spirit and Uses of the Mathematical Sciences* (New York, McGraw-Hill, 1955), pp. 281–301.

[4] We can thank especially Hans-Georg Gadamer (*Truth and Method*) and Hannah Arendt (*Life of the Mind*) for calling attention to the practical consequences of Kant's idea of judgment, elucidated in his third critique.

Notice that these are all actions of a sort, things that we *do*, not processes that simply occur in our minds when we are confronted with a phenomenon. Kant explains that reason is a faculty whose nature is to be active and autonomous. Passivity belongs to the heteronomy of reason, also called prejudice. According to Kant, the greatest prejudice of all is to see the world and its workings as beyond the grasp of human reason. This picture, Kant says, renders us intellectually inert, enslaved by and obligated to the authority of others. A man whose mind has been enlarged, on the other hand, however limited his natural gifts, can be educated to disregard the "subjective private conditions of his own judgment, by which so many others are confined, and reflect upon it from a universal point of view (which he can only determine by placing himself at the standpoint of others)" (Kant 1951, p. 137). This is why the second maxim is crucial. Enlightenment means being able to see clearly that each and every one of us, insofar as we are human beings, has starting points or assumptions that are, from someone else's point of view, contingent and can reasonably be called into question. If there is no such thing as a passive exercise of reason, then the foremost goal of education must be to activate its use in the learner. And the way to do this is by making him grapple with thoughts that are not his own and the existence of which he must somehow integrate into his thinking (which might, of course, take the form of rejection, but only after it has been duly thought through). Autonomous reason is always active in the sense that it entails engagement, an effort to resist the pressures of one's own inclinations, on the one hand, and the assumed authority of others or "common sense," on the other. The third maxim, viz., that of consecutive thought, "is the most difficult to attain, and can only be achieved through the combination of the both former, and after the constant observance of them has grown into habit" (Kant 1951, p. 135–138).

Kant calls the first of these maxims "the maxim of understanding" because understanding is, as it were, something of which we are all already capable to a greater or lesser degree. The question is how to use our understanding, and Kant's answer is that thinking is something that we have to do ourselves. Nobody can do it for us. The second, "the maxim of judgment," requires a challenge to that understanding, its cultivation or refinement. This requires shifting our perspective by trying to understand our own ideas from another point of view. The third entails a sustained self-critique regarding how well we have followed the first and second maxims, which is to say the thinker's critical examination of his own thoughts. This "maxim of reason" tells us to be always on alert that we may have erred somewhere. Taken together, they are Kant's recipe for autonomous thought and action. On a Kantian account, then, what a higher education can do for students is to offer them an intellectual experience that makes them think: actively, impartially, and logically. They are to be lead to see that their own thinking is conditioned, to interrogate those conditions, and to learn to address those conditions critically and correct any erroneous conceptions arising out of them.

Notice here that enlightened thought as described here is not itself a subject matter (say, "critical thinking"). It cannot be taught and learned as a doctrine or method, because then it would not follow the three maxims for the proper conduct of the mind. It is rather a kind of comportment or bearing that can be engendered through practice in any discipline requiring a theoretical understanding. In this respect, all academic subjects are "universalistic" insofar as they strive to make every student think for himself, look at the problem he is trying to solve from a variety of possible approaches and perspectives, and subject his attempts at solving it to strict demands for coherence and clarity. Impartiality in our evaluations and universality in our reasoning are not givens but regulative ideals for leading the life of the mind.

A university education can offer innumerable occasions for exercising the students' capacity to think: Swedish tax law, axioms of non-Euclidean geometry, Swahili syntax, and Kant's three Critiques—all provide opportunities for activation. The crucial part is the insight that certain things are difficult to understand; they require industry and focus, and they take time. Perhaps the most recalcitrant and bewildering aspect of this ideal for education is that to be "rational," "enlightened," or "cultivated" in this sense has nothing to do with the content of learning. It's not concerned with any particular hypotheses, facts, doctrines, or theories as such but with the ultimate aim of the teaching and learning taking place, which, on this view, is to make the student pay attention to the conditions of his own thinking, the grounds for his own judgments, and the use of his own reason. Thus the essence of higher education is, in a way, not acquisition but negation: it is about engendering and enhancing the capacity for reason, which is to say, intellectual self-correction. To be clear, this form of thinking can only be actualized substantially, that is, by learning how to parse a sentence in Greek or prove a theorem in calculus. But without the capacity for autonomous thought, the student is not actually thinking, which means that he doesn't actually understand what he takes himself to know just because he "learned it" at college.

Confrontation with alien thought (which, as mentioned, can be everything from the intricacies of tax legislation to higher mathematics to the syntactic properties of an ancient language) means learning how to deal with the intellectual challenges posed by difficult tasks and texts. Taking our bearings from Kant's third Critique then, education means training in a rigorous kind of self-discipline in which the student is consistently challenged to think and think again. The first step is to get her to *hesitate*: to see that she does not know very well what she takes herself to know intimately (for instance, her native language) and make her understand what is required of her to know more. The second is to force her to recall and articulate what she might know very well without realizing it (her local surroundings, for instance) in such a way as to make her knowledge communicable and comprehensible to others and explicit to herself. Finally, she should deal with any and all cognitive dissonance that emerges from her attempts to assimilate foreign ideas, methods, or concepts. As Kant points out in a footnote, even if enlightenment might seem to be quite a simple matter, in practice it is very difficult to accomplish; it is both arduous and slow.[5] It takes *time*.

Not to allow one's reason to remain passive but to attain and maintain genuine agency and self-regulation is something that is often accompanied by the desire to

---

[5] Kant, *Critique of Judgement*, p. §40, p. 137, ftnte. 32

move beyond what is strictly speaking possible to know, and, importantly, there is no dearth of self-appointed authorities who will claim to be able to satisfy that desire. The single most demanding part of enlightenment is to acknowledge that its constitution is only "negative." Its essence is the application of one's reason to one's judgments: sustained self-regulation and self-correction, nothing more. But thinking and understanding require confrontation with a world of other minds and other thoughts (including, among other things, our best attempts at formulating, say, the laws of nature). This encounter ought to begin with what is so immediate that it is barely noticed, like the air we breathe. Therefore, the alpha and omega of learning and intellectual development, in an engineering program as in a course in Latin, is *paying attention*.

Learning How to Pay Attention

In our current cognitive climate of post-truth and fake news, the question of what constitutes grounds for sound judgment is ubiquitous. There is a sense that if we cannot say something with absolute certainty, then nothing anyone says is, strictly speaking, a question of knowledge or reason or understanding, but just different "identities" and "alternative narratives." The lesson of the passus in the *Critique of Judgement* cited above is that thinking can be characterized as the activity of making adequate judgments, the procedure for which entails not merely the possibility of failure, but the actuality of it. I can only learn, that is, correct an error in my thinking, if I've made one. I can only recognize a mistake on the basis of having made one before, just as I can only feel satisfied that I've made a proper judgment on the basis of recognizing what it means to do so. As Wittgenstein's reply to Moore's "Defense of Common Sense" in *On Certainty* is intended to show, all of our ostensible certainties themselves rest on myriad prior judgment calls:

§124 I want to say: We use judgments as principles of judgment.

§128: From a child up, I learnt to judge like this. *This is* judging.

§162: In general, I take as true what is found in textbooks, in geography for example. Why? I say: All these facts have been confirmed a hundred times over. But how do I know that? What is my evidence for it? I have a world-picture. Is it true or false? Above all, it is the substratum of all my enquiring or asserting. (Wittgenstein 1969)

What Wittgenstein is discussing here is how almost everything we learn can be doubted or questioned bit for bit, but we would hardly be able to doubt it all at once, since then we wouldn't be able to identify what it is we are doubting in the first place nor what the grounds, themselves now dubious, are for doubting. What we can do, however, is *recall* what we have previously taken, probably implicitly, as evidence for believing that X is Y. We are *focusing* on something that we haven't had reason to notice or consider before. What we are then doing is *paying attention* to the grounds of judgment, checking to see (a) if we have any and what they might be and (b) if they satisfy "the demands of subjective truth," that is, if they dissipate any reason we may have to begin to doubt what we thought we know about X or had learned about it. This is entirely a matter of focus and attention. On what? On *our own thinking*, instigated by the intrusion of the world—the introduction of something unknown, unfamiliar, or foreign.

"Being certain" of something is not a matter of "certain facts" or "objective knowledge" but rather of my own relation to a phenomenon, problem, or claim when there is no room for doubt: either because it would be in most cases not real doubt to begin with ("am I right in thinking that I am talking right now?") or because the causes of real doubt have been put to rest once I have weighed the evidence at hand to the best of my ability and all the relevant evidence seems to be in order. Does that mean that some new observation or piece of information cannot call the belief into question? To the contrary, that would mean the end of all thinking and learning. But certain questions can be allayed for the time being for the simple reason that everything speaks against and nothing speaks in their favor (say, a madman's claim that the Earth is 150 years old).

Thus, on the one hand, we have to start *somewhere*, and that place is everything we have learned since childhood, including our native language, our systems of dividing up the world into, say, foodstuffs, means of transportation, furniture, etc., but also methods of confirmation and falsification, recognized institutions for assessment and adjudication of dispute, and so forth. On the other hand, we come to a point in our lives when we are considered, legally, morally, and intellectually, adults, when we are held responsible for our thoughts and actions and have to make all sorts of difficult judgments in our personal, professional, and political lives. We have various terms for this cut-off point, which differs from time to time and place to place: let us call it broadly the "age of majority." Higher education exists in the service of that responsibility.

We do not accept the defense of the incompetent doctor that he was distracted by worries at home that week in medical school when they were going through that bit about the nervous system, nor the inept lawyer who says that he just found contract law really dull and couldn't be bothered to learn it all, nor the language teacher whose students never learn how to conjugate strong verbs, shrugging her shoulders and excusing herself by admitting that she, like everyone else, hated learning German grammar and the important thing anyway is just to get a "feeling" for the language. In each of these cases, were it a matter of 12-year-old children, we would be inclined to think that it is up to the parents and teachers to see to it that the future doctor had someone to talk to about her problems, to find a way of getting the jejune jurist to become more interested in her studies, and to make the young linguist understand that if you can't master basic grammar, you cannot learn the language properly, much less teach it to others. In this respect, higher education means learning how to take ownership of one's intellectual capacities and defects, which means in turn concentrating on what one knows and doesn't know, grasps and fails to grasp. It is, as Kant says, an arduous and uncomfortable task, and it takes time.

To have a clear idea means being capable of coming into possession of the reasons for having it and, consequently, implicitly presupposes that there is such a thing as reasoning and the possibility of communicating intelligibly (which includes arguments, demands for proofs and justification, and so forth) about a common world. To have ideas, to form judgments, is to acknowledge the authority of reason in this sense. Unlike desires and inclinations, which we all have with us from childhood, ideas and insights are arrived at through deliberation and discernment, which is a laborious effort of self-directed thought revision, requiring a matter to be interrogated and analyzed in the first place.

A Time and Place for Thinking

In a spirit not entirely different from Wittgenstein's in his remarks about "worldviews" cited above, Ortega y Gasset also stresses that education, properly speaking, is always "general" in the sense that it concerns culture (see Rider 2018).[6] A culture is "the system of ideas concerning the world and humanity" which forms the "effective guide of existence" at any given time. To be "cultured" or "educated," then, is to have a grasp of this system in a general way. In this respect, education is something entirely different from "professional training," on the one hand, or research, on the other. Both can be conducted without "culture" in this fundamental sense, and, indeed, Ortega's worry is that this is precisely the direction that higher education has taken. "Basic distribution requirements" in the liberal arts and the like constitute a "last miserable residue of something more imposing and more meaningful." An ornamentation, it "serves no end at all." "A vague desire for a vague culture," he says, "will lead us nowhere" (Ortega y Gasset 1946, pp. 42–43).

Ortega's point here is that the continuation of science ("the grandest creation of man," among its "most sublime pursuits and achievements") requires that the scientist understands something of the nature of this formidable institution, aside from its current practical utility and techniques, so that this comprehension can be communicated to the next generation. Modern society needs scientists, and it needs professionals. But further, it needs competent citizens, whose exercise of judgment affects or influences others. If the university is supposed to provide training for the kind of profession that requires sound practical judgment grounded in the knowledge produced by theoretical work (research), then that training should include an education in the "general system of ideas" about the world and man as far as theoretical investigation has taken us. This, according to Ortega, is the basic function of the university, "what it must be above all else." The professional who lacks understanding of "what we now know" about the world from modern physics, genetics, history, or

---

[6] Parts of the discussion of Ortega are, in slightly altered form, borrowed from S. Rider, "Truth, Democracy and the Mission of the University," in *The Thinking University: A Philosophical Examination of Thought and Higher Education*, Ron Barnett & Søren S.E. Bengtsen (eds) (Springer, 2018).

philosophy, and has no inkling of how "we" have come to know it, is not educated. Being uneducated, she will be a less competent doctor, judge, pharmacist, teacher, or engineer, for the simple reason that she will be constrained by her limited awareness and comprehension of the world in which she is to fulfill her function.

But notice that a culture here is something *specific*. It is not everything at once, a hodgepodge of this, that, and the other. It has a definition and focus (indeed Ortega has an entire program of higher education in mind). We will not be concerned here with the content of that focus. I am more concerned here with the idea that certain elements of higher education are central, while others are peripheral. When I say this, I mean regarding the form, not the subject matter. And what is central, I have argued, is the capacity for self-correction, which is what allows for the possibility of taking responsibility (I can't be responsible for something over which I exercise no power). In order to ground my judgments, I have to learn to exercise my own reason, which entails acknowledging the absolute necessity of attention to new, difficult, and perhaps even disturbing ideas—ones that "rock my world." But that doesn't mean that all principles of thought or action are of equal value. Some are the result of reason exercised over generations. Such rules, Simone Weil says, one must take, as it were, "on authority," not looked upon as

> something strange or hostile, but loved as belonging to those placed under its direction. They should be sufficiently stable, general and limited in number for the mind to be able to grasp them once and for all, and not find itself brought up against them every time a decision has to be made...Just as the habit, formed by education, of not eating disgusting or dangerous things is not felt by the normal man to be a limitation on his liberty in the domain of good. Only a child feels such a limitation. (Weil 1952, p. 13)

What we are looking for in education, then, is the capacity to recognize *the roots* of one's own thinking and subject these to scrutiny, when necessary. Self-correction becomes second nature, a habitual frame of mind in which the effort of thinking required is felt by the individual not as some externally imposed limitation but as a power or potential, an expression of what Kant called the individual's character or personality.

I spoke earlier of the conditions of one's thinking as contingent. By this I meant the language in which one was introduced into the world, the social conditions in which one was raised, the characteristics of the natural environment in which one lives. These all could be otherwise, but they are the absolute starting points for a human being. These are the soil out of which her beliefs, desires, inclinations, and basic suppositions grow. A formal education that is not rooted in and derived from the actual determinate conditions of thinking cannot constitute a refinement of it. At best, it will be just more "information," not anchored in the student's own thought but added onto it, like a dangling appendage. Weil remarks:

> A lot of people think that a little peasant boy of the present day who goes to primary school *knows more* than Pythagoras did because he can repeat parrot-wise that the earth moves around the sun. In actual fact, he no longer looks up to the heavens. The sun about which they talk to him in class hasn't for him the slightest connection with the one he can see. He is severed from the universe surrounding him... (Weil 1952, p. 69)

She complains that schoolchildren study geometry as a game, or to get good marks, not to seek any truth in it:

> The majority of them will always remain ignorant of the fact that all our actions, the simple ones as well as the judiciously combined ones, are applications of geometrical principles; that the universe we inhabit is a network of geometrical relations, and that it is to geometrical necessity that we are in fact bound, as creatures enclosed in space and time. This geometrical necessity is presented to them in such a way as it appears arbitrary. Could anything be more nonsensical than an arbitrary necessity? (Weil 1952, p. 69)

Now we don't have to embrace Weil's Platonic view of geometry to acknowledge that the presentation of geometry (or arithmetic, for that matter) as just one technique among others makes it look as if it is not absolutely necessary, for our way of thinking, for the simple reason that this *is* how we calculate. The necessity is real for us, just as the idea that there can be alternative geometries or base systems required that we are first familiar with what it means to add or measure in the plain sense found in school books.

Does this mean that education should strive always to appeal to the student's personal experience? Hardly, if that means eschewing, say, demonstrations. For the demonstrations *are* geometry. If these are omitted, all that is left are formulae with no real interest for the students. Formal demonstration and lived experience are not at odds with one another. Rather, the former takes the latter as its starting point. Weil offers an example of what that kind of instruction would look like. The instructor would say:

> Here are a number of tasks to be carried out (constructing objects fulfilling such and such requirements). Some of them are possible and some are impossible. Carry out the ones that are possible, and as regards the ones you don't carry out, you must be able to force me to admit that they *are* impossible. (Weil 1952, p. 69)

What this accomplishes, according to Weil, is this: the adequate execution of the possible task is sufficient proof; for the impossible task, there is no proof, which means that a justification, that is, a demonstration, is necessary. This makes the "impossible" concrete for the student. Through demonstration, she sees the difference between "I can't" and "it can't be done" and feels the force of conceptual necessity.

In the examples above, there is no difference between thinking or thoughtfulness and simply paying attention to a matter at hand. Thinking is here a question of focus, of noticing and acknowledging limits or boundaries, as real (earlier, this was called the search for truth). We have now come full circle back to my original remarks about philosophy being discourse about discourse, talk about talk. We began with Socrates, who famously grounded the entirety of his philosophy in the recognition of his own ignorance as the beginning of wisdom. To be committed to learning means seeing that our standard opinions and preconceived notions are a largely a mixed bag of errors, failures of understanding, misconceptions, and sheer ignorance. Thinking arises out of something that forces us to admit that failure and ignorance, with regard to something that impinges upon us from the world: a "necessity," in Weil's terminology. So thinking is always in relation to something; there is some thing that thinking is "about," even when our thoughts are mistaken, confused, or just vague. The starting point for thinking is the assemblage of prior judgments out of which it emerges, which themselves depend on the inevitable particularity and limited perspective of the individual's standpoint, the place one is in. Attentiveness to that particular "place" is not at odds with the learning or advancement of general truths, methods, or principles. It is the condition for the possibility of all thinking and learning, especially at a higher level. When I used the word "truth" to describe the acknowledgement of bounded thought as a condition of expanded thought, what I meant was quite simply whatever the state of affairs that we are trying to understand, the problem is that we are trying to solve, the "pragma," as Aristotle would say. It is not some eternal or unchanging transcendence, but the matter to which we turn our attention.

In this paper, I have tried to turn the reader's attention to the need to remind college students of what it means to pay attention, to commit oneself to getting things right. That might mean showing the teacher and oneself that one knows how to work a problem out without being told how; it might mean showing the teacher that it can't be done. And, in some rare and blessed cases, it might even mean showing oneself and one's teacher that having considered the pragma thoroughly, from one's own personal point of view but taking in all that instruction has had to offer in the way of authoritative knowledge, there is something of importance that hasn't been noticed and deserves more attention. This is not something that can be achieved by turning the page, scrolling the screen, or flipping channels as soon as the work gets difficult or tedious. It is the satisfaction of bringing oneself out of confusion and into clarity. Once achieved, that sense of autonomy, of having within oneself the resources to understand, can lead to the felt need to experience that state as much and as often as one can. In that sense, it is addictive—it can become a life-long habit. One might think that the university ought to be the place where that habit is formed and ingrained.

References

Arendt, H. (1981). *The life of the mind*. San Diego: Harcourt Brace Jovanovich.
Buber, M. (1945). The philosophical anthropology of Max Scheler. *Philosophy and Phenomenological Research, 6*(2), 307–321.
Buber, M. (1965). *The knowledge of man: A philosophy of the interhuman*. New York: Harper & Row.
Cassirer, E. (1944). *An essay on man: An introduction to a philosophy of human culture*. New Haven: Yale University Press.
Gadamer, H.-G. (1989). *Truth and method*. London: Sheed and Ward.
Kant, I. (1951). *Critique of Judgement* (J.H. Bernard, Trans.) New York: Hafner Publishing.
Kant, I. (2006). *Anthropology from a pragmatic point of view* (R. Louden, Trans.) Cambridge: Cambridge University Press.
Ortega y Gasset, J. (1946). *Mission of the University*. London: Kegan Paul, Trench and Trubner.
Piper, A. (2012). *Book was there*. Chicago: Chicago University Press.

Ricoeur, P. (2016). *Philosophical anthropology: Writings and lectures* (D. Pellauer, Trans.) (Vol. 3). Cambridge: Polity.
Rider, S. (2018). Truth, democracy and the mission of the university. In R. Barnett & S. S. E. Bengtsen (Eds.), *The thinking university: A philosophical examination of thought and higher education*. Cham: Springer.
Scheler, M. (2008). *The human place in the cosmos* (M. S. Frings, Trans.) Evanston: Northwestern University Press.
Turkle, S. (2015). How to teach in an age of distraction, *The Chronicle of Higher Education*, 2 October 2015.
Weil, S. (1952). *The need for roots. Prelude to a declaration of duties toward mankind* (A. Wills, Trans.). New York: Routledge.
Weyl, H. (1955). Insight and reflection. In T. L. Saaty & F. J. Weyl (Eds.), *The spirit and uses of the mathematical sciences* (pp. 281–301). New York: McGraw-Hill.
Wittgenstein, L. (1969). *On certainty*. (G. E. M. Anscombe & G. H. von Wright, Trans.). New York: Basil Blackwell.
Wolf, M. (2018). Skim reading is the new normal. The effect on society is profound, *The Guardian*, August 25 2018.

Sharon Rider is Professor of Logic and Metaphysics at the Department of Philosophy, Uppsala University, where she was Vice-Dean of the Faculty of Arts in Uppsala 2008-2014. She is a member of the Royal Society of the Humanities at Uppsala, and was the first recipient of the Swedish Humtank Prize for eminent scholars in the humanities who have brought research beyond the academy. A philosopher by training, with an emphasis on later modern European thought, she has published on issues connecting epistemology to education, including themes such as the relationship between linguistic competence and mathematical reasoning, the idea of a university, and the cultural conditions of rational judgment. Her current focus is on how the very conditions of possibility for thinking, understanding and learning, often understood in terms of subjectivity, are often misconceived as limitations and barriers in current educational research and policy. Rider's most recent book is *World Class Universities: A Contested Concept* (Springer 2021).

Chapter 7
In Search of Student Time: Student Temporality and the Future University

Søren S. E. Bengtsen, Laura Louise Sarauw, and Ourania Filippakou

Introduction

The Covid-19 pandemic is a challenge to the universities' organisation in time and space, but do we actually want to return to the functional and linear temporality that characterised the pre-pandemic university?

As we write this chapter, it feels as if the entire world has closed down and time has stopped. Due to the pandemic with its constant threat of the Covid-19 disease, societies around the world have closed down most public institutions, public spaces, and national borders. No one can get in or out of the country. We cannot move in the known physical world.

The inner life of the individual university may, to some degree, be maintained, and the status quo may be upheld. In the early phase of the pandemic, most events and classes were cancelled. However, as the situation prolongs itself into an indefinite and unforeseeable future, courses, meetings, exams, and conferences are being moved to online spaces. However, the usual time schemes and physical learning spaces are gone and are currently reinvented anew. Spaces no longer need to be continuous, and temporalities can flow forward, backward, and stop. Some may

---

S. S. E. Bengtsen (✉)
Danish School of Education (DPU), Aarhus University, Aarhus, Denmark
e-mail: ssbe@edu.au.dk

L. L. Sarauw
Roskilde University, Roskilde, Denmark

O. Filippakou
Department of Education, College of Business, Arts & Social Sciences, Brunel University London, Uxbridge, UK

© The Author(s), under exclusive license to Springer Nature Switzerland AG 2021
S. S. E. Bengtsen et al. (eds.), *The University Becoming*, Debating Higher Education: Philosophical Perspectives 6,
https://doi.org/10.1007/978-3-030-69628-3_7

dream of a quick fix return to their pre-pandemic routines, but, for many students and teachers, the situation reveals a crucial need to rethink time and space in higher education.

In many cases, the exemption of daily routines has produced a questioning of the desirability of resuming academic life as it was organised before the pandemic, and, for many students and teachers, it has produced new kinds of openness, albeit uncertainty, about when and where to go next and whether something permanent would be ever available.

To that end, the pandemic has re-actualised discussions about the temporal organisation of the pre-pandemic university. Gibbs and colleagues (2015) have argued that time and temporality need to be understood anew in higher education, as the linear and functional temporalities of neoliberal policies and managerialism agendas do not align well with the temporalities of student and teaching practices and the identity work connected to formation and personal growth. Furthermore, in the current situation of Covid-19, the international frameworks of qualification for higher education, which are based on fixed time schemes such as the European Credit Transfer System (ECTS) and students' compliance with predefined learning outcomes, may prove unfruitful.

In this chapter, we set out to explore the notion of student time and temporality in the wake of recent policy reforms with a special focus on the national contexts of Denmark and the UK. Furthermore, to challenge the linear conceptions of time and progression that we find implicit in these reforms, we explore alternative ways of thinking and organising time in higher education. In addition to previous research on time and temporality in higher education (Gibbs et al. 2015; Shahjahan 2018; Ulriksen and Nejrup 2017), the chapter offers a comparative empirical exploration of how particular notions of time are currently fostered and cultivated in educational policies and institutions. A key finding emerging from this analysis is that the Bologna Process and related national reforms embrace a capitalist worldview, which is not limited to the economic system and has significant implications for the daily lives of students and teachers. For this reason, in the third and final part of the chapter, we aim to move the discussion beyond the widespread binary vocabulary of 'functional time' versus 'lived time' and discuss an imagined third way in the light of the current pandemic situation.

Firstly, we explore how recent higher education reforms in Denmark and the UK, particularly in England, have influenced the understandings of study and teaching time and student identity. We do so with focus on the Study Progress Reform initiated in Denmark in 2014 and the Teaching Excellence Framework (TEF) introduced in 2016 by the UK government. The two countries make an interesting comparison, since these reforms tap into two historically different academic traditions, namely, the Humboldtian (Denmark) and the Anglo-Saxon (England).[1] Furthermore, England is an example of a marketised, neoliberal governance, while Denmark

---

[1] It is difficult to claim whether there ever was a UK higher education system as the Scottish tradition has deviated in critical ways from the English model: wider social access, four-year degrees, and broader degree programmes (Filippakou et al. 2012).

exemplifies what we see as a quasi-marketised, yet neoliberal, governance with no tuition fees and a generous public grant and loans scheme for the students. Regardless of these differences between the two countries in terms of university funding and governance, we argue that an institutional understanding of linear, functional, and instrumental time has become dominant. This temporally frames curricular planning and design, student and teacher mindsets, and understandings of progress and career trajectories in similar ways (Sarauw and Madsen 2016a, b; Nielsen and-Sarauw 2017). We argue that temporalities embedded within these higher education policies constitute a 'closed ontology' (Nørgård et al. 2019), which may limit students in developing creative and future-oriented forms of knowledge, competences, and skills.

Secondly, to challenge this 'closed ontology', we explore alternative ways of thinking and organising time in higher education and elsewhere. In doing so, we emphasise the notion of 'lived time' originally drawn from the philosophy of temporality by the French philosopher Henri Bergson (1998, 2001). Against this background, we discuss a series of studies in current research arguing for time and temporality in higher education to be seen as an embodied, experienced, lived, and non-linear process (Gibbs et al. 2015; Barnett 2007). In this endeavour, we are inspired by the philosophical studies by Barnett (2004) and Biesta (2006) that open up for the possibility of a freer and unbridled approach to student learning. To the current literature in the field, we add an analysis that takes into account higher education policy *and* practices and how they are entangled and cannot be separated. Also, we aim to overcome the sometime binary analysis of functional and lived time and learning in higher education and argue that a complimentary perspective and approach is needed to move higher education curricula out of the gridlock. As part of imagining an alternative future for the post-pandemic university, we discuss possible trajectories in relation to student time and temporality that are based on an 'open ontology' (Nørgård et al. 2019). We suggest that higher education practice, the more so in the light of the Covid-19 pandemic, has its strengths in learning for the unknown (Barnett 2004; Bengtsen and Barnett 2017). For the future university this will imply going beyond narrowly preset and predefined learning goals and outcomes.

Functional Time

The ideology of markets and state control in the history of the quality agenda in higher education has helped to permit a whole range of institutionalised activities to be gathered together under the concept of 'time' to the point where serious epistemological, ethical, and political confusions are occurring. In the last three decades, the idea of quality in higher education has been repositioned discursively: there are statements, which suggest that now many more systems than before can and should be implementing quality assurance, that it is very useful and relevant as a guide to academic standards, and that it has a strong and obvious immediacy in terms of its ability to come to grips with the European Bologna Process (Filippakou 2017, pp. 185–98).

In this section, we explore the temporal dimension of contemporary higher education policy discourses and practices in Denmark and the UK. Based on recent developments in the two countries, we show how particular temporal logics prevail as an onto-epistemic grammar that forms particular ways of thinking and being in academia. We argue that the prevalent functional time perspective should be seen in the context of a series of recent reforms in higher education. Such reforms challenge the currently dominating understandings of academic achievement, in that students' time optimisation becomes an objective in itself and quite separated from the educational and learning processes of students.

ECTS Time

In a Danish context, the European Credit Transfer System (ECTS) is a good place to start if one wants to understand how a quantitative and accumulative, yet finite, temporality has gained international dominance in higher education. In the Bologna Process, ECTS credits are counted on the basis of the workload required of students in order to achieve the expected learning outcomes. On average, one ECTS credit point equals 25–30 working hours, and 60 credits are the equivalent of a full year of study or work. In combination with a shared degree structure for all Bologna member countries, the ECTS has enabled joint standards for how much time students should take to complete their entire study programmes as well as the individual components, such as modules, course units, dissertation work, internships, and laboratory work (EU's ECTS User's Guide 2015, p. 36). The ECTS plays a key role in the economy of many universities as a performance indicator in the national funding system. For example, the so-called taximeter models award the universities according to the number of ECTS accumulated by the students while incentivising the universities to make more students complete their exams at a faster pace. For many students, the ECTS implies a similar personal economy in which they continuously benchmark the time that they allocate to their studies against an idea of academic achievement, which is determined by the clock (Nielsen 2015; Sarauw and Madsen 2020).

The Accelerated Curriculum

In Denmark, the ECTS has been a driver of recent reforms with the aim to speed up students' degree completion. The objective of the so-called Study Progress Reform (2014) was to reduce the average completion time of university students in Denmark with 4.3 months before 2020. The reform required compulsory enrolment of all students in subjects and exams equivalent to 30 European Credit Transfer System

(ECTS) per semester. Delay was sanctioned both individually and on an institutional level. Universities who did not manage to reduce the time it took their students to complete their degrees would be given a fine. Public grants were withdrawn from students who delayed for more than 30 ECTS, whereas students who completed their studies before the prescribed time were awarded with extra grants. Due to a series of changes in the curricula as well as the everyday life of teachers and students, the political objective of an average reduction of students' completion times by 4.3 months before 2020 was accomplished three years before expected. From 2014 to 2017, the average time students in Denmark required to complete a university degree was reduced by 4.7 months – from an average delay of 11.4 months in 2014 to an average delay of 6.7 months in 2017 (Danish Ministry of Higher Education XE "Higher education" 2018).

The success of the reform, however, had a price, which was paid by students and teachers. According to a survey from the Danish Union for Academics and PhDs (2017), 43% of the university teachers believed that the students' possibilities for developing reflexive analytical skills were reduced, and 31% of the teachers felt that they were themselves incentivised to lower the academic standard on their courses, so the students could pass on time. Analogously, students became less explorative and more instrumentally oriented towards passing their exams (Sarauw and Madsen 2016a, b, 2020; Sarauw and Frederiksen 2020). Now, a no-risk strategy prevailed, where students would increasingly opt out academically demanding modules, internships and studies abroad, extracurricular activities, and particularly part-time work (ibid.).

In parallel, most study programmes chose to reform the curriculum. A linear, accumulative understanding of progression, which implied that the students have to pass their exams in a given pace and order, became prevalent (Sarauw and Andersen 2016). To make more students pass their exams at a quicker pace, large modules were often cut-up in smaller bits (down to 5–10 ECTS). For many students this implied an increased number of exams, which meant that their workload was more evenly distributed throughout the semester, but their time for independent and self-directed learning was reduced (ibid.). Generally, the students now allocated more hours to their studies than before the reform. However, many students felt that they did not have the sufficient time to pursue deep learning, because they had to make sure to pass all courses within the given time frame. Furthermore, some mentioned that the cut-up of modules in smaller bits implied that their learning had become more fragmented (Sarauw and Madsen 2020; Sarauw and Frederiksen 2020).

Study Intensity and Micromanagement of Students' Time

Another key driver in reducing the time that university students in Denmark take to complete their degrees has been the idea that all students should be full-time students, i.e. allocate approximately 43 h a week to their studies. The government's Expert Committee on Quality in Higher Education and the Danish Evaluation

Institute (EVA) argued that students who allocated more hours to their studies would automatically gain a higher learning outcome (Quality Committee 2015; EVA 2016). Therefore, if the universities could make their students allocate more hours to their studies, the students would all be able to complete their degrees in a quicker pace without compromising quality and learning outcome (ibid). Consequently, to support their students in allocating more hours to their studies, universities and university colleges in Denmark have developed different time management frameworks for the students. All university colleges in Denmark plus one of the eighth universities have implemented the so-called study activity model, which is a framework that suggests relevant study activities for the students to undertake, when they are on their own outside the lecture halls. The activities are based on an estimate of the students' workload, recalculated in clock hours in correspondence with the number of ECTS allocated to the module (Keiding et al. 2016). While this framework leaves it up to the individual student to decide the order of the activities, the University of Copenhagen has started to distribute what look like a conventional school scheme to all undergraduate students. This scheme prescribes activities for the students in a sequential workflow from eight o'clock Monday morning to Friday afternoon.

While these frameworks have proven to be helpful for some students (Sarauw and Andersen 2016), they have also introduced a new language, or onto-epistemic, that the students are encouraged to use about themselves when performing the role as a student. This grammar is based on a functional understanding of time, which limits the meaning 'studying' to subjecting oneself to activities with a particular extension in time and space that are predefined by the university. The grammar does not apply evenly to all students, and previous studies show that socio-economic factors as well as the ways in which the idea of managing students' time is taken up by the study environments do play a role for the ways in which it influence the students' daily lives (Sarauw and Andersen 2016; Saraw and Madsen 2020; Sarauw and Frederiksen 2020). In combination with the fixed learning outcome that was introduced in continuation of the Bologna Process, however, many students and teachers feel that that non-performative ideas of studying, such as contemplation or open-ended self-directed learning, are no longer approved (ibid.).

The Quality Agenda and the Commodification of Time

Quality mechanisms in the UK are designed to collect information, link with institutional and other data, and evaluate the teaching and learning infrastructure of higher education institutions. Of themselves some of these processes are not new. More recently in British higher education policy discourse, there is an ongoing debate on time with a particular focus on 'contact hours' and 'learning gains' (BIS 2016; UUK 2016). Currently these debates are taking place within the context of the new Teaching Excellence and Students Outcomes Framework (TEF) and the newly established Office for Students (OfS) (Adonis 2018). On a regional level, such understandings of time are linked to the discourse of the knowledge economy, where OECD and EU initiatives also encourage and drive higher education metrics, the skills agenda, and other forms of performativity (Filippakou 2017). Commonly the present initiatives concerning the increase of teaching intensity draw from a quantifiable understanding of intensity to be worked into demands for more hours on site in the classroom and institutionally organised extracurricular activities (usually aiming, particularly in the UK, to enhance students' employability skills).

What is new and politically sensitive as seen in the proposed TEF is the combining of the teaching quality and the commodification of time. The ready justification for this endeavour is that as follows: 'The TEF will increase students' understanding of what they are getting for their money and improve the value they derive from their investment, protecting the interest of the taxpayer who supports the system through provision of student loans. It should also provide better signalling for employers as to which providers they can trust to produce highly skilled graduates' (BIS 2015, pp. 12–13). The political significance of the framework was summed up by Jo Johnson, the Minister of State for Universities and Science, who commented:

> While there is a lot of excellence, there is also, as the sector acknowledges patchiness and variability in and between institutions. We're helping the sector address that patchiness so we drive up the quality of teaching for everybody … Students should come out of their university years feeling they've got value for money for their time there. (Adams, Guardian 6 November, 2015)

The most contentious topic in the consultation of the TEF was the proposal to introduce a new measure of 'teaching intensity' in subject-level TEF (OfS 2018). The model was essentially one of efficient 'delivery' by the provider, and, as planned, it did not factor in, for example, assessment of the part the student plays in acquiring the learning. Among the proposals in the government consultation document was the addition of a 'supplementary' measure of 'teaching intensity', on the hypothesis that '…excellent teaching is likely to demand a sufficient level of teaching intensity in order to provide a high quality experience for students' (OfS 2018, pagex). The idea that a student is entitled to a number of hours of actual teaching or feedback from academic staff in return for the fee paid was first floated in a series of HEPI publications. It had the attractiveness of simplicity, and it encouraged students to complain that they were getting too few 'contact hours' a week for their high tuition fees. In 2011 in an effort to clarify matters, the Quality Assurance Agency (QAA) published helpful guidance entitled 'Explaining Contact Hours'. However, expressions of student disquiet about getting 'value for money' when fees are so high have grown still louder since.

Similar to the time management frameworks for students at the Danish universities, this raises one of the central questions arising from the design of the TEF in general: What responsibilities for their own learning do students have? How far in higher education should the student actively meet the teacher halfway in learning, rather than merely receive the instruction delivered? In the UK student contracts commonly list what the 'provider' and the student are, respectively, expected to do. For example, that the student 'will take responsibility for her own learning and development, working in partnership with staff to become a self-reliant, independent learner' is an expectation in Bristol University's Student Agreement (2017–2018). But this reciprocal requirement of student participation does not seem to be measured in the planned subject-level TEF. Yet the detailed 'TEF Guidance for Providers' in its version released in January 2018 goes in some detail into the complexities of the ways student response to teaching may take place, including the problem of so-called 'asynchronous online teaching', where a student may visit the online teaching at any time and perhaps many times and the teacher may not be present at all. Is this a contact hour (or hours)? How is it to be measured in terms of value for money? How is 'teaching intensity' to be quantified?

Respondents strongly disagreed with this in the consultation, and, given this, teaching intensity will be taken forward by the OfS outside of the TEF. The OfS suggested that they will explore how students should be provided with more direct information about the amount and different forms of teaching they can expect from their chosen course. They will also explore 'how providers currently meet existing consumer law obligations to provide course information to prospective students and whether this could be improved'. As the UK government recognised, the higher education market is now seen to require a 'robust framework' if they are to carry out their work with the active support of its key stakeholders such as students and universities. Thus, the discourse of time is elevated to the status of a sine qua non of the marketisation project. For students this can be construed as a discourse regarding the use of the teaching quality information, where the key question is the relationship between, on the one hand, their interests as consumers over that information (BIS 2015: 59) and, on the other hand, the interests of the universities, employers, and the state.

From this perspective, one of the most notable political consequences of the uncertainties surrounding the new quality agenda has been the adaptation of regulatory forms to include expert committees dealing with, and pronouncing on, the economic implications of higher education. Their purpose is to routinise the discussion of the economic rationality of higher education and provide an authoritative means for resolving political struggles (Filippakou 2017). Alongside the legitimisation of quality in HE, new discourses emerge around social mobility and widening participation (cf. BIS 2015, p. 36). However, system stratification tends to reinforce social stratification (Marginson 2016), and the intended differential levels of institutional income, deriving from different TEF evaluations, and the greater institutional hierarchies that these are likely to bring should lead to a rise in social inequality.

Lived Time

Following Shahjahan, the functional time implies a calculating way of being that has an anthropocentric orientation and is forward looking, constantly focused on an imaginary ahead, and obsessed with the steps that are needed to achieve that 'teleological end point' (2019, p. 292). In a similar vein, Manathunga (2019) argues that higher education temporalities are implicitly favouring some cultural identities and norms over others. Manathunga points out that we currently witness chronological and bureaucratic approaches to higher education 'timescapes (...) which positions [certain] candidates as lacking the capabilities, organisational skills and commitment deemed necessary to fit with dominant temporalities' (Manathunga 2019, p.11). In this section we explore possible alternatives to the functional decontextualized temporalities of teaching and learning in higher education. Commonly these alternatives emphasise educational timescapes' entanglement with personal, social, cultural, and political realities and trajectories of embodied and *lived* time.

The notion of lived time reaches back perhaps most strongly to the philosophy of time and temporality by the nineteenth-century French philosopher Henri Bergson (1998, 2001). Bergson objected to the increasing focus on mechanistic and quantitative time in industrialised societies with the continued fragmentation of time into still smaller, measurable quanta. In order to understand the human formation process and personal growth, Bergson stressed that it would 'no longer do to shorten future duration in order to picture its parts beforehand; one is bound to *live* this duration whilst it is unfolding' (2001, p.198). Bergson objects against the possibility of understanding time and temporality from outside the lived experience itself. When we live through and experience learning, the process of growth has its own time, which cannot be compared and quantified. In this sense, learning outcomes cannot be predicted but have to be lived and experienced by each individual student. Bergson distinguished between time flowing and time flown and argued that creative thinking and 'the free act takes place in time which is flowing and not in time which has already flown' (2001, p. 221). This perspective strongly challenges the functional understanding of study intensity and the increase in quantitative time (adding still more 'study hours') and instead argues that study intensity is not about the amount of time spent but the quality of the learning experience endured or lived through.

Following Bergson, the learning process cannot be reduced into quantifiable units in an ECTS credit framework but is a 'qualitative multiplicity, with no likeness to number; an organic evolution (...)' (Bergson 2001, p. 226). There is a paradox in the way that the humanities and social sciences (but perhaps other disciplines too) use a functional temporal framework in order to manage study processes of social and cultural phenomena, which themselves are acknowledged to not be reduced into neatly ordered, quantifiable units of reality. When students study the social and cultural realities that take place in the situated flux of time, the flow of the learning process itself and 'flowing reality' (Bergson 1998, p. 344) of the wider formation trajectory should be recognised as well.

Following Bergson's argument, the mechanisation and schoolification of higher education study practices threaten the creativity often connected with academic learning. The *lived* time of student learning is 'not an interval that may be lengthened or shortened without the content being altered', and the duration of the student's work is 'part and parcel of his work' (Bergson 1998, p. 340). To separate the learning process and learning outcome is impossible. As Bergson argues, 'the time taken up by the invention, is one with the invention itself' – they cannot be separated – and the 'progress of a thought which is changing in the degree and measure that it is taking form. It is the vital process, something like the ripening of idea' (ibid.). With Bergson's perspective on the temporality of human development and growth, the notion of functional time as the key framer and driver in our higher education institutions seems severely misplaced.

In her work on conflicting temporalities of academic knowledge production, Finnish researcher Oili-Helena Ylijoki (2015, 2016) distinguishes between what she terms project time and process time. Her definition of project time encapsulates the descriptions of functional time practices above, where time 'is rooted in clock time that represents a linear, standardized abstract, homogeneous, measurable and decontextualized perception of time' (Ylijoki 2015, p. 95). Hence, the study schedules with fixed boxes set aside for specific learning and study tasks (described above) are formed on the basis of an underlying project time mindset and trajectory. According to Ylijoki, the notion of project time conflicts severely with the actual experienced learning processes by students of higher education. Experiential temporalities of learning processes are defined by what Ylijoki terms 'process time', which is 'non-linear involving periods of standstill, deceleration, [and] acceleration' (Ylijoki 2015, p. 96). Here, the temporality of learning is not progressing neatly and linearly but is often characterised by 'setbacks when work gets trapped, making it necessary to move backwards'; and often there may be 'periods of routine work when nothing much happens', and yet again there may be phases when 'research makes rapid leaps forward entailing energizing moments of 'eureka', inspiration and spark' (ibid.). The notion of process time is not compatible with the idea behind progress reform initiatives and study intensity and wider forms of managerialism agendas in higher education policymaking. Ylijoki's points about study time as 'slow time', where the 'tempo and rhythm of work is not determined by the schedule but the task at hand' (Ylijoki 2015, p. 97), chime in well with contemporary research into higher education temporalities.

As Aaen (2019) has shown, feelings and experiences of boredom and confusion in higher education may lead to uncertainty and even a standstill initially. At the same time, however, such feelings allow for spaces for creativity and imagination that suddenly and unexpectedly propels the learning forward in ways standardised learning schedules could not otherwise have done. Within the emerging field of the philosophy of higher education, there has been an increasing awareness of the so-called darkness of learning (Barnett and Bengtsen 2019; Bengtsen and Barnett 2017; Dall'Alba and Bengtsen, 2019). Here, the argument is that the understandings of functional time and learn*ing* in higher education policies and strategies implicate correspondingly functional understandings of learn*ers* and knowledge forms. To sustain the diversity in the student segment, it is important to sustain the diversity in study temporality as well. The notion of functional time 'fosters a narrow ideal of good learning processes as clean and rational, when for many students they are highly messy, deeply confusing and exhausting, and at times downright unpleasant' (Bengtsen and Barnett 2017, pp. 124–125).

Contrary to the implications of the functional approach to study time, this philosophical argument proposes that having time to study is not always a pleasant and productive situation, and sometimes the time itself causes stress, procrastination, uncertainty, and fatigue. However, entering into detours, blind alleys, and dead-ends in the learning process is central for building resilience and developing agency in the studying and wider academic identity formation. Dall'Alba and Bengtsen (2019) argue for the necessity of an occasional radical standstill in the learning process as a necessary impetus for a more creative form of active learning. The authors argue that 'by allowing students the possibility of reaching a 'point zero' of knowing—the point of nothingness—we allow them to form their own thinking and understanding, claiming ownership of their learning process' (Dall'Alba and Bengtsen 2019, p. 1483). Knowledge does not emerge in neat packages but is acquired by learners often through much labour and hard work. Knowledge is 'surrounded with a penumbra of darkness, which separates the known form the mysterious' (Barnett and Bengtsen 2019, p. 105). This makes the learning process towards obtaining that knowledge equally unpredictable and non-predetermined.

Glimpsing Ecological Time

In the introduction, we welcomed the Covid-19's exemption from the linear and functional notions of temporality as an opportunity to revisit the organisation of time and space academia. From our argument until now, we have seen that student time may be divided into two opposing temporal frames – functional and lived time. The binary opposition has served an analytical purpose, but in this last section we aim to move beyond the constructed temporal duality and to discuss an imagined third way. We suggest that time, like a grammar in any language, is *inside* and *part of* the learning outcome and knowledge creation. Student time and temporality are not outside and separate from the learning process, nor the learner, but deeply interwoven with, and even embedded or nested within, the learning trajectory. This way seen, student learning is never completed, or finished, but is the very unfolding. This perspective implies that student time cannot be reduced to either functional or lived time but should be seen in a multiple view, where many different times and temporalities influence on the learning process – personal time, social time, societal and political time, cultural time, curricular and intellectual time, material and embodied time, etc. There is an ontological openness and multi-directedness at work, which resists the temporal hegemony and favouritism of some temporalities over others.

In a similar vein, Barnett (2018) and Wright (2016) argue that higher education institutions and their curricula cannot be understood isolated from their social, political, and cultural surroundings and are inescapably interwoven with wider societal and global conditions and realities with which they form an ecology. According to Wright, the university is embedded within symbiotic relations with its surrounding societal, political, and cultural contexts and should not be seen as separate or in opposition to such but as an interwoven part and a 'liveable landscape' and 'a "liveable university"' (Wright 2016, p. 66). To Wright the temporal hierarchy of functional time should be broken and a 'symbiotic [temporal] ecology' (Wright 2016,

p. 74) should be formed, where the various stakeholders of higher education would realise that they are dependent on each other and need each other in order to sustain a greater whole. This way seen, higher education is not a finished packaged product but rather something that is shaped and formed by every student in every interaction with the (representatives of) the institution inside and outside for as long as they are studying. Provoked by the pandemic, the current educational situation could, therefore, provide an opportunity to interweave culture and institutional frameworks with the social dimension of being human.

One way to do so could be to pay more attention to students' experience of wavering between different coexisting temporalities (Nielsen and Sarauw 2017; Ulriksen and Nejrup 2017). Barnett argues that there is a living, organic temporal life of the thinking process itself, a 'time in the knowing' (Barnett 2015, p. 126), which may only be sustained through a careful and sensitive temporal listening into the 'time signatures' (ibid.) of advanced knowledge creation processes. Such temporal signatures of higher education learning are not static and standardised but mirror the living academic community responding to a surrounding world constantly in fluctuation economically, socially, and politically. According to Barnett a temporal signature 'changes over time, it has its own dynamics, with varying rhythms for different epistemic tasks' (Barnett 2015, p. 131), and closely anchored within local institutional, national political, and global ecological contexts.

During the pandemic, the use of digital technologies and products has contributed to warping our notions of space and time. Spaces no longer need to be continuous, and temporalities can flow forward, backward, and stop. In our point of view, this is not an ideal situation for teaching and learning, but it is indeed a token of the possibilities for (instant) change. What we have learned from the pandemic so far is that there is nothing natural about the temporal organisation of the pre-pandemic university. In other words, the pandemic shows us an openness in the heart of what and how we do, and for many of us this knowledge comes with a freedom to think and act differently. Furthermore, the pandemic has conveyed an unpredictability in the lives of many students and teachers. New restrictions on our practices of teaching and learning can occur from one day to another, and at the same time the economic crisis implies that many more are facing uncertain careers. For these reasons, the pandemic calls for a greater focus on temporal sustainability – not merely favouring educational practices with immediate economic cash-in but promoting policies and practices, which may aid and sustain our societies also in time of crisis and change. This call comprises new higher education policies that do not only address the need for progress and quantifiable intensity measurement scales but acknowledge and recognise that speed and volume in itself will not improve the quality of learning and ensure the most valuable forms of knowledge creation.

When societal and political realities change, as we are encountering during the Covid19-pandemic, pre-planned progress markers and a streamlined curriculum fall too short – the pandemic may be an opportunity that educating for a known future and job market may not be the most desirable route. On the institutional level, we acknowledge that translating progress policies into school schemas and learning cubicles and quanta may provide structure and platforms in an otherwise open and open-ended learning process. However, the temporal hierarchies make schematic learning prior to more open-ended and non-linear learning journeys. In an ecological understanding, higher learning is not a commodity to be purchased but a possible outcome of social engagement and communal responsibility. Learning is not a receiving but happens when students give of their time and themselves – when time is being spent (and not bought) and offered to a greater cause raising beyond the individual learner. Student time and temporality are, ultimately, not to be saved and increased but to be used, and used up, in the contribution to other times, and others' time. Student time is the opportunity to give of whatever time you may have. That form of giving, we call learning.

References

Aaen, J. H. (2019). *Student darkness. An inquiry into student being at the university*. Aarhus: Aarhus University. PhD dissertation.
Adonis, A. (2018). Office for Students? It's the office against students and it is not going to last. *The Guardian*. Available at: https://www.theguardian.com/education/2018/jan/23/office-for-students-andrew-adonis. Accessed 11 Apr 2018.
Barnett, R. (2004). Learning for an unknown future. *Higher Education Research & Development, 23*(3), 247–260.
Barnett, R. (2007). *A will to learn. Being a student in an age of uncertainty*. Berkshire: Open University Press.
Barnett, R. (2015). The time of reason and the ecological university. In P. Gibbs, O.-H. Ylikoji, C. Guzmán-Valenzuela, & R. Barnett (Eds.), *Universities in the flux of time: An exploration of time and temporality in university life*. London: Routledge.
Barnett, R. (2018). *The ecological university. A feasible utopia*. London/New York: Routledge.
Barnett, R., & Bengtsen, S. (2019). *Knowledge and the university. Re-claiming life*. London/New York: Routledge.
Bengtsen, S., & Barnett, R. (2017). The dark side of higher education. *Journal of Philosophy of Education, 51*(1), 114–131.
Bergson, H. (1998). *Creative evolution* (A. Mitchell, Trans.). New York: Dover Publications.
Bergson, H. (2001). *Time and free will. An essay on the immediate data of consciousness* (F. L. Pogson, Trans.). New York: Dover Publications.
Biesta, G. J. J. (2006). *Moving beyond learning. Democratic education for a human future*. London/New York: Routledge.
BIS (Department for Business, Innovation & Skills). (2015). *Fulfilling our potential* (The green paper). London: BIS.
BIS (Department for Business, Innovation & Skills). (2016). *Success as a knowledge economy: Teaching excellence, social mobility and student choice*. London: BIS.
Dall'Alba, G., & Bengtsen, S. (2019). Re-imagining active learning: Delving into darkness. *Educational Philosophy and Theory, 51*(14), 1477–1489. https://doi.org/10.1080/00131857.2018.1561367.
Danish Ministry of Higher Education. (2018). Press Release [Pressemeddelelse] fixme https://ufm.dk/aktuelt/pressemeddelelser/2018/universiteterne-har-faet-has-pa-de-lange-studietider
Danish Union for Academics and PhDs/Dansk Magisterforening. (2017). *Survey among university teachers*, online 2017. http://magisterbladet.dk/magisterbladet/2017/042017/042017_p20 (December 2019).
Filippakou, O. (2017). Towards a new epistemic order: Higher education after neoliberalism. In J. Nixon (Ed.), *Higher education in austerity Europe*. London: Bloomsbury.

Filippakou, O., Salter, B., & Tapper, T. (2012). Higher education as a system: The English experience. *Higher Education Quarterly, 66*(1), 106–122.

Gibbs, P., Ylikoji, O.-H., Guzmán-Valenzuela, C., & Barnett, R. (Eds.). (2015). *Universities in the flux of time: An exploration of time and temporality in university life*. London: Routledge.

Keiding, T. B., Mølgaard, H., Quortrup, A., Kim, C., Dolmer, G., & Klok, J. (2016). Studieaktivitetsmodellen, Systime Profession.

Manathunga, C. (2019). 'Timescapes' in doctoral education: The politics of temporal equity in higher education. *Higher Education Research & Development*. https://doi.org/10.1080/07294360.2019.1629880.

Marginson, S. (2016). The worldwide trend to high participation higher education: Dynamics of social stratification in inclusive systems. *Higher Education*. Available from: http://link.springer.com/article/10.1007/s10734-016-0016-x. Accessed 15 Apr 2020.

Nielsen, G. B. (2015). *Figuration work: Student participation, democracy and university reform in a global knowledge economy*. New York: Berghahn Books.

Nielsen, G. B., & Sarauw, L. L. (2017). Tuning up and tuning in: How the European Bologna process is influencing students' time of study. In S. Wright, & C. Shore (Eds.), *Death of the public university? : Uncertain futures for higher education in the knowledge economy* (pp. 156–172). New York: Berghahn Books.

Nørgård, R. T., Mor, Y., & Bengtsen, S. (2019). Networked learning for, in, and with the world. In A. Littlejohn, J. Jaldemark, E. Vrieling-Teunter, & F. Nijland (Eds.), *Networked professional learning. Emerging and equitable discourses for professional development* (pp. 71–86). Cham: Springer.

Office for Students (OfS). (2018, October). *Teaching excellence and student outcomes framework: Subject level government consultation response*. Available at: https://assets.publishing.service.gov.uk/government/uploads/system/uploads/attachment_data/file/750411/TEF_government_response.pdf. Accessed 1 Oct 2018.

Sarauw, L. L., & Andersen, H. L. (2016). Målstyring og fremdrift – Soppedidaktik og fremtidens vidensarbejder. *Dansk Pædagogisk Tidsskrift, 1*(2/2016), 5.

Sarauw, L. L., & Frederiksen, J. T. (2020). Universitetet som plan B: studietvivl som copingstrategi blandt universitetsstuderende. *Dansk Pædagogisk Tidsskrift, 1*(1/2020).

Sarauw, L. L., & Madsen, S. R. (2016a). *Studerende i en fremdriftstid: Prioriteter, valg og dilemmaer set i lyset af fremdriftsreformen*, 1 udg. København: DPU, Aarhus Universitet, 2016.

Sarauw, L. L. & Madsen, S. R. (2016b). Editorial summary: Findings from a survey on the Danish study progress reform: Students' views, priorities and dilemmas based on survey data from 4500 student respondents in April 2015, Aarhus University, 2016, pp. 1–11.

Sarauw, L. L., & Madsen, S. R. (2020). The risks of timely degree completion: Student perspectives on following non-straightforward patterns in higher education in the paradigm of speed. In *Learning and teaching: The International Journal of Higher Education in the Social Sciences (LATISS)* (Vol. 13). Oxford: Berghahn Books.

Shahjahan, R. A. (2018). Re/conceptualizing time in higher education. *Discourse: Studies in the Cultural Politics of Education*. https://doi.org/10.1080/01596306.2018.1550041.

Shahjahan, R. A. (2019). From 'geopolitics of being' towards inter-being: Envisioning the 'in/visibles' in the globalization of higher education. *Youth and globalization, 1*(2019), 282–306. https://doi.org/10.1163/25895745-00102005.

The Danish Evaluation Institute [EVA]. (2016). *Styrk de studerendes udbytte – Inspiration til at arbejde med de studerendes studieintensitet*. https://www.eva.dk/sites/eva/files/2017-08/Styrk%20de%20studerendes%20udbytte_inspirationskatalog_1.pdf (December 2019).

The Danish Expert Committee on Quality in Higher Education [Udvalg for Kvalitet og Relevans i de Videregående Uddannelser]. (2015). xXX fixme.

Ulriksen, L., & Nejrup, C. (2017). *Quality and time – The time budget of university students*. Conference paper, European Conference of Educational Research 2017, Network 22. Research in Higher Education, online: https://static-curis.ku.dk/portal/files/193960107/EERA_Quality_And_Time_The_Time_Budget_Of_University_Students.pdf. Accessed Aug 2020.

UUK. (2016). *Student experience: Measuring expectations and outcomes*. London: Universities UK.
Wright, S. (2016). Universities in a knowledge economy or ecology? Policy, contestation and abjection. *Critical Policy Studies, 10*(1), 59–78. https://doi.org/10.1080/19460171.2016.1142457.
Ylioki, O.-H. (2015). Conquered by project time? Conflicting temporalities in university research. In P. Gibbs, O.-H. Ylikoji, C. Guzmán-Valenzuela, & R. Barnett (Eds.), *Universities in the flux of time: An exploration of time and temporality in university life* (pp. 94–107). London: Routledge.
Ylioki, O.-H. (2016). Projectification and conflicting temporalities in academic knowledge production. *Theory & Science, 38*(1), 7–26.

Søren S. E. Bengtsen is an associate professor in higher education at the Department of Educational Philosophy and General Education, Danish School of Education (DPU), Aarhus University, Denmark. Also, at Aarhus University, he is the co-director of the research centre 'Centre for Higher Education Futures' (CHEF). Bengtsen is a founding member and chair of the international academic association 'Philosophy and Theory of Higher Education Society' (PaTHES). His main research areas include the philosophy of higher education, educational philosophy, higher education policy and practice, and doctoral education and supervision. Bengtsen's recent books include *The Hidden Curriculum in Doctoral Education* (Palgrave Macmillan, 2020, co-authored with Dely L. Elliot, Kay Guccione, and Sofie Kobayashi), *Knowledge and the University: Re-claiming Life* (Routledge, 2019, co-authored with Ronald Barnett), *The Thinking University: A Philosophical Examination of Thought and Higher Education* (Springer, 2019, co-edited with Ronald Barnett), and *Doctoral Supervision: Organization and Dialogue* (Aarhus University Press, 2016).

Laura Louise Sarauw's field of expertise is the intersection between policy reforms, educational development, and practice in the field of higher education. She holds a PhD from the University of Copenhagen in the field of higher education policy reform and its implications for curricula. Her first postdoc explored the implications of the Danish study progress reform for students' conduct, and the second explored the implications of the Danish Code of Conduct for Research Integrity. Sarauw's research has a strong foundation in post-structuralist and actor-networked theory, and she has worked with both qualitative and quantitative methods. Her current research interests revolve around time matters, soft skills, and post-student-centred approaches to teaching and learning in higher education.

Ourania Filippakou is Reader in Education and Director of Teaching and Learning. She did her first degree in Education at University of the Aegean and, then, obtained a scholarship from the Academy of Athens to do her postgraduate studies at the UCL Institute of Education. Her main interest is in the politics of higher education with particular reference to comparative historical analysis, a perspective that seeks to combine the methods of history with social sciences theories and concepts. She has published in a wide range of journals including *Discourse: Studies in the Cultural Politics of Education, Higher Education, Higher Education Policy,* and *Higher Education Quarterly* and edited (with Gareth Williams) *Higher Education as a Public Good* (Bern: Peter Lang, 2014). She is co-editor of the British Educational Research Journal (BERJ) and was a council member of the Society for Research into Higher Education (SRHE).

Chapter 8
A Kantian Perspective on Integrity as an Aim of Student Being and Becoming

Denise Batchelor

Formula of Humanity

> Now I say: a human being and generally every rational being *exists* as an end in itself, *not merely as a means* for the discretionary use for this or that will, but must in all its actions, whether directed towards itself or also to other rational beings, always be considered *at the same time as an end* (Kant 2012: 40).

> So act that you use humanity, in your own person as well as in the person of any other, always at the same time as an end, never merely as a means (Kant 2012: 41).

Introduction

What special insights might Kant's Formula of Humanity bring to bear on integrity as an aim of student being and becoming in higher education? I suggest that the ways in which the Formula elucidates the concept have the potential to inform our understanding of student formation, by probing the nature of personhood, informing criteria for thinking about and acting well towards oneself and others, clarifying the grounds for assigning value, determining the extent and use of personal freedom and assessing the centrality of a rational nature.

Student being and becoming partly concern progressively realising a state of integrity. 'Realising' signifies not only engaging with the theoretical meanings of integrity but also translating that theoretical understanding into each dimension of students' practical experience in higher education. My focus in this chapter is to examine certain theoretical understandings of the concept of integrity, and

---

D. Batchelor (✉)
Surrey, UK

© The Author(s), under exclusive license to Springer Nature
Switzerland AG 2021
S. S. E. Bengtsen et al. (eds.), *The University Becoming*, Debating Higher Education: Philosophical Perspectives 6,
https://doi.org/10.1007/978-3-030-69628-3_8

preliminary connections are established with practice in the contemporary higher education context. These references are necessarily abridged here for reasons of space, but their detailed implications will be developed in a separate paper.

I chose to explore integrity through the lens of the Formula of Humanity because I believe the ideals expressed there illuminate its meaning. Integrity is a ubiquitous term in higher education, but its interpretation can be elusive. Reading the Formula for the first time made a powerful impact on me. As I began to imagine the radical personal, interpersonal and institutional implications of seeking to express its precepts in a present-day higher education context, the idea of living and working with integrity emerged as a possible way of capturing certain of its meanings. This chapter evolved from an attempt to engage with some of them.

My interest in student being and becoming arose whilst working as a teacher and personal tutor in a post-1992 higher education institution, where I tried to develop my understanding of the idea of a student and what it might mean for a student to have a voice (Batchelor 2006). In this endeavour I was especially sustained by the writing of Barnett (1994, 2007) and Taylor (1991, 1996). The generic delineations in the institutional framework of 'the student experience' did not quite capture for me some of the possibilities for being and becoming latent within the concepts of student-hood and student formation.

The chapter is structured in three parts:

- The Formula of Humanity: examination of core terms
- Understandings of integrity through the Formula's lens
- Conclusion: a possible Kantian theory of integrity

The Formula of Humanity: Examination of Core Terms

The term 'integrity' is not specifically mentioned in the *Groundwork* and the *Doctrine of Virtue*. Rather than manufacture artificial links with the expression itself, I examine what integrity might look like from the perspective of ideas articulated in those texts and especially in the light of the Formula.

Kant's Formula of Humanity is one expression of the Categorical Imperative, '…act only according to that maxim through which you can at the same time will that it become a universal law' (Kant 2012: 34). Its three core terms, 'end', 'means' and 'humanity' interact to enable agents to treat themselves and others always as ends, never only as means.

Humanity and Being an End

The conditions of humanity and being an end are interconnected. 'Humanity' denotes both a state of being and a way of responding to and acting towards oneself and others always as an end, never only as a means. It is an end through being the source and location of unconditional value in itself, and it engenders the capacity to set and realise ends as goals not only for oneself but also to support others in setting and realising their ends: 'The autonomous being is both the agent and the repository of all value…' (Scruton 2001: 86).

Humanity and its resulting orientation towards self and others are grounded in the rational nature which characterises human beings. Kant uses 'humanity' and 'rational nature' as interchangeable synonyms (Korsgaard 1996: 110). The hallmark of a rational nature is its capacity to propose ends to itself. These are generated by the will, which Kant (2012: 27) defines thus: '…the will is nothing other than practical reason'. Ends should not be determined by instincts, inclinations or desires but always by reason. Setting an end concerns a purpose which is the object of a free choice emerging from a freely adopted maxim. A maxim is both a subjective principle and a motive.

Being an end is connected with, but not derived from, the ends in the sense of goals that someone embraces. If they are important and valuable to him, he must by association be important and valuable by virtue of having chosen and endorsed them. But they are not the source of his value as an end. Because of his humanity, he is a value-conferring agent. His humanity is a source of unconditional value in itself and assigns value to his ends through acts of rational choice.

Humanity is common to everyone and independent of individual characteristics and proclivities. It is impersonal and universal, not located in ephemeral and variable characteristics such as achievements, failures or appearance. Nor is it connected to how people compare in these respects. Inner worth and dignity are neither competitive characteristics nor contingent upon other variables. Every person possesses value simply by virtue of his humanity, the rational nature located in his will. Being an end has nothing to do with his deserts.

Kant's terminology equating humanity with the unconditional value of the human person in himself enabled me to formulate more clearly a difficulty with the idea of a student as defined in parts of contemporary higher education. Students are offered an array of prefabricated, ready-to-use definitions expressing conceptions of being a successful self in the present and becoming a successful future self. These images may confirm or ignite students' own aspirations or indeed offer them a reassuring degree of security. A risk is that the language itself, however well-intentioned, functions as a limitation on their becoming if they find they cannot match its criteria. Barnett (1994: 55–153) examines the human cost for higher education of embracing a new vocabulary of skills and vocationalism, competence and outcomes and capability and enterprise at the expense of a lost vocabulary of understanding, critique, interdisciplinarity and wisdom.

The powerful idea of each person as a source and location of unconditional value in herself opened up more complex ways of thinking about building a student's confidence and self-esteem, particularly when she experiences significant failure: a series of rejected journal submissions perhaps, failed examinations or the inability to flourish on a wrongly selected course. Adhering in adversity to a bedrock of belief in one's intrinsic value as a person, whatever the external difficulties, contributes to restoring a sense of composure and dignity and engenders the energy and courage to try again. Where it exists, the personal tutoring provision (in its pastoral rather than individual tuition sense) offers a potential open rather than pre-scripted space to listen to students non-judgementally, with an attitude of unconditional positive regard for their intrinsic worth and dignity as persons (Rogers 1967). Barnett (2007: 131) alludes to personal tutoring as one of the expressions of institutional solicitude through which a university demonstrates care for its students.

Treating Oneself Always as an End or Only as a Means

Kant locates the primary root of being an end in the freedom that reason leads to: 'If only rational beings can be an end in themselves, this is not because they have reason, but because they have freedom. Reason is merely a means…through reason we grasp the rules that we need to follow in order fully to realise our freedom as autonomy…' (Guyer 2006: 178).

He proposes that '…rational beings are called *persons*, because their nature already marks them out as ends in themselves, i.e. as something that may not be used as a means…' (Kant 2012: 40). Things may be regarded only as means, but persons may not (Scruton 2001: 86). Treating oneself as a means expresses a reifying, dehumanising attitude towards the self which rejects the innate value derived from my humanity, that rational nature which makes me an end in myself, a person rather than a thing. It misuses personal freedom. This speaks to concerns about the objectification and commodification of individual personhood within a marketised system and the risk for students of internalising these descriptors. Watson (2009) charts the inner conflicts they generate, not only in students but also in teachers.

Treating oneself as an end involves fulfilling obligations owed to one's humanity. Duty and obligation are not synonyms. Whereas a duty means a required action, an obligation refers to the requiredness of an action, '…to its normative pull' (Korsgaard 1996: 44). A person is impelled to action by experiencing the normative force of an obligation. He feels bound, here by the obligations prescribed in the Formula of Humanity. His response is then expressed through specific attitudes and acts.

Kant (1996: 175) conveys the idea of regarding oneself as an end, and its resulting behaviour, through a taxonomy of duties to the self. Its two principles are '…*preserve* yourself in the perfection of your nature…' and '*make yourself more perfect* than mere nature has made you…'. Obligations of self-maintenance and self-improvement are owed to one's humanity and expressed through treating oneself as an end: '…there is more to making humanity our end than merely not acting against it; humanity includes capacities that must be *developed*...Our humanity is both a predisposition and a potential, something that we must both preserve and promote' (Guyer 2006: 187).

An aspect of promoting one's humanity is the cultivation of talents. Kant (1996:194) proposes recognising and developing one's capacities as a person's duty to himself: 'A human being has a duty to himself to cultivate (*cultura*) his natural powers (powers of spirit, mind, and body), as means to all sorts of possible ends. – He owes it to himself (as a rational being) not to leave idle and, as it were, rusting away the natural predispositions and capacities that his reason can someday use'. Deciding to treat oneself as an end emerges from reasoning and reflection. Self-knowledge is necessary, which Kant (1996: 191) elevates as the '...First Command of All Duties to Oneself'.

The process of identifying, setting and realising one's own goals develops through growing self-knowledge, which, in the quotation above, emerges from reasoning and reflection. These are demanding and sometimes painful and protracted undertakings which are liable to setbacks. A student's sense of self is in danger of disintegrating, leaving her vulnerable. Kant's idea of her humanity as a source of unconditional value in itself preserves intact a core of inner self-belief which is immune to external threats.

Treating Another Always as an End or Only as a Means

Kant (1996: 30) proposes that everyone has an innate right to freedom, rooted in his humanity, provided it does not erode another's freedom:

> *Freedom* (independence from being constrained by another's choice), insofar as it can coexist with the freedom of every other in accordance with a universal law, is the only original right belonging to every man by virtue of his humanity.

This freedom entails an obligation not to use others for one's own ends, treating them as a means for one's own purposes rather than respecting their dignity as persons of equal worth, because of their humanity, with oneself. Treating another as an end involves supporting him in setting and realising his own ends. The Formula of Humanity raises the question of whether to endorse another's ends if I disagree with them.

Kant indicates that to sanction another's ends they must be morally permissible. Otherwise they violate the humanity both of the person setting them and the person supporting him. Treatment of self and others is inextricably connected: 'Our commitment to the value of humanity constrains our own choices, by limiting us to pursuits which are acceptable from the standpoint of others, and extending our concern to the things which others choose' (Korsgaard 1996: x). Encouraging others to pursue acceptable goals entails not only supporting them in realising specific ends but also preparing the ground beforehand by nurturing in them powers of reasoning that enable them to formulate and choose worthwhile ends. Someone's humanity becomes degraded if corrupt ends are embraced. They must be of a calibre such that everyone could adopt them without harming the humanity within themselves or others.

When another's ends are morally permissible but different from one's own, Kant counsels understanding. Encouraging another to set and realise his own ends does not mean pressurising him to adopt the ends I think he ought to have. Promoting another's self-fulfilment must not mean taking him over in a domineering way, thus robbing him of the independence that is a hallmark of his humanity. Only each person himself can set and fulfil his own ends: '...he *himself* is able to set his end in accordance with his own concepts of duty; and it is self-contradictory to require that I do...something that only the other himself can do' (Kant 1996: 150). Personal freedom lies at the heart of the Formula of Humanity, but it is not an unbounded freedom. 'The constraint on our freedom is that we must respect the freedom of all' (Scruton 2001: 86).

Even if I disagree with someone's goals, my duty is to think the best of him and remember that I may not fully understand the reasons for his choice. It is inappropriate to condemn him by denying the moral value inherent in his humanity (although condemnation is fitting when someone chooses ends that violate humanity). I may condemn his act, but not the humanity in his person. A generous disposition is ready to make allowances. In giving him the benefit of the doubt, I show him respect.

Kant advocates empathy and lack of feelings of superiority towards the other. I should honour the reality that he is a source of value in himself and therefore my equal as an independent, free human being capable of using his rational nature to set ends for himself and strive to realise them. Treating him only as a means denies his autonomy and capacity for self-governance. It is expressed through attitudes and actions which refuse him the dignity that is his due by virtue of his rational nature. It entails undermining and devaluing everything that comprises the status of being an end, using him in an instrumental way – not as in straightforward transactions where the terms and conditions are clear – but by prioritising one's own purposes over his through deliberately misleading him, thus limiting his freedom to choose how to respond.

How might these initial thoughts about the Formula of Humanity and its central triangle of terms, 'humanity', 'end' and 'means', relate to integrity? Tentative pointers towards a possible Kantian theory of integrity have begun to emerge, concerning criteria for thinking about and acting well towards oneself and others, grounds for assigning value, the extent and use of personal freedom and the centrality of a rational nature. However firmer connections cannot be established before considering different understandings of integrity through the Formula's lens.

Understandings of Integrity Through the Formula's Lens

In everyday discussions in a higher education institution, integrity is often mentioned in terms of its absence rather than presence: an approach to grade allocation lacks integrity, a research methodology is deficient in integrity, or a curriculum design demonstrates inadequate integrity. Watson (2014: 29) indicates the wider implications for higher education institutions of the presence and absence of different dimensions of academic integrity, and Macfarlane (2004, 2009) demonstrates its centrality to teaching and researching. What is this enigmatic value, and how might it relate to student being and becoming?

Halfon (1989: 6) describes a complete understanding of integrity as being '…deeply elusive and exceedingly complex, because there are numerous uses of the term and a wide variety of objects to which we may attribute the property of integrity'. Cox et al. (2016: section 5) capture this conceptual complication by considering the meaning of integrity under six headings:

1. Identity
2. Self-constitution
3. Standing for something
4. Virtue
5. Self-integration
6. Moral purpose

Each of these interpretations contributes a particular dimension of meaning to the process of student being and becoming. For reasons of space alone, just four of them are considered here, 'virtue' at greater length.

1. Identity

The Formula of Humanity pivots on what lies at the core of a person's identity, the humanity she shares with everyone: she owes this a responsibility to use it always as an end, never only as a means. Integrity as identity concerns adhering resolutely to commitments such as '…intentions, promises, convictions and relationships of trust and expectation', including undertakings to '…people, institutions, traditions, causes, ideals, principles, projects …' (Cox et al. 2016: section 2). They may be public or private, deep or superficial.

What kind of commitments are centrally important to a person's integrity and to which he is expected to remain faithful? One answer is to delineate integrity by those undertakings he identifies with most profoundly and which are at the heart of his life. Williams (1981: 12) calls these 'identity-conferring commitments' or 'ground projects'. They constitute '…the condition of my existence, in the sense that unless I am propelled forward by the conatus of desire, project and interest, it is unclear why I should go on at all...'. Students sometimes discover such ground projects through research interests which develop into lifelong passions.

But certain ground projects potentially violate another's humanity. If their only criterion is that someone identifies with them completely and they express most fully who she is, what if she adopts morally inadmissible projects? Through the Formula's lens, this cannot constitute integrity. It sets firm criteria for moral acceptability through its doctrine of ends and means. Its yardstick for integrity is treating others as ends equal to oneself: certain ground projects are morally restricted by this requirement.

2. Self-constitution

Integrity as self-constitution is the fundamental premise of being an agent. Failing to live with integrity equates to failing to be a self or to live as a person. Threats to integrity should be suppressed not in order to be morally estimable but to be a unified and whole person. The processes involved in having a personal identity and being a rational agent are forms of work, and success or failure in this means that someone is good or bad at being a person (Korsgaard 2009). This interpretation concerns not only someone's present self but also her future self. She must act in the present on precepts which her future self could accept and support.

Integrity as self-constitution uncovers the link between personhood and agency. Although 'integrity' is a noun, its implications are preponderantly verbal: integrity refers to my activity. It is about something I do to constitute myself as the person I am now in the present and the person I hope to be in the future. Becoming a person is a project which is simultaneously both goal and work-in-progress.

3. Standing for Something

Integrity as standing for something is a social virtue, determined by a person's relationship with others (Calhoun 1995). Someone with integrity stands up for her beliefs in a wider community of people who are also seeking meaningful and valuable convictions and practices. Standing for something means that persons of integrity need to respect each other's views. This guards against regarding fanatics as having integrity.

The Formula indicates a preferred way of standing for something. The seriousness with which I take my own cause should not lead me to disrespect another's support for his cause, even if I disagree with him. I must empathise with the earnestness with which he holds his views rather than disparage his opinions and denigrate his worth as a person. I should never lose sight of his humanity, which I share. Integrity as standing for something always requires respect for the dignity and sincerity of someone with a different outlook. This attitude is inherent in the Formula and is a way of treating the other as an end. Developing one's own voice as a student cannot be at the expense of denigrating the other person's voice.

The dispositions and activities involved in identity formation, self-constitution and standing for something are central to students' being and becoming. Examining all their complexities lies beyond the scope of one chapter, but the capacity for critical thinking is a common denominator permeating them.

Davies and Barnett (2015) provide a valuable map to the literature in this field. Papastephanou and Angeli (2007: 611) advocate '…what we call an 'aporetic' (i.e. question raising) stance toward knowledge or the cultural material that shapes people's subjectivities'. Their focus on the vulnerability of the aporetic quality in critical thinking is of special interest in a higher education context where performativity is stressed and mechanistic learning outcomes are sometimes narrowly and tightly specified. Recognising aporia acknowledges the uncertainty and doubt in identity formation and self-constitution, or listening to a different perspective and seeking to understand rather than dismiss it out of hand. Critical thinking is likely to provoke difficult questions which invite complex responses. It requires self-interrogation and an admission of one's own ignorance These are significant features of students' being and becoming.

4. Virtue

There are different understandings of integrity as a virtue. Scherkoske (2012) classifies integrity as an epistemic rather than a moral virtue, which tends towards characteristic thoughts or motivations, whereas epistemic virtues do not. Cox et al. (2016: section 6) suggest that integrity is a cluster concept linking together other virtues and qualities of character. Understanding integrity this broadly could mean the definition lacks precision, making it difficult to assess the integrity of specific individuals and situations. They propose that what connects its associated virtues and traits is the disposition to take one's life seriously, entailing self-examination and self-monitoring. The Formula of Humanity offers an inclusive way of taking one's life seriously through responding wholeheartedly to its invitation to conform to a special orientation towards the self and others.

The Formula elucidates integrity as a cluster concept for other virtues and qualities of character by being simultaneously broad in vision yet precise in application. It expresses a powerful fusion of universality in reaching out to include every person within the range of its injunction and implied specificity in intimating the manifold ways of responding to it in private and public situations and relationships. Very different people embedded in different lives and contexts may all potentially aspire to fulfil its precepts. It is impersonal in its sheer scope and deeply personal when its implications are translated into the choices and decisions that compose the texture of individual lives.

Kant rejects understanding virtue as a belittling obsession with petty details. Rather, virtue is an all-embracing way of life which takes someone over in a positive way: '...not as if a human being possesses virtue but rather as if virtue possesses him' (Kant 1996: 165). Integrity as an all-pervasive common denominator infuses every aspect of someone's being, guiding his thoughts, motives and actions.

The Formula is both a standard for virtue and a signpost towards it. It sets the bar high. There is a danger that the ideal it contains is so elevated as to become a daunting deterrent, inviting discouragement rather than inspiring hope of ever adequately meeting its stipulations. Kant is uncompromising in setting a demanding target but realistic about the difficulties involved in making progress towards it. His depiction of virtue is not so remote and esoteric as to be beyond the reach of ordinary human beings, attainable only through superhuman efforts. He recognises human limits. Virtue is grounded in 'human finitude' (Grenberg 2005: 53).

Nevertheless the Formula is uncompromising and unambivalent. It confronts the agent with tough choices about his attitudes and actions. It pivots on tension: the potential for conflict always exists when deciding whether to treat oneself and others as ends or means. Kant indicates that the fight to overcome one's inner resistance is an essential ingredient of virtue and a crucial factor in understanding it. Virtue is hard-won; constant vigilance is needed to maintain it. McFall (1987: 9) notes the potential fragility of attaining and maintaining integrity: 'Where there is no possibility of its loss, integrity cannot exist'. The agent in the Formula is always vulnerable to the possibility of being unable to live up to its demands. It is a Formula shot through with the risk of failure. It elucidates the provisional nature of integrity, its precariousness if the agent's will is weak.

The endeavour embodied in the Formula is one of striving to realise a goal through the medium of personal weakness as well as strength. The agent is prone to setbacks and likely to experience and surrender to temptation, which Halfon (1989: 44–47) suggests is a form of adversity. Yielding to temptation is human and understandable. Kant advises empathy, compassion and understanding as generous responses to the inevitable failures involved in trying to treat oneself and others always as ends and never as mere means.

Given these challenges, is integrity as a complex virtue better understood as a project of self-formation continuously developing through the formulation and reformulation of aspirations, choices and actions, or is integrity the goal of that process? Kant suggests that virtue is simultaneously the unreachable goal and the conflictual and sometimes fragile characteristic of the process engaged in to attain it. The course of striving to realise the ideal of virtue is not linear but erratic. Moving towards the goal entails radical revisions, always starting over and being permanently vulnerable to setbacks:

> Virtue is always *in progress* and yet always starts *from the beginning*...it is an ideal and unattainable...virtue can never settle down in peace and quiet with its maxims adopted once and for all but, if it is not rising, is unavoidably sinking. (Kant 1996: 167)

Achieving equilibrium is a strenuous, uncertain project, prone to slippage. The difficulty in enacting the Formula's implications makes a tranquil progression from intention to realisation unlikely. It represents a potential moral minefield. For Kant this struggle is the hallmark of being human. Achieving virtue is not an all or nothing battle but a matter of degree, an incremental, gradual and lifelong process: 'It is a human being's duty to *strive* for this perfection, but not to *reach* it...and his compliance with this duty can, accordingly, consist only in continual progress' (Kant 1996: 196). The project of matching one's thoughts and behaviour to one's ideals, and reconciling one's inclinations to one's will, is marked by continuous renewals of intention and motivation.

The ideals which a person strives to realise may undergo re-evaluation. Commitment to a goal for someone of integrity does not entail its unreflective, blinkered pursuit. Integrity allows for flexibility and development, which indicate '...not inconsistent behaviour, but a capacity to change and grow' (Halfon 1989: 18). 'The capacity for self-criticism and ability to reassess one's roles and relations may also help to distinguish the person of integrity from the ideologue or dogmatist...a person of integrity should exhibit a willingness to re-examine and perhaps abandon previous commitments' (Halfon 1989: 19). Cox et al. (2003: 41) call this practice of reassessment '...a kind of continual remaking of the self...'.

A Kantian perspective on integrity as a virtue might differ from this rather open-ended and flexible approach to holding ideals, but also not fit with ascriptions of rigidity and blinkered dogmatism. Halfon is suggesting that for someone of integrity, ideals and principles are provisional and revisable. For Kant a latitude for reconsideration of one's commitments does not exist in the same way. Certainly the initial pledge to the Formula entails making further choices to confirm it. These may falter, but their immutable parameters have already been set by the original commitment. The Formula remains the unwavering pilot light guiding the agent's course in both his successes and failures to reach its demands. The quality of his responses may fluctuate, but holding the Formula as an ideal never does. It expresses a guiding principle which is stable, unchanging and difficult, but inspiring partly because of its uncompromising rigour.

Each of these interpretations of integrity brings to light further meanings within the Formula of Humanity. The intersubjective dynamic the Formula expresses has fundamental implications and consequences for the integrity of interpersonal relationships in higher education, between students, teachers, researchers, counsellors, personal tutors, supervisors, mentors, managers and administrators. In the multiple possibilities for the Formula's application, it holds out ideals of self-fulfilment, equity, equality, respect, humility, understanding and tolerance.

Conclusion: A Possible Kantian Theory of Integrity

From a Kantian perspective, integrity is a common denominator infusing every aspect of someone's being, expressing an overarching moral virtue which engenders characteristic thoughts, motivations and actions. It is denoted by fidelity, commitment and consistency and is repeatedly constituted and refined through an inner conversation, a process of self-legislation in the light of the Formula resulting in choices expressing its injunction. Integrity is a capacity which enables someone to think about and act towards the humanity in herself and others always as an end, never merely as a means. It expresses an orientation of the whole person and emanates from her deepest motivations and intentions. It is like a vein running through her, connecting every aspect of her thought and action into a unified structure of response. It is about wholeheartedness.

However it is not about just any unified and wholehearted stance, regardless of what that orientation might be. There are boundaries of moral acceptability. At its core must be respect for the humanity in oneself and others. This generates the motive to think and act in ways which foster a developing understanding of what respect for humanity means.

Integrity is an inspirational and aspirational ideal. As a source of inspiration, it represents an ideal that is ultimately unrealisable – not through being an escapist fantasy but because it entails a lifetime's striving towards it. Attaining and maintaining integrity involves an unremitting struggle within the self to achieve a worthwhile goal. As an aspirational ideal, its realisation is anchored in empirical experience and approached through choices and decisions activated by a strong will informed by a firm moral purpose. A Kantian theory of integrity is as an ideal that is simultaneously broad in vision yet practical in application, ultimately unreachable yet accessible momentarily. Its distance from attainment is not so great as to be demotivating. Its conception through the imagination translates into practical footholds towards it.

Integrity is not sustained by desires and inclinations but by strength of will. Although aspirations arise from desire as well as the will, integrity depends for stable continuance on the will to keep striving towards the ideal even when someone feels like giving up or succumbing to temptation or is overwhelmed by adversity. His will re-animates desires and aspirations. His striving may rarely entail grand heroic gestures, consisting rather of a myriad small, private and unglamorous choices about his attitudes and actions towards himself and others. Together these generate the increments of integrity.

Integrity concerns being in harmony with what is at the heart of our identity, what makes us most deeply who we are. Being true to oneself, being authentic, involves respecting the humanity in oneself and everyone else. Being and becoming cannot remain purely individualistic and solipsistic endeavours. The Formula is permeated by the implications of the interrelationship between the self and others: their treatment is intimately connected. Its concern is not solely introspective but extends outwards to others in an expression of altruism. One meaning of integrity is 'intactness'. The self's intactness must be continuously broached through immersion in the complex challenges of engaging with others as ends, not means, within the concrete circumstances of actual life. The tone and quality of this engagement contribute to self-constitution. Integrity cannot rest on a base of inequality of power, whether tacit or overt: everyone must be treated in the same way, as ends not means.

Integrity is more than the six meanings indicated earlier. It denotes the fundamental personal orientation which pulls them together and points beyond them, enabling someone to preserve her sense of self, personhood and chosen responses even in adversity. It concerns the inner freedom to be one's own person, self-regulating and autonomous no matter how constraining the external circumstances.

The Formula's concentration on a shared humanity accentuates what respect for oneself and another person could mean and the profound demands it would make. Its perspective interrogates understandings of equality, equity, diversity and inclusiveness and carries complex implications for the relationships that are central to higher education activities.

In a logic textbook edited under his supervision, Kant added a fourth question to the three already posed in the *Critique of Pure Reason:* 'What can I know?', 'What should I do?' and 'What may I hope?' This question was: 'What is a human being?' (Guyer 2006: 7). Integrity is axiomatic to human being and becoming and a fundamental factor in the quality of a student's knowing, doing and hoping as she finds her own voice as a person and enables others to do the same.

References

Barnett, R. (1994). *The limits of competence*. Buckingham: The Society for Research into Higher Education & Open University Press.
Barnett, R. (2007). *A will to learn: Being a student in an age of uncertainty*. Maidenhead: Society for Research into Higher Education and Open University Press.
Batchelor, D. (2006). Becoming what you want to be. *London Review of Education, 4*(3), 225–238.
Calhoun, C. (1995). Standing for something. *Journal of Philosophy, XCII*, 235–260.
Cox, D., La Caze, M., & Levine, M. P. (2003). *Integrity and the fragile self*. Aldershot: Ashgate.
Cox, D., La Caze, M., & Levine, M. P. (2016). Integrity. In *The Stanford Encyclopaedia of Philosophy*. https://plato.stanford.edu/archives:win2016/entries/integrity/. Accessed 27 Mar 2020.
Davies, M., & Barnett, R. (Eds.). (2015). *The Palgrave handbook of critical thinking in higher education*. New York: Palgrave Macmillan.
Grenberg, J. (2005). *Kant and the ethics of humility*. Cambridge: Cambridge University Press.
Guyer, P. (2006). *Kant*. London/New York: Routledge.
Halfon, M. (1989). *Integrity: A philosophical inquiry*. Philadelphia: Temple University Press.
Kant, I. (1996). *The metaphysics of morals* (M. Gregor, Trans.). Cambridge: Cambridge University Press.
Kant, I. (2012). *Groundwork of the metaphysics of morals* (M. Gregor, Trans.). Cambridge: Cambridge University Press.
Korsgaard, C. M. (1996). *Creating the Kingdom of ends*. Cambridge: Cambridge University Press.
Korsgaard, C. M. (2009). *Self-constitution: Agency, identity, and integrity*. Oxford: Oxford University Press.
Macfarlane, B. (2004). *Teaching with integrity: the ethics of higher education practice*. London: Routledge Falmer.
Macfarlane, B. (2009). *Researching with integrity: the ethics of academic enquiry*. Abingdon: Routledge.
McFall, L. (1987). Integrity. *Ethics, 98*, 5–20.
Papastephanou, M., & Angeli, C. (2007). Critical thinking beyond skill. *Educational Philosophy and Theory, 39*(6), 604–621.
Rogers, C. (1967). *On becoming a person*. London: Constable.
Scherkoske, G. (2012). Could Integrity be an Epistemic Virtue? *International Journal of Philosophical Studies, 20*, 185–215.

Scruton, R. (2001). *Kant: A very short introduction*. Oxford: Oxford University Press.
Taylor, C. (1991). *The ethics of authenticity*. Cambridge, MA/London: Harvard University Press.
Taylor, C. (1996). *Sources of the self*. Cambridge: Cambridge University Press.
Watson, D. (2009). *The question of morale*. Maidenhead: Open University Press.
Watson, D. (2014). *The question of conscience*. London: Institute of Education Press.
Williams, B. (1981). *Moral luck*. Cambridge: Cambridge University Press.

Denise Batchelor taught in higher education, and is interested in the concept of 'voice' in that sector. Her current research is into vulnerability as a factor of intersubjectivity, and the values and qualities which contribute to developing a disposition and voice of vulnerability as part of responding to another. Her work is anchored in the writing of Kant and Levinas.

Chapter 9
An Entrepreneurial Ecology for Higher Education: A New Approach to Student Formation

Wesley Shumar and Søren S. E. Bengtsen

Introduction

In many parts of the developed world, the university is in crisis. Many scholars have sounded the alarm over the neoliberalization of universities and the education they provide (Ball 2012; Canaan and Shumar 2008; McGettigan 2013; Newfield 2008; Nussbaum 2010; Shore 2010; Shore and Wright 2017; Slaughter and Rhoades 2004). This neoliberalization has been a response to the financial crisis that has largely been caused by the reduction of state support for the funding of universities. And in the neoliberal economic model, one is selling a service or a production – a thing – to a consuming public. Neoliberalism's emphasis on the reification of the process of learning and knowledge production so that it can be effectively sold, ironically, threatens to destroy the culture and activity that makes universities so dynamic and what David Noble (personal communication) once called a national treasure. Scholars have been concerned about how the cult of numbers has emphasized the auditing and accounting for knowledge accumulation as if it were a coin that we could measure not only the dimensions of but how many we are able to place in one hat (Shore and Wright 2000, 2015). But overall, this economization of the university has led to a question of what are the core values in a university and what is the university becoming.

W. Shumar (✉)
Department of Communication, Drexel University, Philadelphia, PA, USA
e-mail: shumarw@drexel.edu

S. S. E. Bengtsen
Danish School of Education (DPU), Aarhus University, Aarhus, Denmark
e-mail: ssbe@edu.au.dk

© The Author(s), under exclusive license to Springer Nature Switzerland AG 2021
S. S. E. Bengtsen et al. (eds.), *The University Becoming*, Debating Higher Education: Philosophical Perspectives 6,
https://doi.org/10.1007/978-3-030-69628-3_9

If the Humboldt vision was a creative imagining of what the university could become, the current vision is one of institutional survival. The modern German university, which so greatly influenced the development of research universities around the world, was built upon principles and an imagination that was expansive when thinking about what the individual and what the nation could become (O'Boyle 1983; Kwiek 2006). It was also very much a vision of the relationship of the state to knowledge production and intellectual work. The contemporary status of the university is very hollow by comparison. Neoliberal economic theory suggests that the market is the most efficient way to organize most all institutions in social life. And therefore, there should not be a state relationship with institutions, like education. There should only be a market relationship. This ideology has brought about a tremendous reduction of state support for universities. This ideology along with demographic shifts has indeed forced educational institutions to become very "lean." It has forced universities to focus primarily on their own survival and not a robust focus on knowledge creation and learning.[1] The focus on finances and efficiency has brought about a new state in the university where the focus is in just surviving as an institution. What is lost is any sense of a higher purpose. It is our hope that this paper, through a reevaluation of the concepts of value and entrepreneurship, might help us move toward a more contemporary sense of purpose for the university.

The university did not lose its sense of purpose all on its own. From the early days of the development of the modern capitalist economy, executives and policy makers saw the value of university research for the economy and the value of a university education for training an advanced workforce for the developing technological economy. Ironically, this potential for the university to support invention, new technologies, and advanced legal managerial and business practices came about because the university was committed to the pursuit of basic research and the practice of academic freedom. It was an unintended consequence that this pursuit was so beneficial to the growing advanced industrial economy (Rider 2018). But as that benefit became clearer, the goal to instrumentalize university practice and make it more beholden to serving the economy grew over time (Noble 1977). And as the university becomes more instrumentalized, the desire to make it a self-supporting independent industry grew as well, especially as the cold war was winding down and state investment in universities seemed less important.

---

[1] Ironically, the pressure to survive, as it has pushed educational institutions away from their core focus, has also driven the movement to account for learning and knowledge production. An efficient market means that there is also value for dollar. And measuring value for dollar means that one has to further distort what learning and knowledge production are, as they need to become reified, things, in order to put them within a numerical accountability scheme. And so, accounting and economics become the dominant discourses which frame the imagination of what a university is, what knowledge is, and what learning is. These pressures in the end are all very contradictory. And in the case of Britain (and much of Europe), a different process as the national state was more central to the British system of higher education. At the same time, the current COVID-19 pandemic is a crisis that has made us aware of how important university training and research are for the safety and well-being of people around the world.

This historical trend is then followed up by the rise of neoliberal ideology discussed above. While Barnett's assessment of the historical development of the university's legitimation crisis is very helpful (Barnett 2015; Habermas 1975), it is also important to realize that in the larger capitalist economy, we went from the Fordist/Keynesian model in the postwar that saw a large role for the state in society to the current era of neoliberalism where state intervention into any aspect of society is seen as a negative.[2] As state support declines for universities, all but the most elite institutions' survival is threatened. The top concern then for universities became: how can an institution remain viable and not go bankrupt?

The Entrepreneurial Turn in Higher Education

Burton Clark (1998), in his central work on entrepreneurship in the university, demonstrated with several examples in the UK how entrepreneurial universities might be a solution to part of the financial crises that modern universities faced. And he also showed (although this is not necessarily his purpose) how universities shifted to a focus on survival. For Clark, entrepreneurship was not a way to solve the crisis of meaning and purpose but rather as a way to address the economic challenge of the modern university. From his research on five institutions in Britain and Northern Europe, he was able to show how institutions that could look at their circumstances and take an entrepreneurial approach to providing training and knowledge development to fit the economy were successful in that strategy (Rhoades and Stensaker 2017a, b). Clark's supporters saw this as a way forward for many institutions of higher education as they attempted to find their place in the twenty-first-century landscapes. For his critics, the local enterprising response to market conditions was perhaps a weak response rather than a larger solution for the problems that universities face (Marginson and Considine 2000; Rhoades and Stensaker 2017a, b).

But Clark also shows us a reality as well. As states around the world withdraw some (or most) of their investments in universities, universities have been forced to focus on survival and compete within a neoliberal framework. This work is so intensive that many institutions do not feel they can focus on a more basic mission. In fact, surviving and meeting the needs of the local, regional, and global economy become the reason for the university. And as such, the neoliberals would argue that then universities should be efficient and disciplined by the market. But what is lost in this discourse of survival and economization is: what is a university for? Maybe even what is an economy for? Universities are the place where we discuss and question our values and think deeply about what a society should value. It is a place of

---

[2] Ironically, we are currently seeing the foolishness of neoliberal ideology during the COVID-19 pandemic. Many societies that took this neoliberal approach do not have the resources built up to fight the new coronavirus as the national health institutions have been stripped of resources and power. The states that are doing well are those where the state has stepped up and put a large amount of resources toward the fight.

thinking about becoming: what do we want to become? And a place to think about the ethics of the things we do and the people we do become. It is one of the main institutions in modern society where value and values meet in a dialogue. And creating value that we value is an entrepreneurial activity but maybe one that is inclusive of, but larger than, venture creation.

In this chapter, we too will take up the notion of the entrepreneurial, thinking about an entrepreneurial ecology. But our conception of an entrepreneurial ecology is one where the issue is not just producing revenue streams to support the existing institution. That would not take us out of the "legitimacy crisis" that so many universities find themselves in (Barnett 2015). Following Shumar and Robinson (2018, 2020), we take up a broader notion of entrepreneurial and entrepreneurship to think about what value is and the role of universities in value creation. Key questions include the following: What should universities value? How can they go about engaging in the production and evaluation of a set a values that have been carefully thought out, discussed, and agreed upon? Martin Lackéus cites a definition of entrepreneurship articulated by the Danish Foundation for Entrepreneurship.

> Entrepreneurship Education is defined from a broad understanding of entrepreneurship: Entrepreneurship is when you act upon opportunities and ideas and transform them into value for others. The value that is created can be financial, cultural, or social. (Vestergaard et al. 2012, p.11, cited in Lackéus 2016:3)

Lackéus's interest in his chapter is entrepreneurship education, but here we want to focus on the second part of the quote that define entrepreneurship. While most work in entrepreneurship focuses on venture creation, and value is primarily thought of as economic value, there is an increasing literature that looks at the creation of value more broadly. And if we look carefully at this definition, the emphasis is on turning ideas and opportunities into *value for others*. We will come back to this critical idea of value being social and transferable to others a little later.

This broader view of value creation is very strong in Scandinavia, but it exists in Britain, the USA, and other parts of the world (Blenker et al. 2012; Gibb 2002; Pittaway et al. 2017; Steyaert and Katz 2004). The question of a broader sense of value creation raises both the question of what value is and how value is determined in a society. There are many philosophers and social scientists who have addressed those questions, but not usually in relationship to the concept of entrepreneurship. Our goal in this chapter is to not attempt a broad review of this thinking about value but rather to move out from notions of economic value to think about how economic value is connected to other forms of value and valuation. We will also give a few examples of some of the thinking in this area. Ultimately, our purpose is to focus on how thinking about value, and the university's role in both value creation and the evaluation of value can be an important path forward. We hope this work will contribute to thinking about a new sense of purpose for the university that both fits with global society and also looks beyond and puts limits on economic value as the ultimate form of value. We will come back to this progressive entrepreneurial thinking, but first we will look at what value is.

What Is Value?

John Dewey (1939) thinks of value as something that is psychological and individual. It is a behavioral reaction to experience and as such is concrete and linked to experience. He sees value as rooted in a very immediate behavioral reaction: we either like something and think it is good, or we do not like it and think it is bad. Value judgment for Dewey is then an effort to rationalize our valuing. Value judgment is rational and a form of evaluation. These two moments of value production for Dewey are part of his concept of valuation. While we will want to move to a more sociological conception of value, it is useful to think about Dewey's two moments, what are immediately attracted to and think is good and then how we evaluate that attraction.

David Graeber (2001, 2013) has thought a lot about how the human societies produce value and how they think about value. Further he has thought about the relationship between economic value and societal values. Graeber, in his central anthropological work on value, suggests that Polanyi (1957) begins to address the question of the relationship between economic value and societal values with his concept of formalist and substantivist economics. Polanyi, looking at a number of tribal and smaller scale societies, commented on the fact that in these societies, the economy is not a separate part of the society and economic activity is fully integrated into the other realms of social life such that one cannot separate easily what is economic value from other forms of value. Of course, most anthropologists were aware of this fact, as subsistence cultures often do not have a market and see goods and services more in terms of gift exchanges rather than purchase. This insight goes all the way back to Marcel Mauss's classic work *The Gift* (2001). But Polanyi was trying to systematically think about how we can then theoretically frame the idea of value given this huge gulf between subsistence cultures and market societies. For Polanyi, a substantivist economy is one where economic activity is fully integrated with other aspects of social life. The formalist economy is one where the economy has developed separate institutions forming a separate structural level within society and hence is separate from other aspects of social life. This separation not only describes existing societies, but the difference emerged historically. Polanyi saw this historical development as problematic in that it changed the relationship of economic activity to other aspects of society and in a sense removed the economy from normal societal evaluation.

Graeber (2001, p.12) suggests that Polanyi opened the question of the relationship of economic value to societal values, but the question was never fully answered and is still a living debate as seen in Mazzucato's (2019) recent work and her argument that value has been lost to economics itself as a discipline. Graeber suggests that anthropologists (and others) largely abandoned the question of what value is cross-culturally rather than pursuing it to a final solution. It is to that larger question that Graeber addresses himself in his work on value. Drawing on the work of mentors like Nancy Munn and Terrence Turner, Graeber suggests that ultimate values in a society are the activities that people do that are the most valued, and they produce the things that people most highly value. In a sense, value is framed by the ultimate concerns of people in a particular society. This is true of money in a capitalist society and Kula objects in the Trobriand Islands. For Graeber, value is always comparative and also social. It is a social imaginary. As he says:

> One aspect of this approach that has been largely overlooked is the critical role of imagination. Insofar as value is social, it is always a comparison; value can only be realized in other people's eyes. Another way to put this is that there must always be an audience. (Graeber 2013:226)

Graeber points out that in every society, it is human social activity that produces value. And people decide what they ultimately value because they will accept the products of that activity in exchange. The tokens will be held in high esteem. As so every society, market-based or reciprocity based, makes decisions about what activity is most important, what objects that activity produces, who gets to control the circulation of those objects, and so on. Graeber then leads us to the realization that these questions of what value is, how does one accumulate it, and who holds high esteem in the eyes of others are all political questions. And they are ones that a society must work out, often through struggle and conflict (Graeber 2001, p.88, 2013, p.228).

This notion, that value is based in human activity and is a product of the imagination leads us back to the concept of entrepreneurship and the notion of an entrepreneurial ecology. In *Disclosing New Worlds*, authors Spinosa et al. (1997) suggest that entrepreneurs are a special group of individuals. They are able to focus on what the authors call the "disharmonies" of the way of life that a group of people are living. And by remaining focused on those disharmonies, they are then able to imagine ways of solving those disharmonies which would not only create new things but would in fact bring about a different world. All we have to do is think of smart phones as an example of an object that changes the world we live in. Spinosa, Flores, and Dreyfus's work draws heavily on the work of Martin Heidegger *Being and Time*. And while for Heidegger (1962/1927) most humans are trapped in their everyday worlds and cannot imagine their becoming, for Spinosa, Flores, and Dreyfus, entrepreneurs are those unusual individuals. Entrepreneurs can think about a specific arena of human activity, what they call a "disclosive space" where particular kinds of practices go on and they can remain focused on what does not work in this space, what they might call a disharmony. The entrepreneur can then begin to imagine a life beyond a disharmony and how the practices of a group of people might change in that particular arena. Interestingly for Spinosa, Flores, and Dreyfus their model of seeing the disharmonies, imagining solutions, and then creating solutions and moving toward new worlds is a process they see in entrepreneurs as well as individuals engaged in democratic action. For them it is about a more self-conscious history making, a focus on becoming.

It is in the spirit of focusing on becoming that we see as the potential for the university to regain the ground of legitimacy and to be called to an ultimate purpose. By engaging students and faculty in a focused approach to the larger community's disharmonies and seeking solutions to those disharmonies by looking to the world in the process of being remade from an entrepreneurial stance, that university practice can become central to a democratic society's well-being. Returning to Dewey, this social and discursive process would have two parts to it, the focus on value creation and also the focus on evaluation – if these values are good and right.

In order to think about this process of value creation and reevaluation, we examine two other conceptions of entrepreneurship, that of absence and alienation. These for us are exemplary rather than complete. In the spirit of Heidegger's notion of "worldhood" and the notion of a disclosive space, there are at least two additional things the university must focus on. One is that the university is a space where many "others" come together who do not share a common culture. And as such they must find a way to mutual recognition (Rider 2018). And then further, there are needs that cannot be anticipated and so a social imagination must come to deal with that which is not knowable. It is to these concerns that we turn next.

Entrepreneurship of Absence

Entrepreneurship, in our version, shows itself as an ethical activity in the recognizing and acknowledging value(s) we do not necessarily fully understand ourselves but may be important for others. To act as a means in the creation of values that may be foreign to ourselves reveals the meaning of an ethical entrepreneurship. Following Emmanuel Levinas (2003), ethics is the ability to resist the temptation of turning the values what we do not know, understand, and care for ourselves into our own image and something we *do* care for, understand, and wish to protect – thus assimilating the other person, social identity, or belief system into my own. In a Levinasian perspective, value creation lies in assisting the other in her creation of values which may be strange to us. In this perspective, entrepreneurship is not the creation, harnessing, and growth of values we are constituted by, but entrepreneurship lies in the very welcoming of the "strangeness of the Other, his irreducibility to the I, to my thoughts and my possessions" (Levinas 2003, p.43).

Entrepreneurship may then become a formation of communities between strangers and a connection (and not assimilation) of value systems that cannot be reduced to each other's socio-material and sociopolitical premises for meaning making. We argue that entrepreneurship may be understood as the obligation to enter into processes of value creation I do *not* understand (Levinas 2000). Our notion of deep entrepreneurship or depth entrepreneurship is ethical in its core semantics. Entrepreneurship, in this sense, moves beyond struggle, conflict, and violence when opposing value systems meet and interact. Entrepreneurship as a form of ethics, rests on the idea that "[p]aradoxically it is qua alienus – foreigner and other – that man is not alienated" (Levinas 2000, p.59) and that the true possibility for creation of ethical value lies in the openness to the other and the possibilities for change, in the deepest sense of the term, that lie in wait.

Building on the work of Alphonso Lingis (1994), Gert Biesta (2006) argues that listening and responding to what is other, and finding one's own voice through that response, is the deepest form of learning. According to Biesta, true learning is not the ability to copy or reproduce what already exists but happens when the student "responds to what is unfamiliar, what is different, and what challenges, irritates, or even disturbs" (Biesta 2006, p.68). In this mode "learning becomes a creation or an invention, a process of bringing something new into the world: one's own, unique response" and learning builds "the community of those who have nothing in common" (ibid.). In this mode of learning and studying, we are letting the thoughts and voices of others speak *through us*. We create value from the *other's* point of view. We are invoking an entrepreneurship of absence when we allow what is often missing or kept in the margins of our societal awareness, debates, and cultural belief systems. We engage with the entrepreneurship of absence when we are, in our value creation, led by the moral imperative of speaking for "the silent and for the silenced" and when we say "what others would say if they were not absent, elsewhere, or dead" (Lingis 1998, p.136). Seen this way, learning is not only about finding my own voice, but finding the voices of others, who are not allowed or able to speak, or who are not here anymore to tell their stories and to be heard and included into the societal and cultural realities constituted. Through academic studying, whether it is the study of texts in the library, theoretical or empirical study, or through various forms of action research, we seek understandings, occurrences, events, and phenomena otherwise undetected, marginalized, suppressed, or perhaps lost and forgotten.

We use the term entrepreneurship here because we argue for student learning not only as a way of enriching the learner herself but to open up wider social and cultural realities and value systems otherwise not accessed and acknowledged. Acquiring academic knowledge is to "form a language with which to speak about a topic, and to inhabit the topic through imparting one's own voice" (Barnett and Bengtsen 2019, p.86). As argued by Barnett and Bengtsen, knowledge lets us not only understand but also engage with and even "step inside dimensions of reality and experience afresh different aspects of the world," and through knowledge creation processes, we may be able to see through the eyes of the "space-traveller, or the prisoner of war, or listen with the ears of the diplomat or feel with the hands of the mountaineer. Knowledge is traversing life" (ibid.). In this view, student learning and knowledge creation are not chained to the university as particular socio-material and socioeconomic institution, and through knowledge "we take on a heightened sensitivity to others and the place of others" (Barnett and Bengtsen 2019, p.89). The notion of absence helps us refine the meaning of entrepreneurship we are after in this chapter, a social and even ethical value creation that takes its form and being not from what I or we need but from what *others* see, understand, and need.

Alien Entrepreneurship

As we are writing this chapter, we find ourselves in the middle of the COVID-19 pandemic, where it has become clear that entrepreneurship falls short if it targets only the creation of values that are understandable and relevant from what we know, from the current time and situation. As our idea of entrepreneurship should not only include the recognition and acknowledgement of values in the margins societally, culturally, and historically, we also argue, further, for an alien entrepreneurship – the creation of values that are unknown and perhaps even strange to us now but are values for what is to come. This is an entrepreneurship of the not-yet-ness, an entrepreneurship of fecundity, where value creation becomes the terroir of possible futures, for societies and generations yet to come.

According to Friedrich Nietzsche, one of the most important aspects of our culture is the creation of values for a society and a culture, which do not yet exist. Only this way do we keep our cultural horizon open and build up our personal and cultural courage to meet yet unknown challenges such as we see now with the climate and health crises. As alien entrepreneurs, we must be able to "use of a rare and singular measuring-rod, almost a frenzy" and to contain "the feeling of heat in things which feel cold to all other persons" to enable "a diving of values for which scales have not yet been invented: a sacrificing on altars which are consecrated to an unknown God" (Nietzsche 2006, pp. 49–50). As we enter an era of posthumanism and the Anthropocene (Gildersleeve and Kleinhesselink 2019; Lysgaard et al. 2019), we find that "[d]ichotomies such as human-nature and human-Earth, no longer work or fit" (Gildersleeve and Kleinhesselink 2019, p.5). Values for a future yet to come do not rest on the "centrisms" of the past century: anthropocentrism, eurocentrism, and other forms of segregation and protectionism. The values for the future seem to lie in the ability to dissolve borders and boundaries between nation states, cultural value paradigms, genders, social divides, and even previously sociopolitically natural (and before that sacred) divisions between not only races but species as well.

An alien entrepreneurship not only includes innovation as a way of improving already existing social and cultural spheres of life but seeks the value experiment, where universities and institutions for higher education may become like "hothouse[s] for strange and choice plants" (Nietzsche 1968, p.478). Alien entrepreneurship is a form of value creation, where the horizon of meaning does not close down and form a totality, a hegemony. On the contrary, with Nietzsche, we argue for a "Higher education: (…) and excess of power (…) [to] constitute a hothouse for the luxury cultivation of the exception, the experiment of danger, of the nuance" (Nietzsche 1968, p.492). This excess of power is the core drive for universities to overcome the shackling of learning to narrowly and instrumentally defined preset learning goals sustaining knowledge practices and forms of student formation relevant for the current state of things (and the present job-market layout). In Bengtsen's (2020) Nietzsche interpretation, the hothouse metaphor aims to counter negative ecologies, cultural pessimism, and value paralysis, and the "image of the hothouse points towards exotic ecologies and relationships between universities and their surroundings – perhaps even a new dawn for higher education" (Bengtsen 2020, p.20). Similarly, Paul Standish's (2011) Nietzsche reading calls for the university of the day after tomorrow, which will "demonstrate its essential public place in the democracy to come" (Standish 2011, p.164).

Alien entrepreneurship calls for a learning for the unknown and to be able to create what Barnett (2004) terms "epistemological gaps" (p.251), which are "epistemological interventions in turn disturb the world, so bringing a new world before us" (ibid.). Students of higher education must learn that creativity and innovation in their knowing efforts do not only aim at finding secure and sustainable solution for the society and world we know but also to destabilize the known world, which is "knowing-in-and-with-uncertainty. The knowing produces further uncertainty" (ibid.). Alien entrepreneurship requires an imaginative approach within the learning designs and curriculum planning that recognizes that imagination is not merely about finding solutions to already existing socioeconomic problem but allows the view that "the imagination has a power to see into things, to feel into things, [and] to be at one with things anew" (Barnett 2013, p. 25).

Our institutions have to be able to support and nurture the imagination encouraged and hoped for in the learning and student formation processes. The universities themselves have to be able to enter the space of uncertainty, where they educate for not only a known but also an unknown future. To enter the space of epistemic as well and institutional uncertainty requires "thought about the university outside the fatalistic binary that places the global neoliberal university as the dominating one and the old western collegial university (say) as its subordinated other" (Grant 2020, p.23). As Grant argues, this "binary traps us in an unhappy mix of fury and nostalgia, nostalgia which might be mobilising but is just as likely to be pacifying" (ibid.). To, institutionally, be able to form a future-oriented trajectory, we must understand institutions not an all-comprehensive and cohesive structures but assemblages – a "liberating multiplicity of a thousand tiny universities [for] the future-which-is-now" (Grant 2020, p.24). Alien entrepreneurship requires an alien university (Bengtsen 2018) – an institutionally awry and askew space for learning, entangled in societal futures not yet brought about. The "alien university is not in the future as such, but it is not entirely in the present either. The alien university educates in anomalous and incomprehensible situations" (Bengtsen 2018, p.1541). It takes courage, and a great amount of care, to form institutional and learning spaces around processes of value creation that cannot immediately be translated or exchanged into the social capital or cultural currency currently surrounding us.

Conclusion: Universities as Central Institutions in Contemporary Society

In this chapter, we have interpreted the current condition, challenges, but also possibilities, for the university and higher education through the lens of entrepreneurship and different understandings of value creation.

Firstly, we have argued that the current crisis of universities and higher education is rooted in the historical narrowing of the university's mission to one of supporting economic value creation for a formalist economy, where the economy has developed as a separate structure within society and is separate from other aspects of social life. The underlying trope of formalist economy has, through several phases, resulted in the neoliberal and market-driven contemporary university. In contrast, we have argued, with Polanyi, for a move toward a substantivist economy, where value creation is fully integrated with social and cultural life. To release the university from its neoliberal gridlock, higher education, in turn, needs to be seen as fully embedded within its surrounding social and cultural contexts and not as separate from them. Higher education, like value creation, should seek away from the increasing focus on individual performances and buy-ins and move toward the notion of the common (Szadkowski 2018).

Secondly, we have argued, with Graeber and Spinosa, Flores, and Dreyfus, that value creation is, ontologically seen, the very cross-cultural intersection and, followingly, the disclosing of new worlds (in contrast to constant reinventions of old, or already known, worlds). Higher education may contribute to this form of value creation, not through a reinforcement of already established and societally assimilated cultural understandings and belief systems but through disharmonic and critical encounters with one's own, and one's own cultural, preconceptions and limitations. Higher education, seen in this light, becomes a form of cultural growth itself.

Thirdly, we have argued, with Levinas and Lingis, that higher education constitutes an entrepreneurial activity of value creation through its looping in the social and cultural margins of its surrounding societal and political contexts. We have argued that higher education learning is not only about finding one's own voice and speaking up for oneself – but makes possible a care-for-the-other. Here, higher education reveals its potential as becoming a form of ethical entrepreneurship through speaking with and for others, such as the marginalized, silenced, and silent groups in our societies and our cultural and political history.

Finally, we have argued, with Nietzsche, that any sustainable form of value creation must rest on its entrepreneurial not-yet-ness. Universities and higher education contribute to forms of value creation, where one is concerned not only with the values one already understands and cherishes but also values and belief systems one does not understand or fully embrace. These are values we may yet grow into and which wave to us from a still distant future. Alien entrepreneurship is a form of giving to a future that does not belong to us but belongs to generations and societies yet to come. It even extends beyond the human ken and strives to understand and lay the foundation for what is valuable for other species and geological realms.

These four dimensions of the meaning of value creation form, together, an ecological entrepreneurship connecting economy to culture, universities to societies, and higher education to societal responsibility. Further, part of this value creation is the reflexive discourse of evaluation – if these forms of value are good and right. As universities and higher education form a central pillar within the notion of ecological entrepreneurship, the institutions, research, and learning and teaching practices will become essential in order to ensure sustainable social and cultural futures.

References

Ball, S. J. (2012). *Global education inc.: New policy networks and the neoliberal imaginary*. Milton Park/New York: Routledge.

Barnett, R. (2004). Learning for an unknown future, Higher Education Research & *Development*, 23:3, pp. 247–260.

Barnett, R. (2013). *Imagining the University*. London/New York: Routledge.

Barnett, R. (2015). Higher educational legitimation crisis. In *Thinking and rethinking the university: The selected works of Ronald Barnett*. Milton Park/New York: Routledge.

Barnett, R. & Bengtsen, S. (2019). Knowledge and the university. Re-claiming life. London/New York: Routledge.

Bengtsen. (2018). The alien university. *Educational Philosophy and Theory, 50*(14), 1541–1542. https://doi.org/10.1080/00131857.2018.1462452.

Bengtsen, S. (2020). Nietzsche (1844–1900). The will to power and the university. In R. Barnett & A. Fulford (Eds.), *Philosophers on the university. reconsidering higher education* (pp. 13–25). Cham: Springer.

Biesta, G.J.J. (2006). Beyond learning. Democratic education for a human future. Boulder/London: Paradigm Publishers.

Blenker, P., Frederiksen, S. H., Korsgaard, S., Müller, S., Neergaard, H., & Thrane, C. (2012). Entrepreneurship as everyday practice. *Industry and Higher Education, 26*(6), 417–430.

Canaan, J., & Shumar, W. (Eds.). (2008). *Structure and Agency in the Neoliberal University*. New York: Routledge.

Clark, B. R. (1998). *Creating entrepreneurial universities: Organizational pathways of transformation*. Bingley: Emerald Group Publishing Limited.

Dewey, J. (1939). Theory of valuation. In *International encyclopedia of unified sciences* (Vol. 2 No. 4). Chicago: University of Chicago Press.

Gibb, A. (2002). In pursuit of a new 'enterprise' and 'entrepreneurship' paradigm for learning: creative destruction, new values, new ways of doing things and new combinations of knowledge. *International Journal of Management Reviews, 4*(3), 213–233.

Gildersleeve, R. E., & Kleinhesselink, K. (2019). Introduction: The anthropocene as context and concept for the study of higher education. In R. E. Gildersleeve & K. Kleinhesselink (Eds.), Special Issue on the Anthropocene in the Study of Higher Education, *Philosophy and Theory in Higher Education* (Vol. 1(1), pp. 1–15). New York: Peter Lang.

Graeber, D. (2001). *Toward an anthropological theory of value: The false coin of our own dreams*. New York: Palgrave Macmillan.

Graeber, D. (2013). It is value that brings universes into being. *HAU: Journal of Ethnographic Theory, 3*(2), 219–243.

Grant, B. (2020). The future is now: A Thousand Tiny Universities. In Bengtsen, S. & Barnett, R. (Eds.). Imagining the Future University. *Special Issue in Philosophy and Theory in Higher Education, 1*(3), 9–28.

Habermas, J. (1975). *Legitimation crisis*. Boston: Beacon Press.
Heidegger, M. (1962/1927). *Being and time*. New York: Harper and Row.
Kwiek, M. (2006). *The classical German idea of the university revisited, or on the nationalization of the modern institution*. Center for Public Policy Research Chapter Series Vol. 1. http://www.cpp.amu.edu.pl/pdf/CPP_RPS_vol.1_Kwiek.pdf.
Lackéus, M. (2016). *A 'value' and 'economics' grounded analysis of six value creation based entrepreneurial education initiatives*. Chapter for 3E ECSB Entrepreneurship Education Conference. Leeds, UK, 11–13 May, 2016.
Levinas, E. (2000). *Otherwise than being or beyond essence* (A. Lingis, Trans.). Pittsburgh: Duquesne University Press.
Levinas, E. (2003). *Totality and infinity. An essay on exteriority* (A. Lingis, Trans.). Pittsburgh: Duquesne University Press.
Lingis, A. (1994). *The community of those who have nothing in common*. Bloomington/Indianapolis: Indiana University Press.
Lingis, A. (1998). *The imperative*. Bloomington/Indianapolis: Indiana University Press.
Lysgaard, J. A., Bengtsson, S., & Laugesen, M. H.-L. (2019). *Dark pedagogy. Education, horror, and the anthropocene*. London: Palgrave Macmillan.
Marginson, S., & CONSIDINE, M. (2000). *The enterprise university: Power, governance and reinvention in Australia*. Cambridge/Melbourne: Cambridge University Press.
Mauss, M. (2001). *The Gift. The form and reason for exchange in archaic societies*. London/New York: Routledge.
Mazzucato, M. (2019). *The value of everything. Making and taking in the global economy*. London: Penguin.
McGettigan, A. (2013). *The great university gamble: Money, markets and the future of higher education*. London: Pluto Press.
Newfield, C. (2008). *Unmaking the public university: The forty year assault on the middle class*. Cambridge, MA: Harvard University Press.
Nietzsche, F. (1968). *The will to power* (W. Kaufmann & R. J. Holingdale, Trans.). New York: Random House.
Nietzsche, F. (2006). *The gay science* (T. Common, Trans.). New York: Dover Publications.
Noble, D. F. (1977). *America by design: Science, technology, and the rise of corporate capitalism* (1st ed.). New York: Knopf.
Nussbaum, M. C. (2010). *Not for profit: Why democracy needs the humanities*. Princeton/Oxford: Princeton University Press.
O'Boyle, L. (1983). Learning for its own sake: the German university as nineteenth-century. *Comparative Studies in Society and History, 25*(1), 3–25. Published by Cambridge University Press. Stable URL: http://www.jstor.org/stable/178570. Accessed 28 Nov 2014, 13:50.
Pittaway, L., Aïssaoui, R., & Fox, J. (2017). Social constructionism and entrepreneurial opportunity. https://doi.org/10.4324/9781315625454-4.
Polanyi, K. (1957). *The great transformation: The political and economic origins of our times*. (Original publication 1944). Boston: Beacon Press.
Rhoades, G., & Stensaker, B. (2017a). Bringing organizations and systems back together: Extending Clark's entrepreneurial university. *Higher Education Quarterly, 71*(2), 129–140.
Rhoades, G., & Stensaker, B. (2017b). Bringing organisations and systems back together: Extending Clark's entrepreneurial university. *Higher Education Quarterly, 71*(2), 129–140.
Rider, S. (2018). Truth, democracy, and the mission of the university. In S. S. E. Bengtsen & R. Barnett (Eds.), *The thinking university: A philosophical examination of thought and higher education*. Cham: Springer.
Shore, C. N. (2010). Beyond the multiversity: Neoliberalism and the rise of the schizophrenic university. *Social Anthropology, 18*(1), 15–29. https://doi.org/10.1111/j.1469-8676.2009.00094.x. URL: http://hdl.handle.net/2292/10824.
Shore, C., & Wright, S. (2000). Coercive accountability: The rise of audit culture in higher education. In M. Strathern (Ed.), *Audit cultures: Anthropological studies in accountability, ethics and the academy* (pp. 57–89). London: Routledge.

Shore, C., & Wright, S. (2015). Governing by numbers: audit culture, rankings and the new world order. *Social Anthropology, 23*, 22–28. https://doi.org/10.1111/1469-8676.12098.

Shore, C., & Wright, S. (Eds.). (2017). *Death of the public university? Uncertain futures for higher education in the knowledge economy*. Berghahn Books. ISBN 978-1-78533-542-6.

Shumar, W., & Robinson, S. (2018). Universities as societal drivers. Entrepreneurial interventions for a better future. In S. Bengtsen & R. Barnett (Eds.), *The thinking university: A philosophical examination of thought and high er education* (pp. 31–46). Cham: Springer.

Shumar, W., & Robinson, S. (2020). Agency, risk-taking and identity in entrepreneurship education. *Philosophy and Theory of Higher Education, 1*(3), 153–173.

Slaughter, S., & Rhoades, G. (2004). *Academic capitalism and the new economy: Markets, state, and higher education*. Baltimore: The Johns Hopkins University Press.

Spinosa, C., Flores, F., & Dreyfus, H. L. (1997). *Disclosing new worlds: Entrepreneurship, democratic action and the cultivation of colidarity*. Cambridge, MA: MIT Press.

Standish, P. (2011). Teaching in the university the day after tomorrow. In R. In Barnett (Ed.), *The future university. Ideas and possibilities*. London/New York: Routledge.

Steyaert, C., & Katz, J. (2004). Reclaiming the space of entrepreneurship in society: Geographical, discursive and social dimensions. *Entrepreneurship and Regional Development, 16*, 179–196.

Szadkowski, K. (2018). The common in higher education: A conceptual approach. *Higher Education*. https://doi.org/10.1007/s10734-018-0340-4.

Vestergaard, L., Moberg, K., & J.rgensen, C. (2012). *Impact of entrepreneurship education in Denmark –2011*. Odense, Denmark: The Danish Foundation for Entrepreneurship – Young Enterprise.

Wesley Shumar is a professor in the Department of Communication at Drexel University. His research focuses on higher education, mathematics education, and entrepreneurship education. His recent work in higher education focuses on the spatial transformation of American universities within the consumer spaces of cities and towns. From 1997 to 2018 he worked as an ethnographer at the Math Forum, a virtual math education community and resource center. He continues to do research into the use of online spaces to support mathematics education. He is author of *College for Sale: A Critique of the Commodification of Higher Education*, Falmer Press, 1997, and *Inside Mathforum.org: Analysis of an Internet-based Education Community*, Cambridge University Press, 2017. He co-edited, with Joyce Canaan, *Structure and Agency in the Neoliberal University*, Routledge/Falmer, 2008. He also co-edited, with K.Ann Renninger, *Building Virtual Communities: Learning and Change in Cyberspace*, Cambridge, 2002.

Søren S. E. Bengtsen is Associate Professor in higher education at the Department of Educational Philosophy and General Education, Danish School of Education (DPU), Aarhus University, Denmark. Also, at Aarhus University, he is the Co-Director of the research centre 'Centre for Higher Education Futures' (CHEF). Bengtsen is a founding member and Chair of the international academic association 'Philosophy and Theory of Higher Education Society' (PaTHES). His main research areas include the philosophy of higher education, educational philosophy, higher education policy and practice, and doctoral education and supervision. Bengtsen's recent books include *The Hidden Curriculum in Doctoral Education* (Palgrave Macmillan, 2020, co-authored with Dely L. Elliot, Kay Guccione, and Sofie Kobayashi), *Knowledge and the University. Re-claiming Life* (Routledge, 2019, co-authored with Ronald Barnett), *The Thinking University. A Philosophical Examination of Thought and Higher Education* (Springer, 2019, co-edited with Ronald Barnett), and *Doctoral Supervision. Organization and Dialogue* (Aarhus University Press, 2016).

Part III
The Idea of the Future University

Chapter 10
Philosophy for the Playful University – Towards a Theoretical Foundation for Playful Higher Education

Rikke Toft Nørgård

Introduction: Gamified Higher Education

Although higher education today is focused on creativity, imagination, innovation and personal growth, this is largely embedded within frameworks of marketisation, knowledge production and performance economies. Over the past 40 years, the university and higher education worldwide has found itself subject to a neoliberal agenda of corporatisation, up-skilling, future workforce and accountability. As a consequence, higher education institutions and academic life are being reconfigured and corporatised to account for these shifts growing out of 'new capitalism' and 'the knowledge economy' (Whitton and Langan 2018; Koeners and Francis 2020; Jayasuriya 2015; Shumar 1997; Wright 2016). It is the university's responsibility to produce the right students with the right competencies and skills that enable them to occupy the right jobs that will ensure the right socio-economic growth. As such, there are production schemes and measurement tools in place to ensure that students are produced at ample speed and with desirable employability (Nørgård et al. 2019). Thus, the university has become a professional competence factory, complete with branding strategies, corporate culture, accelerators, incubators, strategic communication and so on (Barnett 2011). This constitutes what could be termed 'the accelerated university', where students are driven through higher education as fast and efficiently as possible in order to be put to hard work in society.

Koeners and Francis (2020) point out how this performativity-based approach to higher education 'penetrates deep into the classroom, affecting both teachers and students alike and thus provokes both individual and collective stressors [which] present us with an urgent need to consider alternative educational philosophies to

R. T. Nørgård (✉)
Aarhus University, Aarhus C, Denmark
e-mail: rtoft@edu.au.dk

© The Author(s), under exclusive license to Springer Nature Switzerland AG 2021
S. S. E. Bengtsen et al. (eds.), *The University Becoming*, Debating Higher Education: Philosophical Perspectives 6,
https://doi.org/10.1007/978-3-030-69628-3_10

protect educational authenticity and what Stephen Ball aptly names the "teachers' soul"' (Koeners and Francis 2020: 143–144). One manifestation of the accelerated and streamlined university is the appearance of gamification and gamified higher education. Here, games and gamified tools and tactics are employed to enhance learner motivation and satisfaction as well as boost performance and competitiveness. This focus on games, gamification and gamified higher education is problematic as:

> The engagement strategies used typically by educational games and gamification techniques focus on providing extrinsic rewards for measurable performance, which simply echoes the systems and structures of an increasingly metric-driven higher education sector in an increasingly quantified society (Whitton 2018: 2).

Accordingly, even though gamified higher education is often utilised to improve motivation, circumvent stressors and combat poor student experience, it simultaneously also accentuates a culture of competition and performance by the very nature of games. An increasing number of studies have confirmed that the use of game elements such as badges, levels, leader boards, points, competitions, prices, rewards, etc. have a detrimental effect on intrinsic motivation, creativity, risk-taking and experimentation (Whitton 2018; Pink 2009; Deci et al. 2001). Furthermore, there is little evidence that these initiatives and strategies foster academic enjoyment or deep thinking and learning. Rather, gamified higher education encourages students to "do education" through manipulation of point-based incentive systems or what is sometimes called "gaming the system" (Baker et al. 2008; Nørgård et al. 2017).

All in all, gamification strategies and gamified higher education runs the risk of turning higher education into a game system where you can lose or win, level up and monitor your progression as points – something far removed from the soul of the university and higher education.

The State of Play: From Gamified to Playful Higher Education

While digital games for the last 30 years or so have been regarded as a (somewhat) approved activity for adults and for the last 20 years have been the subject of serious academic research, it is a different matter when it comes to play and playfulness in adulthood. And, while the study of play and playful learning in childhood is widely acknowledged and have a longstanding history within theory and research, the role of play, playfulness and playful education is still thoroughly underdeveloped and under-acknowledged as a separate field of study (Whitton 2018; Walsh 2018). Today, there is an abundance of literature – when it comes to science, research, theory, educational development and practice – both within the field of digital games and gaming in adulthood as well as within the field of play, playful learning and playfulness in childhood. However, the field of play in adulthood in general and play/playfulness in higher education in particular are more or less non-existent.

Overall, playful higher education lacks robust theoretical and conceptual foundation (Nørgård et al. 2017; Whitton 2018; Koeners and Francis 2020; James and Nerantzi 2019). While digital games in adult education as well as playful learning in childhood are considered serious subjects with mature fields that have their own journals, conferences, book series and sprawling specialised subfields that could fill a library, works on play and playfulness in higher education is scarce and without its own conferences, journals or developed subfields. As a field, playful higher education is still in its infancy – even more so when it comes to foundational theories or conceptual frameworks.

This is partly due to the fact that playfulness in higher education is routinely positioned as a form of "relaxation", "break", "social event" or "pause" from the seriousness and duties of higher education. In the present reality of the accelerated university, there seems to be no time to play around within the curriculum. Consequently, play is positioned as a frivolous or unserious activity that might relieve stress, give a breather or create fun extracurricular activities outside serious academia and real work. This circumstance is addressed by play scholar Alison James that describes how play and playfulness as serious higher education provokes strong reactions tied to a sense of professional credibility and the way higher education should be framed and practiced:

> Free play is the most challenging form of play for institutions which need to emphasise value for money and financial accountability [...] for many tutors allowing any loss of control, goal or structure runs counter to their professional sense of identity and to offering a well-designed, high-quality learning experience (James 2019: 12).

However, prominent works on the practice of playful higher education do exist, such as *The power of play in higher education* (James and Nerantzi 2019), *Playful learning – Events and activities to engage adults* (Whitton and Moseley 2019), *Framing play design – A hands-on guide for designers, learners and innovators* (Gudiksen and Skovbjerg 2020), 'The physiology of play: potential relevance for higher education' (Koeners and Francis 2020), 'Playful learning: tools, techniques, and tactics' (Whitton 2018) and 'Playful learning in higher education: developing a signature pedagogy' (Nørgård et al. 2017). Still, these are scarce, scattered and mostly concerned with the practice of playful higher education, activities for playful teaching and learning, case studies on playfulness in higher education or how to design for playfulness – That is, occupied with mapping, describing or inspiring practice rather than developing theoretical foundations or conceptual frameworks for the playful university or playful higher education.

This is problematic, as the current lack of philosophical, theoretical and conceptual grounding of play and playfulness entails that:

> play in adulthood is stigmatised, little understood and lacks a coherent body of research [...] without the necessary background in play in adulthood, study of playful learning in higher education becomes even more complex and difficult. [...] Associations with play as an activity that is childish, frivolous or inauthentic may limit the motivation of learners - particularly adult learners - to engage with playful learning' (Whitton 2018: 9)

Therefore, the present chapter seeks to provide some steps for more thorough consideration of playful higher education and the playful university through contemplating what is actually implied by the words 'play', 'playful' and 'playfulness'. The hope is to advance the field from being largely practice-oriented towards developing a philosophy for the playful university. A groundwork for what it means to be intentionally and substantially playful, that in turn can constitute a well-founded way forward for the university as a playful force in the world. Knowing what play and playfulness is, brings about the possibility of a genuine playful university and spirited – not profane – playful higher education. Or, as German philosopher Eugen Fink puts it: 'As long as, in such trains of thought, one still naively operates within the popular antithesis of "work and play", of "play and the seriousness of life," and so forth, play is not understood in the content and depth of its Being' (Fink 2016: 16–17). What would it, then, imply to have a university that not only accommodates the Homo Faber (the working academic) and Homo Sapiens (the thinking academic) but also the Homo Ludens (the playing academic)?

To Play or Not to Play: On the Distinction Between Play and Playfulness

> Man only plays when he is in the fullest sense of the word a human being, and he is only fully a human being when he plays – Friedrich Schiller 1795, Letter XV

But, what then, is play? Reading into prominent works on play philosophy, play theory and key texts on play and playfulness in higher education, the overall spirit running through these works is an acknowledgement and appreciation of play as a core aspect of curiosity, creativity and communality. Play is not something fun standing outside "serious affairs" or "adult life", but is a life force, elevated thinking, doing and being, a sacred fellowship and a cornerstone in culture and human existence. Within play studies, common definitions of play describe it as an activity or experience that is enjoyable and voluntary (Caillois 1958), involves an in-the-now attitude characterised by immersion and engagement (Huizinga 1938) and promotes fellowship and community (Fink 1957). Furthermore, play is accentuated as integral to human existence, freedom and connected to the quality of life (Schiller 1795), which puts it not outside "adult life" or "the serious activities" of life, but squarely in the heart of life, existence and education as a form of "sacred seriousness" (Gadamer 1966). In the words of play scholar Brian Sutton-Smith: 'The opposite of play is not work – it is depression' (Sutton-Smith 1997: 198).

However, before diving into play philosophies and theories and what these entail for a genuinely playful university, an important distinction between play and playfulness needs to be emphasised. Perhaps the most fundamental and defining aspect of play activities is their autotelic nature. Play activities have their own goal and purpose, meaning that there is no purpose of play outside the activity play. The play activity establishes and unfolds its own purposes within and through play, and as such, no external aims, purposes or intentions can be imported into a play activity. This highlights an insuperable clash between the purpose of play and the purpose of education. Pedagogy and education always have purpose. This purposefulness of pedagogy and education is found in the very etymology of the words as they both mean 'to lead'. Given that pedagogy and education are acts and processes of intentionally leading someone to certain knowledge, competencies, values, beliefs and habits, play abolishes education as education abolishes play. Following from this, it becomes clear that play as an activity may be both subversive and inappropriate for higher education and the university.

Here, play philosopher Miguel Sicart's distinction between "play" and "playfulness" becomes crucial to differentiate between play and playful higher education. The playful university is not a university occupied *by* play or by integrating play activities *into* higher education. Rather, it is a university occupied by *playfulness* and by *playful* higher education:

> We need play, but not all of it - just what attracts us, what makes us create and perform and engage, without the encapsulated singularity of play. What we want is the attitude of play without the activity of play. We need to take the same stance towards things, the world, and others that we take during play. But we should not play; rather, we should perform as expected in that (serious) context and with that (serious) object. We want play without play. We want playfulness - the capacity to use play outside the context of play. Playfulness is a way of engaging with particular contexts and objects that is similar to play but respects the purpose and goals of that object or context. (Sicart 2014: 21)

As a consequence, the playful university and playful higher education is projecting the spirit, structure and culture of play into nonplay activities and contexts. Here, playfulness lacks the autotelic nature of play activities in order to preserve the purpose of the original context or activity it is applied to. However, ungovernability, unpredictability, unknowability and un-usability – the traits of play activities – are still present in the activity or context wherein playfulness is instilled. This entails that the higher education context or activity becomes occupied by play without being destroyed by it. Following Sicart, playfulness implies seeing the university and higher education through the lens of play 'to make it shake and crack because we play with it' (Sicart 2014: 24). In a literature review of play, imagination and creativity, Kuan Chen Tsai comes to a similar conclusion: 'Taken together, the main purpose of those [playful] activities is to "play" your ideas and explore alternative pathways to solve the problems [...] Consequently, this play mood of toying with ideas for the sake of shifting paradigm should be promoted in educational settings' (Tsai 2012: 17).

Overall, three significant play frames arise from play philosophies and theories as well as work within playful higher education: (1) playful curiosity, that is, play as life and force within higher education exploratoriums; (2) playful creativity, or play as form and act within higher education experimentariums; and (3) playful communality, based on play fellowship and play culture within higher education collaboratoriums. These three play frames are instrumental in substantiating the notion of the playful university and constituting a foundation for the emergence of the Homo Ludens within playful higher education.

Playframe 1: Curiosity – Play as Life and Force and HE as Exploratorium

Within the first play frame, four core traits of play come together to constitute the possibility of playful curiosity in higher education: carnivalesque atmosphere, lusory attitude, existential orientation and imaginative nature. Taken together, these traits position the university as an exploratorium or a cabinet of wonders [Wunderkammer], where playfulness manifests itself as and through curiosity. Playful curiosity engulfs, liberates and opens up: In order to play, you must surrender yourself to play, let yourself be guided by play and become playfully wonderful. At its core, higher education as playful exploratorium is founded on the play imaginary and play question of 'what if…?'

Play is carnivalesque through its to-and-fro movement between curiosity and destruction, sense and sensibility, the Apollonian and the Dionysian (Sicart 2014). To be playful requires freedom, an opening up of the institutional world and dismissal of oppressive forces. In *Truth and Method* (1966) – a core work in play studies – Hans-Georg Gadamer highlights how, in play, it is not as much the players that are playing as it is the play that plays the players. In playing, players "play along", that is, play plays the players through orchestrating and framing the play experience and activity within an established playworld (Gadamer 2004). Following Gadamer, we can position the higher education exploratorium as a playful space that draws people into its space, fills them with a playful spirit and opens them up to reality, the world and existence. In the exploratorium, the real subject of play is not the player but playfulness itself. The player is absorbed by playfulness and through this played by the world, reality and existence (Gadamer 2004: 105–109). Consequently, playfulness becomes a force that pilots the player into the unknown, the what-if and the wonder-ful. Playful curiosity simultaneously requires that higher education assume a lusory attitude and brings about the possibility of new insights, wonderings and discoveries.

The lusory attitude in higher education requires, according to play scholar Nicola Whitton, a sacred space where people can take risks, explore, pose what-if questions and wonder openly about the world:

> This ability to enter a world of make-believe and accept alternative rules and realities is crucial to setting free the imagination and considering the possibilities for what might be and the potentials for what should be. This process of fostering imagination and ideation through play can lead to greater creativity and a virtuous circle of play, imagination and innovation. (Whitton 2018: 4).

In higher education, the lusory attitude denotes the ability to allow oneself to be taken over by play and to be put into play. Playfulness creates a thrownness into wonder, imagination and otherness by play. This highlight the "sacred seriousness" of play (Grondin 2001), which is in stark contrast to "profane play" found in the superficial "fun & games" approach, currently permeating higher education.

The lusory attitude required to enter into a mode of playful curiosity points towards the *existential orientation* of play. Play is not only an invocation of curiosity towards the world but also towards ourselves. Being in play is a pathway to exploring ourselves and the world, and through that exploration the possibility of discovering new knowledge, of challenging the establishment and of creating new relations and breaking old ones (Sicart 2014). Philosopher Friedrich Schiller describes the "play drive" as a prerequisite for bildung and being in balance in the world. In the play drive, sense and sensibility works in tandem to allow the human spirit to be curious and find her- or himself (Schiller 1795, Letter XIV). This balancing of sense and sensibility in the play drive is, according to Schiller, what makes humans free and gives humans free will. As a consequence, the playful university would be a place where Apollonian sense (thinking, abstraction and rationalism) and Dionysian sensibility (sensuality, feeling and matter) are in harmonious balance both in the being of the university, in higher education practices as well as in academic life (Homo Ludens).

The above presented come together in the *imaginative nature* of playfulness and the primordial question of play: 'what if…?' What if dogs could fly? What if this old log in the forest was a race car?, What if we pretended that you were a sheep and I was a sheepdog?, What if we used these stones as money in our shop?, What if we invented our own language and country and moved there? Embedded in the seeming silliness of the what-if question lies the opportunity for new discoveries (Bateson 2015), new frameworks (James 2019), moral imagination (Vadeboncoeur et al. 2016) and new forms of knowledge and practice (Nørgård et al. 2017). At the centre of playful, higher education as exploratorium is, then, the constitution of sacred spaces and practices for imagining possibilities, for testing strange ideas, for trying out new forms of knowledge and practices, for crossing boundaries and for engaging in open-ended thinking. This is echoed in 'Creativity as a practice of freedom: Imaginative play, moral imagination and the production of culture' (2017) where the core functionality of playful curiosity is highlighted as thinking and being permeated by an "as if" and "other than" approach which reflect a dialectic between cultural continuity and change through an increasing ability for moral imagination, thinking and action (Vadeboncoeur et al. 2016).

Playframe 2: Creativity – Play as Form and Act and HE as Experimentarium

The second playframe highlights how three core traits of play; play forms, play acts and playworlds, together constitute a safe spaces and brave spaces of playful creativity in higher education. Form, act and world opens up the university as an experimentarium, where playfulness manifest itself through the playful expressions, experiments and creativity of players. Through playful creativity, the player expresses her or his being in the world, act out new ideas and rearrange action and thought. At its core, higher education as playful experimentarium is an oasis of creativity in the form of a playworld, where the desire to play is acted out through the play question 'how can we...'-?

In his seminal book on play, *Man, Play and Games* (1958), French philosopher Roger Caillois established an enduring framework for the different *play forms* that characterises play. Caillois distinguishes between four essential forms of play – agon, alea, mimicry and ilinx – that can play out in a continuum between ludus type play (Apollonian rule-bound play) and paidia type play (Dionysian unruly play) (Caillois 1958). However, no matter the form and type of play, a key ingredient of playing is to play both within and with the rules. Rules are facilitators that create the context of play where players experiment, think, manipulate, change and adjust the rules (Sicart 2014).

The play structure through which play takes place and players play can take on four basic forms. Play can be in the form of competition or combat – *agon* – where the rules are fixed, there are winners and losers and players exercise certain skill-sets (e.g., chess). This is the play form we find in the gamified university where higher education is framed as combat or a competition that can be won (or lost). But play can also take on the form of fortuity or chance – *alea* – where luck, chance and destiny determine the name of the game (e.g., roulette). Here, players surrender themselves to fate or luck that then decides who will win and lose. This is a form of play we find in a destiny-oriented approach to higher education. Dices are rolled, bets are placed and then one hopes for the best. Where the agon play form frames higher education as a form of competition or a game of skill, the alea play form frames higher education as a form of fate, destiny or a game of chance. The third play form is make-believe or imitation – *mimicry* – where play is characterised by imagination, invention and interpretation (e.g., science fiction). It can be in the form of story worlds, theatre, role-play or festivals. Unlike agon and alea, there are no winners or losers, rather players are immersed in imagined or invented worlds, characters and situations. This play frame transforms higher education to a story world, where roles and worlds can be invented, tried on and acted out. The last play form is disorder or vertigo – *ilinx* – wherein players are taken over by their senses, the world or each other (e.g., dancing). It is a play form characterised by strong emotions, such as panic, joy, intoxication, fear or desire. Like mimicry, there are no winners or losers, rather play is here driven by a desire to surrender oneself to the world, the senses or each other. This is a play form that frames higher education as something driven by desire, intoxication and feeling, but also something that can swipe you off your feet, overpower you or make you panic.

Taken together, the four play forms highlight higher education as an experimentarium where players alternate between discipline, skill, fate, fantasy, invention and intoxication to create and experiment with themselves, knowledge and the world. Following Caillois, higher education is not about choosing between one or the other play form, but about creating a world of activities and experiences to play and experiment with.

From the different forms of play arise different *play acts*. To play is, on the one hand, the act of creatively engaging in the world and exploring it through ludic interaction and experimentation and, on the other hand, to create a world to play in with objects, rules, players, situations and spaces (Sicart 2014). In this, lies also the promise of play:

> Play can at one time be experienced as a peak of human sovereignty; the human being enjoys an almost unbounded creativity. He creates productively and without inhibition because he does not produce in the realm of real actuality. The player feels as if he were "master" of his imaginary products. Playing becomes a distinguished – because it is scarcely restricted – possibility of human freedom. (Fink 2016: 26).

Through play acts, old ideas are discarded and new ideas tried on or tried out. Play acts is a way of playfully interacting in the world – or the university – through sacred seriousness. Play is here an open-ended interpretive experience that allows us to experiment and try out new possibilities (Kirby and Graham 2016). Higher education enacted through play acts is characterised by a to-and-fro movement or a 'dance between creation and destruction, between creativity and nihilism [...] a movement between order and chaos' (Sicart 2014: 3). Following play theory, we see how higher education as experimentarium focuses on supporting people in rearranging actions or thoughts, in developing novel ways of dealing with the world and in breaking away from established patterns through combining actions and thoughts in new ways (Bateson 2015). Through play acts people engage in play forms, and through play forms people are called upon to act playfully in higher education and the world.

Play as *playworlds* is, at the same time, interior and exterior in relation to reality and the world. On the one hand, play is always contextual and happens through an entanglement of people, things, spaces and cultures in the world. Play is, in this way, always in and of the world. On the other hand, play is also appropriative in relation to the context where it exists, as it takes over the things, people, spaces and cultures to put them into play. Here, play creates a magic circle or playworld that sets play apart from the world. Through the creation of a playworld or magic circle, play breaks the state of affairs, disturbs our everyday routines and disrupts established conventions (Sicart 2014). But herein lies also the prospect of play. Through establishing a magic circle, play offers us a safe space to be brave, an oasis, in the form of a revitalised and pleasurable present that surrounds and engulfs us: 'In the projection of a playworld the one who plays conceals himself as the creator of this "world". He loses himself in his creation, plays a role, and has, within the playworld, playworldly things that surround him and playworldly fellow human beings' (Fink 2016: 25).

To develop more playful universities or playful higher education is, then, to develop safe spaces in the form of playworlds or magic circles, where people can think, feel and act beyond their immediate present and everyday reality. The university becomes "magical" through moving people beyond their own experiences, beyond the experiences of others and beyond their experience of the world and through this find themselves opened up for other worlds and realities (Vadeboncoeur et al. 2016). Dutch play scholar Johan Huizinga reminds us that school has its etymological roots in "leisure" and "philosophy" and through this points towards education as being essentially playful and transformational (Huizinga 1938, 1949).

Taken together, play forms, play acts and playworlds highlight the transformational nature, otherworldly existence and playful creativity at the heart of higher education as experimentarium. The playful university institutes a safe space in the form of an oasis or magic circle wherein people can be brave and confidently act out their creativity, try on strange ideas or perspectives, embrace diverse knowledge forms, construct alternative worlds or realities and express themselves in and through play. This leads to the third and last play frame, the communality of play. Here, curiosity and creativity come together to breed play fellowships and play cultures. Through conversation, companionship, co-construction and co-operation, people join hands, heads and hearts to playfully imagine ways to open up the world, dance on the border of what is possible and move beyond the limitations of the present reality.

Playframe 3: Communality – Play as Fellowship and Culture and HE as Collaboratorium

The last playframe emphasises how play companions and play collectives together creates fellowship and culture in and through playfulness in higher education. Companions and collectives establish playful cultures at the university and transform higher education from individual performance to co-operative collaboratorium. Higher education as collaboratorium underlines the friendship, solidarity and inter-personality of the playful university where the longing for community, "interplay" and shared experience is fulfilled through the forming of shared spaces and cultures for being and acting playfully together.

In his book, *Play as a symbol of the world and other writings* (1957), German philosopher Eugen Fink points towards play as being inherently interpersonal and intensively social at its core. Even if we play alone, we play within an "inter-personal horizon". In other words, when we become attuned to play and adopt a lusory attitude, we are always amongst fellow-players or *play companions*. Fink, Schiller and Huizinga, all position play as essential and inherent to the constitution of human existence through the forming of playful fellowships and friendships. In play, we play together, and through this, play carries us away from approaching life or higher education as a job or task to be completed. Within the "profane seriousness" of higher education and the neo-liberal university, there is often a drive to fulfil the learning goals, complete the assignments, get the job done and live in the prospect of immanent duties, projects and appointments. Life, and higher education, end up being a trajectory rather than an oasis (Fink 2016). The consequence is that thinking, doing and life at the university becomes isolated, solitary and siloed. Fink points towards play and playful fellowships as something that can help to counter the individualisation and desolation characterising the university and the higher education experience:

> Here a third aspect of the constitution of play can already be stated: the fellowship of play. Playing is a fundamental possibility of social existence. Playing is interplay, playing with one another, an intimate form of human community. Playing is, structurally, not an individual or isolated activity – it is open to one's fellow human beings as fellow-players. (Fink 2016: 23)

Higher education as collaboratorium can facilitate the flourishing of playful fellowships and cultures. This is based on the participant's co-construction of a space that is safe, sacred and shared. As such, the playful collaboratorium is based on mutual trust, freedom to fail, cooperation, communality and denotes a space wherein collectives are curious and creative together through 'what if…?' and 'how can we…?' thinking and tinkering (Whitton and Langan 2018; Whitton 2018; Nørgård et al. 2017). The university as collaboratorium grows out of playful communality, where people have care and concern for each other, a drive towards being playful together, treat each other as equals, engage in joint playful curiosity and creativity, appreciate diversity, heterogeneity and alterity – and through this construct empathic co-operative communities or play cultures (Nørgård et al. 2017).

In Huizinga's *Homo Ludens – A study of the play element in culture* (1938), play is highlighted as a formative element of culture and society. Huizinga believed that *play cultures* are a primary and necessary condition for the generation and flourishing of cultures. Like Fink, Huizinga sees playfulness as a social bond and an initiator of communality and culture. Consequently, a university where people take care of each other, feel part of a collective, are curious and creative together is a university that dares to be playful in and with the world. This is in contrast to higher education and academic life of today that is often experienced as structurally fixed in aiming towards end goals, completion or trajectories of means and ends. When the university is manifested through "profane seriousness", it takes on what Fink terms "the futural character of life" as something only happening for the sake of a final purpose. Conversely, if the university exists through "sacred playfulness", it acquires the character of a "pacified present" or an "oasis" where playfulness is something that "carries us away" (Fink 2016: 20). In 'The physiology of Play: Potential relevance for higher education' (2020), Maarten P. Koeners and Joseph Francis describe how the deprivation of play and playfulness impairs decision-making in novel or challenging contexts, while nurturing play cultures and communal playful activities enhance neural plasticity, intellectual dexterity, adaptability, emotional learning and resilience to depression (Koeners and Francis 2020). When people play, they feel alive and when they feel alive, they play. They argue that a playful university for moving beyond the competitive – or gamified – university is much needed. Such a playful university sees higher education as a collaboratorium focused on 'working together to create what cannot be produced alone, or at least refrain from exploiting each by promoting a capitalistic "winner-takes-all" culture' (Koeners and Francis 2020: 152). In the collaboratorium, cultures and collectives are open towards playing with futures and alternatives through exploring and experimenting in relation to thinking, truth and the world:

> Our classrooms ought to be nurturing and thoughtful and just all at once; they ought to pulsate with multiple conceptions of what it is to be human and alive. They ought to resound with the voices of articulate young people in dialogues always incomplete because there is always more to be discovered and more to be said. We must want our students to achieve friendship as each one stirs to wide-awakeness, to imaginative action, and to renewed consciousness of possibility. (Greene 1995: 43).

Taken together, higher education practised through play fellowships and as play culture carries with it the possibility of more playful higher education futures that work against the current reality of profane seriousness and the gamified university.

Conclusion: Towards a Genuine Playful University

Emerging from the above attempt to read across and connect prominent works within play philosophy, theory and playful higher education, three play frames for a genuinely playful university have been developed: (1) playful curiosity, (2) playful creativity and (3) playful communality. Together, the three play frames are positioned as instrumental in developing a theoretically substantiated foundation for the genuine playful university and comprise a prerequisite for the emergence of the Homo Ludens within playful higher education. In the table below, the three play frames and their core constituents are put together to explicate how they work together to create a framework for the playful university and playful higher education (Fig. 10.1):

PLAYFRAME 1 CURIOSITY	PLAYFRAME 2 CREATIVITY	PLAYFRAME 3 COMMUNALITY
PLAY AS LIFE & FORCE	PLAY AS FORM & ACT	PLAY AS FELLOWSHIP & CULTURE
LUSORY ATTITUDE & 'WHAT IF…?'	LUDIC INTERACTION & 'HOW CAN WE…?'	LUDIC COLLECTIVES & WHAT-IF THINKING + HOW-CAN-WE TINKERING
EXPLORATORIUM	EXPERIMENTARIUM	COLLABORATORIUM
SACRED SPACE	SAFE SPACE	SHARED SPACE
PLAY IMAGINARIES & PLAY DRIVE	MAGIC CIRCLES & PLAYWORLDS	INTER-PERSONAL PLAY & PLAY COMPANIONS

Fig. 10.1 The three playframes – playful curiosity, playful creativity and playful communality – that, together with higher education as exploratorium, higher education as experimentarium and higher education as collaboratorium, establish a framework for the genuine playful university

The framework highlights how playfulness in higher education denotes something fundamentally apart from the "profane playfulness" of relaxing, fun, frivolous or unserious extracurricular activities. It shows playfulness as a simultaneously imaginative and expressive force that cannot be bottled up or tapped, but must be lived through and acted out. The playful university is an accentuation of the ungovernability, unpredictability and unknowability of higher education and the attempt to make it proper and workable through removing the "un-'s" would, at the same time, transform the deep play and sacred playfulness of the university to surface play and profane playfulness. Playful curiosity, creativity and communality is not something that can be implemented, utilised, exploited or measured. Rather, it is something that emerges, sprouts, sprawls and buds through nurturing the core constituents of the genuine playful university.

The hope is that this chapter provides some steps towards this nurturing, as well as a more robust theoretical and conceptual foundation for this nascent field. Overall, the genuine playful university highlights:

> an approach that gives learners and teachers freedom to be playful, freedom to make choices, and freedom towards the world. It is beyond profane seriousness - in the act of being playful, we enrich profane reality by a layer of sacred seriousness [...] Such approaches carry the potential of circumventing some of the present looming problems within education (Nørgård et al. 2017).

This entails that playful universities cultivate an atmosphere and sacred/safe/shared spaces that invite for playfulness in the philosophical sense of the word. This requires, firstly, the development of thinking, concepts, language, discourse, frames and formats that at one and the same time arise from the soul of the university and the heart of play philosophy. Secondly, to advance a genuine playful university, both playfulness and the university must be unleashed – otherwise it cannot be playful in the true meaning of that word. Playful academics (Homo Ludens) and playful higher education evolve and mature through the life of playful universities as environments for people to "play at", "play with" and "play through" in relation to existence, each other, the world, possible futures, deep knowledge and higher education institutions themselves.

Importantly, playfulness should not be operationalised to fix or improve a broken system or practice, but embraced to transform it. The playful university is not a colourful playground filled with fun play materials and relaxing play activities. Rather, the playful university is evoked and materialised through the deeper pedagogical structures, attitudes and approaches emerging from the philosophical and theoretical play frames. As such, the playful university and playful higher education pose a challenge – perhaps even a threat – to the climate, environment and regimes pervading current higher education institutions and practice.

But, concurrently, the idea of a genuine playful university also put forward a promise of potentially more playful futures for the university in the form of what Ronald Barnett calls a "feasible utopia" (Barnett 2011). Here, the three play frames, when put together, offer a tentative blueprint for a feasible playful utopia for the university and higher education:

> [Feasible utopias] have four significant features. First, they are utopias. They are almost certainly not going to be fully realised. Second, they are feasible: that is, in being utopian, they are not fanciful. There are sufficient exemplars already present that show that these utopias could be reached. Third, they contain both optimism and pessimism: they reveal positive possibilities in our present situation but they are confronted with forces in the world such that their coming into being is extremely unlikely. Lastly, utopias are not necessarily all to the good, even if they were realised. As utopias, they look forward to situations that would be mostly beneficial but, as utopias, they often harbour extreme hopes. Dystopias lurk within utopias. (Barnett 2011: 120)

A genuine playful university is, still, a utopia. But it is a feasible utopia. As works within playful higher education show, there are already thinking, practical knowledge and practice present to show that such a utopia could be reached. And as shown in the tension between the present accelerated university and the potential future of the playful university, it contains both optimism and pessimism. Finally, playful higher education in the ordinary sense is not all to the good, as the balancing of, on the one hand, superficial profane playfulness and gamified higher education, and, on the other hand, deep sacred playfulness and playful higher education in the philosophical sense testify.

Overall, the feasible utopia of a genuine playful university evokes acts of playfulness in the form of academic "dreamcasting" or "wish-ful thinking". It is an invocation of academic playfellows to come together in inter-personal play, play imaginaries and playworlds in order to "play towards" what they wish to be, wish to do and wish to know. Through insisting on playful curiosity and playful creativity they seek to institute ludic collectives and playful communality. Such concrete enactment of higher education in the form of playful exploratoriums, experimentariums and collaboratoriums, as found within existing works on and practice of playful higher education, open up utopian but feasible opportunities for making the playful university a reality.

References

Baker, R., Walonoski, J., Heffernan, N., Roll, I., Corbett, A., & Koedinger, K. (2008). Why students engage in 'gaming the system' behavior in interactive learning environments. *Journal of Interactive Learning Research, 19*(2), 162–182.
Barnett, R. (2011). *Being a university*. London: Routledge.
Bateson, P. (2015). Playfulness and creativity. *Current Biology, 25*(1), 12–16.
Caillois, R. (1958, 2001). *Man, play and games*. Urbana: University of Illinois Press.
Deci, E. L., Koestner, R., & Ryan, R. M. (2001). Extrinsic rewards and intrinsic motivation in education: Reconsidered once again. *Review of Educational Research, 71*(1), 1–27.
Fink, E. (1957, 2016). *Play as a symbol of the world and other writings*. Indiana: Indiana University Press.
Gadamer, H. (1966, 2004). *Truth and method*. London: Continuum.
Greene, M. (1995). *Releasing the imagination: Essays on education, the arts and social change*. San Francisco: Jossey-Bass.

Grondin, J. (2001). Play, festival and ritual in Gadamer: On the theme of the immemorial in his later works. In L. K. Schmidt (Ed.), *Language and linguisticality in Gadamer's Hermeneutics*. Lanham: Lexington Books.

Gudiksen, S. K., & Skovbjerg, H. M. (2020). *Framing play design:-A hands-on guide for designers, learners and innovators*. BIS-Verlag.

Huizinga, L. (1938, 1949). *Homo Ludens: A study of the play element in culture*. London: Routledge.

James, A. (2019). Making a case for the playful university. In A. James & C. Nerantzi (Eds.), *The power of play in higher education: Creativity in tertiary learning*. Cham: Palgrave Macmillan.

James, A., & Nerantzi, C. (2019). *The power of play in higher education: Creativity in tertiary learning*. Cham: Palgrave Macmillan.

Jayasuriya, K. (2015). Constituting market citizenship: Regulatory state, market making and higher education. *Higher Education, 70*(6), 973–985.

Kirby, C. C., & Graham, B. (2016). Gadamer, Dewey and the importance of play in philosophical inquiry. *Reason Papers, 38*(1), 8–20.

Koeners, M. P., & Francis, J. (2020). The physiology of play: Potential relevance for higher education. *International Journal of Play, 9*(1), 143–159.

Nørgård, R. T., Toft-Nielsen, C., & Whitton, N. (2017). Playful learning in higher education: Developing a signature pedagogy. *International Journal of Play, 6*(3), 272–282.

Nørgård, R. T., Mor, Y., & Bengtsen, S. S. E. (2019). Networked learning in, for, and with the world. In A. Littlejohn, J. Jaldemark, E. Vrieling-Teunter, & F. Nijland (Eds.), *Networked professional learning: Emerging and equitable discourses for professional development* (pp. 71–88). Cham: Springer.

Pink, D. H. (2009). *Drive: The surprising truth about what motivates us*. Riverhead Books.

Schiller, F. (1795, 2004). *On the aesthetic education of man in a series of letters*. Mineola: Dover Publications.

Shumar, W. (1997). *College for sale. A critique of the commodification of higher education*. London: Routledge.

Sicart, M. (2014). *Play matters*. London: MIT Press.

Sutton-Smith, B. (1997). The ambiguity of play. *British Journal of Educational Studies, 46*(4), 482–485.

Tsai, K. C. (2012). Play, imagination and creativity: A brief literature review. *Journal of Education and Learning, 1*(2), 15–20.

Vadeboncoeur, J. A., Perone, A., & Panina-Beard, N. (2016). Creativity as a practice of freedom: Imaginative play, moral imagination, and the production of culture. In V. Glăveanu (Ed.), *The Palgrave handbook of creativity and culture research. Palgrave studies in creativity and culture*. London: Palgrave Macmillan.

Walsh, A. (2018). Giving permission to play in higher education. In *4th International Conference on Higher Education Advances (HEAd'18)*.

Whitton, N. (2018). Playful learning: Tools, techniques and tactics. *Research in Learning Technology, 26*, 1–12.

Whitton, N., & Langan, M. (2018). Fun and games in higher education: An analysis of UK student perspectives. *Teaching in Higher Education, 24*(8), 1–14.

Whitton, N., & Moseley, A. (2019). *Playful learning: Events and activities to engage adults*. Routledge.

Wright, S. (2016). Universities in a knowledge economy or ecology? Policy, contestation and abjection. *Critical Policy Studies, 10*(1), 59–78.

Rikke Toft Nørgård is Associate Professor in Educational Design & Technology at The Danish School of Education, Aarhus University. Nørgård is in the steering group of Centre for Higher Education Futures (CHEF) and board member of the Philosophy and Theory of Higher Education Society (PaTHES). Dr. Nørgård's research focuses on the complexities and interrelationships of technology, culture, education, design and philosophy in relation to future education. She is consortium partner lead in several funded projects with a particular focus on developing future higher education. Projects include 'VASE – Value-Sensitive Design in Higher Education', 'IGNITE – Design Thinking and Making in the Arts and Sciences' and 'STAK – Students' Academic Digital Competencies in Higher Education'. Nørgård has published numerous articles and given keynotes on playful higher education, digital humanities and designs for future higher education with a focus on formats, challenges and potentials for the future university.

Chapter 11
The Migrant University

Ryan Evely Gildersleeve

Migration is fundamental to the planet, and human experience is no exception. Since the emergence of *homo erectus*, and especially as *homo sapien*, movement has defined our experience with, on, toward, and as part of the Earth. Contemporary humankind's dominance and dominion over the Earth is no exception. We are more mobile today than ever, perhaps. Whether measured by the record-setting number of migrants traversing international terrain or the ever-increasing airline flights, or train, bus, and car rides that humans make annually, humankind is a species on the move. Yet, we have built our institutions – including the university – within settlement-based frameworks. That is to say, the contemporary university is understood as a place-based and place-making institution.

Or is it?

Perhaps, our contemporary thinking of the university does not match up especially well with real conditions. After all, both students and faculty are more mobile than ever. The curriculum certainly has not remained static, much less have standards and practices for admissions. And while campuses might remain at the same address for decades or centuries, their borders seem to expand, contract, and multiply – particularly with the onset of new technologies that can seemingly move the university anywhere. Perhaps, it is the predominant place-based understanding of the university that has kept scholars and leaders from effectively speculating the urgent needs of change for the university, at least scholars in the social sciences that tend to dominate scholarship in the United States about higher education.

Indeed, while scholars have noted many challenges to the university and its mission, they have struggled to identify the desired future-university that might meet these challenges. Scholars of the last 25–50 years have increasingly obsessed on

---

R. E. Gildersleeve (✉)
Morgridge College of Education at University of Denver, Denver, CO, USA
e-mail: Ryan.Gildersleeve@du.edu

© The Author(s), under exclusive license to Springer Nature
Switzerland AG 2021
S. S. E. Bengtsen et al. (eds.), *The University Becoming*, Debating Higher Education: Philosophical Perspectives 6,
https://doi.org/10.1007/978-3-030-69628-3_11

present and past-present issues that overwhelmingly stem from economic framings of the institution: student career outcomes, revenue and budget modeling, individual and social return-on-investment, affordability, and productivity. Many scholars have summarized these concerns as the *neoliberal university* (Lipman 2011; Kuntz 2015; Gildersleeve 2016). The neoliberal university is a recognition that the institution is now organized around neoliberal ideals and concepts – neoliberalism has penetrated the fabric of the university. I briefly discuss some of the consequences of neoliberal higher education further below.

These present and past-present studies are most pronounced in research that follows social scientific methodologies. Exceptions to these efforts to diagnose neoliberalism in higher education largely stem from philosophers, many of whom are located outside the United States. For example, Jon Nixon's (2009) *Towards a Virtuous University* outlines philosophical tenets that could become a moral framework for the institution, and he posits a re-evaluation of academic practices. Yet, he does not himself measure or examine such practices. Bruce MacFarlane's (2006) *The Academic Citizen* argues for the value of service in the constitution of a future university. While MacFarlane draws from multiple examples, none of which is necessarily examined systematically through rigorous methodological treatment. Rather, they stand as signs of what MacFarlane would like to see more of, illustrating his ethics of a virtuous institution. Operating within US contexts, Martha Nussbaum's (2016) *Not For Profit* makes compelling arguments for the humanities and the university's role in democracy, particularly within the neoliberal confines of the institution. Again, these are applications of philosophical commitments related to the ethics of democratic life, rather than the application of philosophy within the systematic analysis of the daily life of the institution itself. Perhaps one of the most prolific writers of higher education futures is Ronald Barnett. Barnett's longstanding interest in the university and its potential salvage for the future has made an indelible imprint on the last decade (2011, 2013, 2014, 2017). One of his latest volumes, with collaborator Søren Bengtsen (Barnett and Bengtsen, 2019), breathes new life into imagining a university that takes life as the center of knowledge, reorganizing knowledge and life as inextricably linked constitutionally rather than correlational. It offers powerful ways of thinking the university, but again, it does not provide empirical prescription nor offer an analysis based on practices that have engendered the kind of university they envision. These are not faults in the offerings from the rich philosophical emergence of higher education futures. However, I am seeking a different kind of contribution.

The aforementioned scholars tend to draw from philosophical methods of analysis, without the empirical fieldwork that marks the distinction of the social sciences. This note is not a criticism, but rather acknowledgement that philosophy has outpaced the speculative and productive analysis of higher education futures that the social sciences, like anthropology, seem to struggle to engage. One goal of this chapter is to establish philosophical tools that can be used in tandem with social science traditions for theorizing a future university that might fracture neoliberal confines. Through such interstices, I hope to support affirmative contributions to the knowledge imperative of academe – contributions that reimagine not only what the university might become but how we might engage in practices to achieve it. Or, at least work toward it. As such, I offer an ontological inquiry that entangles some of my prior anthropological work with Latinx (im)migrant communities[1] in US higher education (Gildersleeve 2010, 2017a, b) with my philosophical and methodological work around the knowledge imperative of academe (Gildersleeve 2016, 2020a, b). The knowledge imperative, put simply, is a recognition that the university is the social institution entrusted as the steward of academic knowledge. The university generates knowledge through the faculty's scholarship of teaching, scholarship of research, and scholarship of service and outreach. Ontological inquiry, in this regard, seeks to move away from explaining the *meaning* of practice, but rather explain both the constitution and emergence of practical *being* (St. Pierre 2015; Koro-Ljungberg 2016). Within my methodological tradition, which seeks to operationalize a social research analysis of practice from *process*-ontologies (Jackson and Mazzei 2012), both constitution and emergence serve as one in the same (Koro-Ljungberg 2016).

My prior anthropological work has been theory-driven, but grounded in empirical ethnographic fieldwork with Latinx (im)migrant communities in the United States. This prior work includes ethnographic engagements, participatory action research, and life history projects with Mexican migrant farm-working families in California focused on understanding how migrant students navigate the complex processes of accessing higher education (Gildersleeve 2010). It also includes discursive analyses of policies that directly implicate Latinx and immigrant students (Gildersleeve and Hernández 2012). I also will draw from ethnographic investigations of ritual culture with Latinx (im)migrant students at Hispanic Serving Institutions[2] in California. These efforts have been in response to the systemic underrepresentation of Latinx (im)migrant students in higher education, their persistent struggle with institutional racism and systemic inequality within higher education, and their under-reported contributions to US higher education.

By combining my philosophical, methodological, and anthropological lines of inquiry, I hope to explain the contemporary condition of Latinx (im)migrant communities in US higher education as both normative and as an extension of Latinx (im)migrant families' historic migrations. I provide an analysis of Latinx (im) migrant higher education using Thomas Nail's (2015) system of *kinopolitics* (i.e., the politics of movement) and his theories around the *figure of the migrant*. Through

---

[1] "Latinx (im)migrant communities" is my attempt to signify a social, cultural, and political class of US residents. It includes both immigrant and first-generation family members, those who might migrate to/from Central/South American and some Caribbean countries of origin, and is inclusive of multiple immigration statuses, gender and sexual identifications, expressions or orientations. It seeks to recognize that Latinx (im)migrant cultures are often constituted and practiced in community that transcends or perhaps avoids the nuclear organization of family and community, but not necessarily nor exclusively so. It is an avowedly *American* construction of a social, cultural, and political class of people.

[2] Hispanic-Serving Institutions are colleges and universities where students of Hispanic heritage constitute at least 25% of undergraduate student enrollment.

which I aim to speculatively theorize a migrant university for the future of US higher education.

In sum, there are at least three goals at stake in this chapter:

1. Establish philosophical tools that can be used in tandem with social science traditions for theorizing a future university that might fracture neoliberal confines. (And truthfully, it is far more like experimenting rather than establishing.)
2. Explain the contemporary condition of Latinx (im)migrant communities in US higher education as both normative and as an extension of Latinx (im)migrant families' historic migrations. (Here I lean into the anthropological dimensions of the project, but lend them philosophical support in order to draw out more-than-empirical conclusions.)
3. Speculatively theorize a *migrant university* for the future of US higher education. (Which, in doing so, provide a prescription of principles for future change that emerge from actual practices that make such futures possible.)

Candidly, I admit that the project fails ultimately, but I hope it fails productively and works a bit closer to the kind of fracture that might be valuable in more-to-come future futures for higher education.

Higher Education as Neoliberal, Biopolitical Project, and Latinx (Im)migrant Communities

I begin with a two-pronged premise of US higher education: (a) neoliberal higher education is normative and irreversible and (b) the university is a biopolitical project. Neoliberal higher education, in brief, is marked by an increased corporatization, focusing on activities that generate revenue, more so than knowledge (Lipman 2011). Further, the neoliberal university treats stakeholders as consumers, whether students or alumni or the broader public. Institutional interest in return-on-investment predominates discourses of the university's value proposition. Further still, these corporate brand commodification efforts pit knowledge-builders (i.e., faculty, students, community partners) in competition with one another, dissuading collaboration or coordinated efforts to address society's broadest and most persistent problems (Gildersleeve 2016). A hyper-individualization pervades all dimensions of the institution (Kuntz 2015).

The university as a biopolitical project reflects the larger scale effects of the university on shaping the population (Foucault 2008). As a social institution, the university produces possible people for particular roles in society. It has a heavy hand in making particular bodies for broad sectors of the body politic, which in turn produce other bodies – those who do not attend university – to populate the rest of the social order. Recognizing the economic mobility tied to a university education, and the caste-like determinants of pursuing higher education, it becomes clear that the neoliberal norms of higher education and the biopolitical consequences of the university are entwined.

Measuring US higher education as a biopolitical project in a neoliberal state has led many scholars to recognize that academic knowledge is not in service to an egalitarian society as much as it could be (Gildersleeve 2016; Lipman 2011; Kuntz 2015). The knowledge imperative increasingly faces infringement by political and partisan interests that truncate its potential. In neoliberal terms, this means academic knowledge is truncated by its commodification, the institution's corporatization, our stakeholders' consumerism, and our intra-sector competition. Academic knowledge, then, at scale, reproduces the biopolitical outcomes that neoliberalism is designed to order – an exacerbation of the status quo of inequality.

To be clear, these conditions are reflected in the historical patterns of exclusion from higher education and marginalization from within the institution experienced by Latinx (im)migrant communities.

To answer the distortion of the knowledge imperative, I look to Latinx (im)migrant communities, as I believe they are the future of US higher education. Such a bold statement can be substantiated demographically, recognizing that Latinx communities are some of the fastest growing nationally across the US (Gramlich 2019) and also some of the fastest growing in terms of college attendance, although they remain underrepresented (Bustamante 2020). Latinx students in K-12 schooling districts are also outpacing other groups. Furthermore, Latinx communities can be found in critical mass enclaves across all regions of the United States, no longer relegated to the American Southwest (Gramlich 2019).

Beyond demographics, I mean to recognize that Latinx (im)migrant communities' contributions to US higher education provide a creative cartography for charting US higher education's future course – a course that might effectively navigate through its contemporary neoliberal constraints and break open interstice moments wherein higher education can be refashioned and reconfigured to more egalitarian, social, and public purposes, emphasizing a renewed knowledge imperative for the university. This claim transcends the demographic economy of Latinx (im)migrant participation in US higher education but draws from historic and first-hand anthropological accounts of how Latinx (im)migrant students and communities already engage in such reconfigurations of US higher education.

I draw inspiration from research that has documented the intersections of fluid, technological, *mestiza*, and linguistic subjectivities produced by Latinx migrant communities (Garcia 2014). These dynamic subjectivities foreshadow many expected changes in society, as they are extremely adaptive, creative, and mobile. Further, according to some historians, Latinx communities in the US have led social change in often unmarked, unnoticed ways more so than other social/cultural groups in North America over the past 25 years (see for example, Donato 1997, 2007). Latinx (im)migrant communities have demonstrated tremendous achievement, resilience, ingenuity, and innovation in order to persevere in liminal spaces and preserve treasured cultural heritage in ways that allow for multiplicity (Gibson 2019). In many ways, Latinx (im)migrant communities mirror the tensions found in neoliberal US higher education today. Finally, migration emerges as a more pronounced ontological characteristic in many Latinx communities in the United States due to the colonial heritage and economic relations that have kept movement central to the development of the Americas.

The time to incorporate Latinx lessons, wisdom, culture, and contributions into decision-making and designing social futures – the work of the knowledge imperative in academe – is now!

The Figure of the Migrant and Kinopolitics

A fundamental principle in thinking the migrant university is recognizing migration as a permanent, pivotal, and provocative (yet normal) figuration of the human condition. Furthermore, while the political act of *im*migration might seem to finish by some arbitrary marker (e.g., crossing a border or becoming a citizen), the ontological process of becoming an immigrant itself never ends or completes. Rather, humans always, are ever becoming ... migrant. We are always in movement. Thomas Nail's (2015) system of kinopolitics – a politics of movement – takes these foundations and extrapolates a motion-centered ontology for reconceptualizing two key concepts in political philosophy: the institution of the state and the figure of personhood. In sum, the state generates its power from movement, not stasis. Yet, we have thus far understood statehood and personhood as place-based concepts. This is wrong and does not reflect reality.[3]

In what follows, I briefly outline Nail's system of kinopolitics, applying it to the social institution of the university as an extension of the state apparatus. I begin with Nail's conceptualization of the migrant.

Figure of the Migrant

Nail puts forward a conceptualization of the migrant as the political figure of the twenty-first century. The problem with our current political conceptualization is twofold: stasis and the state. First, we conceive of the human as a figure of *stasis* – a place-bound configuring of the human. This places the migrant in a secondary or subaltern positioning relative to normative humankind. Second, our politics is founded on an agreement of the powerful and place-based *nation-state* that grants

---

[3] Any movement-centered ontology owes some debt and operates to some extent in relation to prior work on space/place. Application of a movement-centered ontology owes debt to prior theories that sought to spatialize education and learning, such as the university. Theorists such as Paul Temple (2014), Ellis and Goodyear (2018), Savin-Baden (2007), and Nørgård and Bengsten (2018) have informed prior thinking on such matters. I do not go into any greater depth or detail of this work due to space limitations and to render focus more closely on the ontology of motion and kinopolotics proffered by Nail (2018).

freedoms and ontological possibilities for becoming-citizens (i.e., fully human/persons). By subverting the ontological foundation of stasis with movement, placing movement as normative rather than exceptional, the figure of the migrant becomes the primary becoming-human figuration and the state becomes less central to subjective agency.

Nail grounds his figure of the migrant within the material and historical conditions of human migration, recent and past. However, he extends the migrant as political figure to include anyone who practices movement (regional, international, economic) in order to participate in society, as well as anyone who is systematically expelled by society's institutions. In short, swaths of marginalized groups and pretty much anyone who experiences some form(s) of precarity in relationship to the state (i.e., government) can be configured as the migrant within Nail's conceptualization.

Kinopolitics and Expansion by Expulsion

Key to understanding the migrant as a political figure is Nail's theorization of *kinopolitics*, or the politics of movement. Nail asks us to consider how we might understand the building of social organization(s) based on the migration of humans. He points out that Western expansion, and the expansion of any Western political project, has always relied upon the expulsion of various groups from social organizations. Movement has always been fundamental to building societies. Nail calls this *kinetic power*. Whether relegating Native Americans to state-drawn land boundaries (e.g., reservations) or using juridical tactics to remove African Americans from civic life (e.g., Jim Crow), the state has expelled groups (i.e., moved them away from) society in some form in order to further state interests. Applied to the becoming-university, histories of higher education are rife with examples of expelling particular cultural groups from participation in order to expand the power, prestige, and, at times, populism of colleges and universities (See Karabel 2005; McDonough 1997). Kinopolitics challenges normative explanations of such exclusion by circumscribing these biopolitical efforts in relation to the political flows and junctions they produce.

Nail's system of kinopolitics relies on the state apparatus to strengthen its power through processes he calls, *expansion by expulsion*. Put simply, the state – or the university, as state institution – builds itself up by determining who is allowed and who must be kept out. For example, in the United States, one way to measure a university's strength is by its rankings in any number of rankings and ratings regimes (Orphan 2021). One way to move up in the rankings is to exclude more students from admission, or crafting a more competitive admissions portrait for the institution. Thus, a university expands its influence (via rankings) by expelling students from its applicant pool, thereby configuring them as undesirable.

However, the practices and philosophies that generate these divisions are anything but simple. Nail articulates four kinetic forces for achieving the expulsion of undesired objects in order to strengthen the state apparatus: centripetal, centrifugal, tensional, and elastic. Each kinetic force makes possible a different figuration of the migrant – the configuring of the undesired object.

Centripetal force expands the university through territorial accumulation. Universities build themselves up and expel the undesired by abandoning them. For example, the land-grant colleges and universities of the mid-nineteenth century in the US gave federal lands to states in order to raise money for technical and agricultural institutions. Many of these have become world renowned research universities, such as Cornell University and Iowa State University. Some of the lands used were the working civilizations of Native American communities, the citizens and residents of which were then displaced and expelled from participation in the university that the sale of their lands funded (Nash 2019). Nail describes the migrant figure created from the expulsion via centripetal force, the *nomad*.

Centrifugal force uses the opposite technique. It expands the political administration of the university and expels undesired objects (e.g., people), through enslavement. Nail describes the migrant figure created from centrifugal expulsion, the *barbarian*. A contemporary example of centrifugal force could be the rise of the for-profit higher education sector in the United States. These institutions typically set tuition-pricing right at the level of federal student loans available to students, encouraging gross debt loads. These same institutions target first-generation and students of color, including Latinx migrant students. Yet, these institutions have far poorer graduation rates than their nonprofit counterparts. The result is an entire caste of students with only some college, but no degree, and unbearable student loan debt – effectively enslaved to the neoliberal economy. They are made into barbarians of society wherein they will only be eligible for work that serves to benefit others and barely affords the noncollege graduates enough to make payments on their student loans.

Tensional force uses a strengthened juridical apparatus to build up the institution. Using contradictory sets of laws and regulations so that the undesired are tossed through the higher education system like a pinball. In-state resident tuition policy for undocumented[4] students is an illustration of tensional force. As I have analyzed with colleagues previously (Gildersleeve and Hernández 2012; Gildersleeve et al. 2015; Gildersleeve 2017a), tuition policies for undocumented immigrant students in higher education vary from state to state and sometimes by institutional type within a single state in the US. One result is that undocumented students' educational opportunity becomes entangled with political whim and will of state legislatures and inconsistent across state lines. At the scale of the population and the broader social institution, the undocumented student is effectively expelled from the

---

[4] The term "undocumented" is commonly used in US-based discourse to describe immigrants without legal status. In relation to students, the "undocumented student" is often understood as someone who was brought into or kept within the United States without legal documentation (e.g., a valid visa and passport) while still a minor and therefore should not be held culpable for the original legal transgression.

university through such tensional force. Nail describes the migrant figure created from the expulsion via tensional force, the *vagabond*.

The fourth kinetic force that the University might exercise is *elastic force*. Here, the university expands and contracts strategically to expand economically and expel undesired objects configuring them into what Nail calls, of the *Proletariat*. University admission, recruitment, tuition, and financial aid policy and programs are examples of elastic force. These practices allow universities to respond to, *and engage in*, market forces to expand their operations while expelling those deemed undesirable. These are practices directly related to revenue that allow the university to target and carve up the potential student body into a preferred demography it desires.

These four kinetic forces enable the university to expand through the expulsion of those it finds undesirable – producing migrants configured as the nomad, the barbarian, the vagabond, and the proletariat. Expelling the undesired expands the power and prowess of the institution. These operations are the quintessential expression of the biopolitical imperative of the university. And neoliberal higher education requires that the institution expand increasingly and inevitably or die.

Pedetic Force – The Power of the Foot

The mobile expulsions practiced by the normative university apparatus also render new possible mobilities. Counterpowers through migrant movements can challenge the status quo. Thomas Nail (2015) refers to these counterpowers as the *pedetic force* of the migrant – the power of the foot. Social movement is never unidirectional, and pedetic powers might help reconfigure US higher education.

Countering the kinetic power of the university, the migrant exercises *pedetic force*, producing new possibilities for social organization by using various strategies that have emerged historically. These strategies include the raid, the revolt, the rebellion, and the resistance. Each strategy maps onto the historically conditioned versions of the migrant as a political figure (the nomad, the barbarian, the vagabond, and the proletariat, respectively). However, each continues to operate today. Indeed, contemporary migrants have each of these four strategies at their disposal in enacting their will on/within the contemporary university. In the sections that follow, I outline how Latinx migrant students and communities have exercised pedetic force in remaking the university. Today's migrants exercise pedetic force in response to all kinetic forces, historic and contemporary, often in hybrid ways. As such, my illustrations below should not be read as mutually exclusive nor static. Rather, they are readings of Latinx migrant activism and advocacy in US higher education – readings of the remaking of the university, even if only momentary or fleeting.

The Raid

In response to centripetal force, the exercise of expansion by expulsion via territorial accumulation, undocumented immigrant students in US higher education and fellow advocates have organized *Dream Centers* at many institutions, especially in the Western United States. These are offices built to provide resources and services to support undocumented students. Some Dream Centers are officially administered by the university; others are unofficial or informal and may include volunteers. The name is an allusion to the acronym for an early attempt at bipartisan legislation in the US Congress that would have provided a pathway to citizenship for undocumented students who arrived in the United States as minors.

Dream Centers can be read as a raid on institutional resources, proclaiming a right to support in spite of (or perhaps in consideration for) ancestral communities' expulsion from Anglo-American westward expansion. It is important to recognize that North American territories were contested across multiple Native/Indigenous civilizations as well as multiple European colonial powers up until the current North American borders were settled in the nineteenth century. Latinx identities are entwined in multiplicity across these ancestral communities. As such, when advocacy yields an established and recognized office for undocumented student support, it might be understood as a *raid* on the institution, like the nomadic migrants historically raided state settlements for sustenance and in response to the territorial accumulation exercised by the mobile state apparatus.

The Revolt

In response to centrifugal forces, which expand the university by strengthening its political administration and expel the undesired through enslavement, configuring the migrant as barbarian, twenty-first century migrants in US higher education have organized their own version of a *revolt*. My own ethnographic examination of Latino Graduation Ceremonies provides an illustration of how these rituals can be read as such a pedetic force (Gildersleeve 2017b). Traditionally, institutional commencement ceremonies center the university, and it seeks to strengthen its power by making students indebted to it for granting them the diplomas they receive.

The Latino Graduation Ceremony uses the same skeleton of the ceremony, clearly marking it in the genre of graduation, but they typically alter some key pieces: they allow individuation in dress, they provide food for families, they make parents, elders, or broader community members the subject of the ceremony in significant ways, and they recognize the biopolitical aberration that the Latinx graduates represent. That is to say, they know that Latinx graduates are exceptional, that US education systems would not predict them to be graduating.

But these dimensions to the ceremony, while adoring and powerful in their own rites, also need to be read within the history of Chicano student activism – specifically, *El Plan de Santa Barbara* (Garcia 2014), which laid out an agenda for Chicano higher education that included, among other things: the increased recruitment and retention of Latinx students and faculty, Chicano Studies as a recognized field of study, and significant rituals and traditions to be built into the fabric of the institution, like the Latino Graduation Ceremony. *El Plan* calls upon the notion of *Aztlan* – an imagined unifying recapture of a thriving Latinx community. I have previously analyzed Latino Graduation Ceremonies in such a manner (Gildersleeve 2017b) and applied within the system of kinopolitics – such ceremony can be understood as a *revolt*. These ceremonies center family, community, and mestiza indigeneity. They claim the protest as place and more-than-place, but a mobile body, a movement from origin to imagined future. In essence, the Latino graduation ceremony seizes the ritual of the commencement ceremony, recreates it in a Latinx migrant image, and then imagines a future-present wherein their ancestors are built into the designs of the university.

The Rebellion

In opposition to the tensional force exercised through juridical domination and the use of contradictory laws to expel the undesired, configuring them into the vagabond, Latinx migrants in Georgia rebelled against the state higher education system and formed Freedom University (Muñoz and Espino 2017). Georgia is a state that within its own borders has different rules and regulations for undocumented student access to higher education. Some universities will not even admit undocumented students, while some community colleges will allow them to attend at out-of-state tuition prices. Freedom University was founded by activist students, faculty, and staff as a counter-university to provide higher education for undocumented students.

While unofficial and unaccredited, classes and supports were formalized by Freedom University, with an emphasis on praxis – education for social change. Freedom University can be understood as a rebellion against the expulsion through juridical domination of the mainstream higher education system. It rebels against the formal, recognized university and operates completely outside of it. Freedom University, as rebellion, remakes the university in the image of the migrant.

The Resistance

In response to the elastic force that economically seeks to expel migrants from the university by forming them into the proletariat, Latinx college students often organize into student groups, such as *Movimiento Estudiantil Chicanx de Aztlán*/Chicanx Student Movement of Aztlán, also known as MECHA. As an activist organization originally founded in the 1960s, MECHA chapters across US universities support migrant students in resisting the normative pathways, expectations, and kinopolitical forces of normative higher education institutions. They use the tools of the university to empower migrants in crafting new modes of participation while meeting institutional expectations.

Through tutoring, support groups, political action campaigns, and other campus activities that bring Latinx communities together in and beyond university spaces, MECHA resists the call to economize migrant bodies for the consumption of the university. Rather, MECHA seeks to mobilize an empowered migrant population to take ownership of the university. They have done this, historically, through movements like *El Plan de Santa Barbara* and the successful establishment of Chicano Studies as a field of study on many US campuses (Rhoads 1997).

The cumulative effect of Latinx migrant communities' pedetic forces can be seen in the growing numbers of Latinx migrants on college campuses, the growing numbers of Chicano Studies programs across US universities, and the increasing number of Latinx faculty members helping shape the institution. Latinx migrant bodies are literally being moved from outside to inside the university, and doing so while retaining the migrant figuration *on their own terms*. Thus, re-positioning the migrant in relation to the kinopolitical state of the university. They become entwined in each other's expansion projects. Yet, simultaneously, the old guard of the university's expansion by expulsion project remains active. The force and counterforces of kinopolitics remain in motion, albeit constantly reconceived and building new opportunities anew, *if paid attention to*.

Nail (2015) cautions, however, that these strategies, are not all-powerful. Rather, they are produced in tension with/against the kinetic power of the university's expansion by expulsion doctrine. Pedetic force, therefore, provides a vehicle for analyzing and making sense of institutional change in relation to migrant participation within higher education. It evokes a dynamic political climate wherein students-as-migrants might become co-constitutive of radical changes to a becoming-university as they enact strategies of pedetic force in new combinations. Contending with such movement might force institutions to reconcile the shortcomings of their traditions in relation to the realities of students' lives.

The Migrant University

The Migrant University is a university built and rebuilt through pedetic forces. In the practical examples I provide above, the university is created in reflection of Latinx (im)migrant communities' cultural practices. Anthropologically speaking, cultural practices are the building blocks of being. Cultural practices are the things humans do that make other things matter. In the migrant university, built within and from a movement-centered ontology, the university is sustainably temporal, illusory, allusive, and elusive from fixity. The migrant university resists the urge to concretize, even as it plants roots within culturally contingent practices. The nature of cultural practices themselves supports such movement-orientation, as cultural practices are mobile in and of themselves. They traverse physical, territorial, social, and political geographies.

As portrayed in this chapter, the migrant university is one that treats Latinx (im)migrant communities as normative, rather than exceptional. Latinx (im)migrant communities act historically. That is to say, their participation is historical; it matters. This positioning of the Latinx (im)migrant community is made possible by recognizing the myriad ways that normative US higher education expels the community, producing them into various migrant figures. I have tried to explicate and illustrate the pedetic re-building of the university into the migrant university by using snippets of Latinx (im)migrant communities' participation and engagement with/in kinopolitical terms in order to push against dominant representations and analyses of Latinx (im)migrant communities relations with US higher education. In this sense, the migrant university depicted here is also a Latinx University, at least to the extent that my prior anthropological work effectively assembles a semblance of Latinx (im)migrant communities' contributions and engagements with the institution.

As the migrant university, Latinx (im)migrant communities' pedetic forces historically re-build the institution as one of radical inclusivity, as shown in the witness bared by the rebellious Freedom University. The migrant university was fashioned from culturally relevant public pedagogies as called for and enacted by the Chicano Student Movement and MECHA. It was established through commitments to community-engagement and community sustainability via the raids of the DREAM Centers for undocumented students. And it was reified into celebration by the revolt perpetrated by Latino Graduation Ceremonies, which not only reached forward but also backward in temporally reclaiming the university as migrant.

Throughout this chapter, I have sought to bring my anthropological work in conversation with Nail's political philosophy of kinopolitics as a way to establish a new tool for examining the knowledge imperative of academe. My hope is that while I might not yet be fully successful, there might emerge glimmers of possibility from using kinopolitics to explain the affective and political consequences of institutionalized practice – that is, of normative US higher education. Certainly, movement and mobility need further attention. Particularly, the generation of practices within an ethics of such movement-centered ontological commitments might be a necessary or helpful next step.

References

Barnett, R. (2011). *Being a University*. London: Routledge.
Barnett, R. (2013). *Imagining the University*. London: Routledge.
Barnett, R. (2014). *Thinking and Rethinking the University: The selected works of Ronald Barnett*. London: Routledge.
Barnett, R. (2017). *The Ecological University: A Feasible Utopia*. London: Routledge.
Barnett, R., & Bengtsen, S. (2019). *Knowledge and the University: Re-Claiming Life*. London: Routledge.

Bustamante, L. (2020). *Education levels of recent Latino immigrants in the US reached new highs as of 2018*. Pew Research Center. Retrieved from: https://www.pewresearch.org/fact-tank/2020/04/07/education-levels-of-recent-latino-immigrants-in-the-u-s-reached-new-highs-as-of-2018/

Donato, R. (1997). *The other struggle for equal schools: Mexican Americans during the civil rights era*. Albany: SUNY Press.

Donato, R. (2007). *Mexicans and Hispanos in Colorado schools and communities, 1920–1960*. Albany: SUNY Press.

Ellis & Goodyear. (2018). *Spaces of teaching and learning: Integrating perspectives on research and practice*. London: Springer.

Foucault, M. (2008). *The birth of biopolitics: Lectures at the Collège de France, 1978–79*. New York: Palgrave Macmillan.

Garcia, M. (2014). *The Chicano movement. Perspectives from the twenty-first century*. New York: Routledge.

Gibson, C. (2019). *El Norte: The epic and forgotten story of Hispanic North America*. New York: Grove Press.

Gildersleeve, R. E. (2010). *Fracturing opportunity: Mexican migrant students and college-going literacy*. New York: Peter Lang Publishers.

Gildersleeve, R. E. (2016). The neoliberal academy of the Anthropocene and the retaliation of the lazy academic. *Cultural Studies-Critical Methodologies*. https://doi.org/10.1177/1532708616669522.

Gildersleeve, R. E. (2017a). Making and becoming in the undocumented student policy regime: A post-qualitative [discourse] analysis of US immigration and higher education policy. *Educational Policy Analysis Archives, 25*(31). https://doi.org/10.14507/epaa.25.2286.

Gildersleeve, R. E. (2017b). Truth-telling, ritual culture, and Latino college graduates in the Anthropocene. *Critical Questions in Education, 8*(1), 101–115.

Gildersleeve, R. E. (2020a). The knowledge imperative in academic waste(lands). *Taboo: Cultural Studies in Education*, Spring, 131–139.

Gildersleeve, R. E. (2020b). Lazy Pedagogy. In N. Denzin & J. Salvo (Eds.), *New directions for theorizing qualitative inquiry: Theory as resistance* (pp. 102–112). Gorham: Myers Education Press.

Gildersleeve, R. E., & Hernández, S. (2012). Producing (im)possible peoples: A critical discourse analysis of in-state resident tuition policy. *International Journal of Multicultural Education, 14*(2). Available at: http://www.ijme-journal.org/index.php/ijme/article/view/517/745

Gildersleeve, R. E., Cruz, C., Madriz, D., & Melendrez-Flores, C. (2015). Neoliberal futures and postsecondary opportunity: The politics of Latina/o college choice. In P. A. Pérez & M. A. Ceja (Eds.), *Latina and Latino college access and choice: Critical findings and theoretical perspectives for a changing demographic*. New York: Routledge.

Gramlich, J. (2019). *19 Striking findings from 2019*. Pew research center. Retrieved from: https://www.pewresearch.org/fact-tank/2019/12/13/19-striking-findings-from-2019/

Jackson, A. Y., & Mazzei, L. A. (2012). *Thinking with theory in qualitative research: Viewing data across multiple perspectives*. New York: Routledge.

Karabel, J. (2005). *The chosen: The hidden history of admission and exclusion at Harvard, Yale, and Princeton*. New York: Mariner.

Koro-Ljungberg, M. (2016). *Reconceptualizing qualitative research: Methodologies without methodology*. Los Angeles: Sage.

Kuntz, A. M. (2015). *The responsible methodologist*. Walnut Creek: Left Coast Press.

Lipman, P. (2011). *The new political economy of urban education: Neoliberalism, race, and the right to the city*. New York: Routledge.

McDonough, P. (1997). *Choosing colleges. How social class and schools structure inequality*. New York: SUNY Press.

Muñoz, S., & Espino, M. (2017). The freedom to learn: Experiences of students without legal status attending freedom university. *Review of Higher Education, 40*(4), 533–555.

Nail, T. (2015). *The figure of the migrant*. Stanford: Stanford University Press.
Nash, M. (2019). Entangled pasts: Land Grant colleges and American Indian dispossession. *History of Education Quarterly, 59*(4), 437–467.
Nørgård, R., & Bengsten, S. (2018). The worldhood University: Design signatures & guild thinking. In S. S. E. Bengtsen & R. Barnett (Eds.), *The thinking University* (pp. 167–183). London: Springer.
Orphan, C. M. (2021). *Life at the "people's universities": Organizational identification and commitment among regional comprehensive university faculty members in the USA*. Higher Education: https://doi.org/10.1007/s10734-020-00629-9
Rhoads, R. (1997). *Freedom's web: Student activism in an age of cultural diversity*. Baltimore, MD: Johns Hopkins University Press.
Savin-Baden. (2007). *Learning spaces: Creating opportunities for knowledge creation in academic life*. New York: Open University Press.
St. Pierre, E. (2015). Refusing human being in humanist qualitative inquiry. In N. Denzin & D. Giardina (Eds), *Qualitative inquiry—past, present, and future: A critical reader* (pp. 103–118). Walnut Creek, CA: Left Coast Press.
Temple, P. (2014). *The physical University: Contours of space and place in higher education*. New York: Routledge.

Ryan Evely Gildersleeve is Associate Dean and Professor in the Morgridge College of Education at University of Denver, United States. His research investigates the relationship between postsecondary education and democracy, working across the philosophical foundations of tertiary education and social research, and the cultural analysis of educational opportunity. His work takes form as philosophy, critical ethnography, and critical policy studies. Gildersleeve's current empirical research investigates the role of income-share agreements in postsecondary education affordability in the US. His philosophical work focuses on the future of the University and a new social contract for higher education globally. In 2019, he was a Senior Visiting Fellow at the Spencer Foundation. Previously, he received honors and awards from the National Academy of Education, American Educational Research Association, National Association for College Admission Counseling, and the Association for the Study of Higher Education. Gildersleeve received his Ph.D. in Education and his M.A. in Higher Education and Organizational Change from UCLA. He is a graduate of Occidental College.

Chapter 12
The Student as Consumer or Citizen of Academia and Academic Bildung

Mariann Solberg

Introduction

Academic Bildung is an idea that has had the function of an ideal for the formation of students in higher education in Scandinavia and northern parts of Europe since the late 1800s (Straume 2013; Fossland et al. 2015; Horlacher 2016). It is often connected to Wilhelm von Humboldt's educational model for the university, which was based on humanist principles and Enlightenment ideals. Humboldt believed that the university should make it possible for students not only to acquire professional knowledge and skills, but also to build autonomy and individual character (Humboldt 1841/1988, 1903/2016). Academic Bildung thus concerns a student's potential for personal development towards academic and personal independence through higher education, connected to, but also beyond, learning of the specific subject matter of a scientific discipline. It has cognitive as well as affective dimensions.

The background for taking up the ideal of the students' academic Bildung in higher education is that the idea since the 1990s has been under pressure due to the growing number of students, the marketization, standardization, and globalization that we see in the sector. Production of skills and working life relevance is the agenda of the day. This development in the sector is international, and it has been widely covered in the literature on higher education (Readings 1996; Shumar 1997; Canaan and Shumar 2008; Biesta 2011; Molesworth et al. 2011; Standish 2013; Marginson 2016; Barnett and Peters 2018). The utility-orientation has also reached Scandinavian higher education, and it has been challenged by appealing to the idea of academic Bildung, in various ways (Kjeldstadli 2010; Solberg 2010; Hagtvet and Ognjenovic 2011; Universitets-og høgskolerådet 2011).

M. Solberg (✉)
UiT The Arctic University of Norway, Tromsø, Norway
e-mail: mariann.solberg@uit.no

© The Author(s), under exclusive license to Springer Nature
Switzerland AG 2021
S. S. E. Bengtsen et al. (eds.), *The University Becoming*, Debating Higher Education: Philosophical Perspectives 6,
https://doi.org/10.1007/978-3-030-69628-3_12

In this chapter, I present a Scandinavian conception of academic Bildung – in Norwegian "akademisk danning or dannelse", in Danish "akademisk dannelse", in Swedish "akademisk bildning" – in order to discuss how these global trends of higher education have met with Scandinavian educational ideals and understandings of academic Bildung. I elaborate on dimensions that are specific for the Scandinavian Bildung tradition of higher education, both theoretically and empirically. I discuss why the personal developmental processes associated with Bildung should be more than a private responsibility for the individual student.

The development toward higher education as a global market has gradually changed the role of the student, from ideally being a citizen of academia, into taking on a role as consumer. What are the consequences of this change? And what can we possibly do about it? I point to the structure of epistemic practices I consider acute for academic Bildung and academic citizenship. But let us first try to unpack the somewhat complex concept of academic Bildung.

Bildung and Academic Bildung

The conception of academic Bildung that I shall espouse is connected to both "a dimension of critical, emancipatory and society-oriented reflection as well as a dimension of ethical-existential and being-oriented reflection" (Solberg and Hansen 2015: 28). For students in higher education, this developmental process thus involves both a striving for autonomy and a striving for authenticity, associated with the search for meaning that is specific to teaching, learning, and research in higher education. However, the notion of Bildung is in use in discourse about all levels of education in Scandinavia, from kindergarten to higher education, and it is a phenomenon not only occurring in formal education. We therefore need to specify what we find to be general traits of the concept of Bildung, and we will then be able to distinguish the specifics of Bildung in a higher education context. I use the term Bildung and academic Bildung because they are terms known also to an English-speaking audience and among philosophers of higher education, but it is the Norwegian concepts "danning" and "akademisk danning" that I have in mind. I will here not trace the similarities and differences between the German and the Scandinavian concepts further.

The concept of Bildung, a notion with German-Scandinavian roots, in general describes personal development processes that a person is going through when he or she meets the world, heading toward something better – a tacit or outspoken ideal, value or vision of ethical, existential, aesthetical or spiritual quality – in an educational setting (Solberg and Hansen 2015: 31). It is a pedagogical concept dating back to the Greek antiquity and the educational program of Paideia and, in a German setting, it is related to the existence of the Bildungsbürgertum of the 1800s (See Koselleck 2002; Straume 2013; Horlacher 2016). In an American setting, we find the related notion of Liberal education (See Løvlie and Standish 2002; Siljander et al. 2012; Horlacher 2016). In a Scandinavian context, however, Bildung relates to welfare state conceptions of education, as well as adult education, people's enlightenment, and enlightenment for life. In English, we often translate Bildung as "formation", "education", or "cultivation", even "edification" (Rorty 1979); in Danish and Norwegian, we use the terms "dannelse" or "danning"; in Swedish "bildning". Whatever term educational philosophers use, and whatever they may mean by the concept, most would agree that Bildung is not identical to a process of socialization into a given culture, as socialization can be passive (Hellesnes 1975). Bildung is more often, in line with Humboldts "Wechselwirkung", presented as a reciprocal process of formation between the individual as a self, and the world, where the individual meets the world actively, with its own subjectivity. In this process, socialization is but one dimension, subjectivation another. Moreover, the idea is that the individual comes out of this interplay, elevated, as a better person. Bildung is thus, through this definition, an inherently normative concept, unlike, e.g., standard definitions of the concepts of learning and teaching, or upbringing.

This development of the capacity for self-determination and self-development is characteristic also in academic Bildung. In a sense, the development process of Bildung of the young is reiterated, but this time the society in question is a specific discipline within academia and often a specific research community. Now the age of the human being is of less relevance. It is through the gradual development of responsibility for your own texts, and gradual development of your own voice, with the support and guidance from an academic authority, that you become a bachelor, a master, or a PhD. It is through the last two of these cycles, the master and the PhD degree, and though the gradual development of responsibility for your own research, that you become a researcher. Through this process, the normative status of the human being, with the achieved self-determination and self-articulation, changes from student to researcher. While I have chosen to focus on these aspects of the academic Bildung here, it must be mentioned that the normative dimensions of university education, often termed character education, is not out of sight (Arthur 2005).

Common for both the process of general Bildung and academic Bildung is that there exist certain normative images that function as goals for the development processes. Opinions on, and ideals of, what it means to be a person and what it means to be a researcher, may vary from community to community, but they are there. It follows from the description that «being a student», a status ascribed in the instance that a human being is enrolled into higher education, is expected to change towards something different. This new status is, at the least, that of being a «student that has graduated», and equipped for research, or, that of being a «researcher».

Lack of a capacity for self-determination will, both in general Bildung and in academic Bildung, imply withheld ascription of normative status. Lack of demonstrated ability for decisional autonomy in academic evaluations will deprive you of graduation, if not at the level of BA, then at the least on the levels of MA and PhD. Independence is an absolute core value of academia, whatever the level. However, in order to be a researcher, originality is a demand. Thus, self-determination is a necessary, but not sufficient, trait of academic Bildung. It is through the gradual development of your own personal ways into the discipline and the subject matter, and through your own unique take on the problems and questions, that you become, and are deemed to be, a researcher.

Thus, when we speak of student being and becoming, we are presupposing that the self can be conceived of as divided between a present and a future state. That which I am, and that which I want to be, or is expected to be. As in this case, that which the student is and that which some authority want or expect them to be. The question for us is now, who is to be ascribed the authority of prescription? Is it the student, the discipline, the supervisor, the research community, the local university, the government of the state, or the Organisation for Economic Co-operation and Development (OECD)? All of these are stakeholders, and the question is who are taking the upper hand in the negotiations.

Unpacking the Scandinavian Bildung Tradition of Higher Education Empirically

As an ideal, academic Bildung does not demand verified empirical existence, and yet some version of this ideal "regulates" our thinking about learning and development in higher education. However, without any experience of it, as a processual phenomenon, state, or cultural practice, whereof we could identify at the least some sufficient conditions for its existence, we could choose to think of the idea as irrelevant, uninteresting, or just a result of wishful thinking. A team of ten Scandinavian colleagues, all active as teachers and academic developers working with ICT in higher education, in 2011, set out to inquire into the question of the existence of academic Bildung in net-based higher education (Fossland et al. 2015). In the study, we scrutinized four different Danish, Swedish, and Norwegian cases. The focus in these case studies were on the possibilities, limitations, barriers, and pitfalls inherent in organizing teaching as fully or partially net-mediated courses. The case studies were describing specific course designs, teaching environments and student activities, and the studies contributed to a discussion about rethinking course design and the use of ICT, all in the light of the ideal of academic Bildung. A sketch of a theoretical grounding for the ideal, on a German-Scandinavian basis, provided a common frame for the case studies (in line with the concept presented in this chapter and in the theoretically grounding chapter of the book) (see Solberg and Hansen 2015). However, we were all at the same time skeptical of the very possibility to operationalize such an elusive and complex conception. The case studies varied in theoretical lenses and themes, but they were all looking out for signs of the presence of academic Bildung. Thirteen different, and to some extent overlapping, instances and interpretations of academic Bildung were found. The authors of the case studies took these traits to be expressions of the empirical existence of academic Bildung. The case studies interpreted academic Bildung as represented (instantiated) in the following traits: (i) professional proficiency, (ii) professional identity, (iii) autonomy in terms of being able to free oneself from didactical design, (iv) ability for perspective expansion, (v) being exploratory so as to achieve deep learning, (vi) being able to take an active part in a democratic society, (vii) being a whole person, (viii) having acquired academic skills, (ix) having acquired academic values, (x) having acquired academic identity and behavior, (xi) ability to think critically, (xii) ability for personal growth and maintenance, and (xiii) having aims of a better society (Solberg et al. 2015: 173). These 13 traits were found to cover both autonomy and authenticity dimensions of academic Bildung. The study thus demonstrates that the ideal of academic Bildung is possible to trace as an empirical phenomenon in the practice of Scandinavian higher education.

The study concludes that different contents and subject matters influence and shape the kind of academic Bildung that potentially can and should be facilitated in a higher education course. This means that all academic disciplines and professions have a Bildung potential. In this way, the different disciplines and the individual teachers will have to reflect on their specific ways into facilitation of student development of academic Bildung in their course or program, in order to succeed. The study also concludes that the teaching and learning environment offered is pivotal for the facilitation of academic Bildung.

Different Conceptions of Bildung in the Daily Discourse on Higher Education

Within Scandinavian higher education, the concept of academic Bildung has been revived repeatedly, in spite of the lack of a clear and concise definition, and different hyphenated concepts of Bildung have been put to use in the everyday language of academia. Instead of talking about the concept of Bildung, one could rather nowadays speak of a multitude of concepts of Bildung, to some extent overlapping with each other in content. Many of the new ways of using the concept, for instance, the use of digital Bildung (no. digital danning) can seem to be far from the concept as Wilhelm von Humboldt conceived of it. According to him, Bildung is about "[to] … give the concept of humanity in our person the greatest possible content. […] This task alone can be solved by connecting our ego to the world through the most universal, living and free interaction" (Humboldt 1903/2016: 180, my translation). The Norwegian educator Lars Løvlie has introduced the somewhat wider notion of techno-cultural formation (no. teknokulturell danning) in order to describe what Bildung can be in a postmodern technological society, where he sees Bildung as analogous to the notion of interface (Løvlie 2003). The meeting between subject and world is in focus in both concepts. In a report released in 2011 by the Norwegian Association of Higher Education Institutions, we find seven different concepts of Bildung (Universitets og høgskolerådet 2011). This repeated revival of the concept of Bildung in Scandinavian higher education, in spite of its notorious lack of clarity, tells us that it captures something that both governments, university management, researchers, and university teachers repeatedly find useful when describing student development in the field of higher education. Not seldom, academic Bildung is upheld as a bulwark against instrumentalism in the sector. And in public debate in and of the higher education sector, it is often connected to the Humboldtian idea of the unity of research and education. In this way, the Bildung processes to be expected in the research university is first of all the processes of subjects engaged in the cultivation of knowledge, and on the search for new knowledge. This engagement is an end in itself and, as Humboldt points out, it is a deeply human endeavor.

Academic Citizen or Consumer?

Academic Bildung, as a normative concept, also addresses political and civic dimensions of life in higher education (Giroux 2002; Arthur and Bohlin 2005; Kuntz 2006). The notion of academic citizenship originally points to membership in the community of teachers and students; in medieval times denoting the university. The university, as a formal institution, has its origin in the Medieval Christian tradition, and the term university is derived from the Latin universitas magistrorum et scholarium, which means "community of teachers and scholars". In Norwegian higher education, the matriculation into this community is symbolized by the academic citizen letter (no. akademisk borgerbrev), a document confirming that the student has been enrolled at a university. However, neither the term itself nor a realization of the content of the concept is very prominent in the everyday life of modern higher education institutions.

These days it is more common that academic citizenship is ascribed only to the teachers, and not to the students. According to a study performed by Bruce Macfarlane (2007), however, modern academics still connect the term with membership in a community. Furthermore,

> Membership of a community also implies duties deriving from kinship in reciprocation of the benefits that membership brings. This was identified by respondents as applying to different groups or communities, such as students and colleagues. Others expressed the view that academic citizenship implied broader requirements in connecting their work with the concerns of society. (Macfarlane 2007: 246)

This means that when the term is employed, not only internal commitments between the faculties is in focus but also a wider civic mission of the university (Macfarlane and Burg 2018: 3).

Moreover, Macfarlane and Burg hold that

> It is widely acknowledged that the displacement of academic self-governance with a more managerial style of leadership in universities can be associated with the decline of academic citizenship. (Macfarlane and Burg 2018: 3)

In this setting, academic citizenship is understood as the third leg of the academic role, and it is a term widely used in higher education to refer to those activities distinct from research and teaching that support and offer services to both the university and wider society. (Macfarlane and Burg 2018: 1)

In a Norwegian setting, the three legs of the academic role is more often referred to as "research, teaching and dissemination", rather than the US and UK "research, teaching and service", and the internal service is not counted directly in, but referred to as "administration".

The notion of citizenship also points to the political role of academics, be it teachers or students. In the theories and vocabulary of Bildung, the political role of the academics is often referred to as democratic Bildung (no. demokratisk danning). This notion implies and presupposes the positioning of the educational system as an important factor within a deliberative democracy.

In light of this, how should we now think of the role of the students? It seems that the students are defined out of the community of the higher education institution. Instead, the role of students as consumers seems to have come to stay. This should be no surprise as tuition fees are more and more common in most countries, and it has been raised as an issue of concern in the literature on higher educations for quite a while.

Students view the opportunity to gain a degree as a right, and a service which they have paid for, demanding a greater choice and a return on their investment. (Molesworth et al. 2011: x)

In a sense, the new role of the student as a buyer of a service may seem to shift the weight of a power balance between professors and students.

What is new and potentially disturbing about the marketisation of education is the attempt to recast the relationship between academics and students along the model of a service provider and customer. (Furedi 2011: 2)

On the one hand, this points towards the role of the student as a role where one is not expected to take part in the internal life of the university, and also a role without responsibility for civil society and public culture, what Jon Nixon has called "the Public Good", and Simon Marginson has called "the Common Good", Marginson pointing also to social solidarity (Nixon 2012; Marginson 2016). On the other hand, this means that the students' perspectives and needs, as students, now, as opposed to pre-1970s, to a larger extent have to be taken seriously by their professors.

Since according to the logic of marketisation, the customer is always right, the university had better listen to the student. (Furedi 2011: 3)

But couldn't this be a good thing on some accounts? In the same period of time, the question of the quality of teaching and learning have been set on the agenda, so have student-centered learning, as well as a demand for enhancing the teaching competence and qualifications of professors through courses in higher education pedagogy. This change may have something to do with the marketization of higher education, and the recast of the relationship between academics and students. However, the situation in the Scandinavian countries, where most higher education has public funding, and is basically free of charge, is not much different when it comes to the student role as citizen or consumer of academia, nor when it comes to the new focus on student-centered teaching and pedagogical qualification of academics. The experience of a greater and growing divide between academics and students is also prevalent in Scandinavia.

How can we meet this situation? Is it possible to reframe the way to think about the role of the students? My suggestion is that we, as faculty and students, in practice work on the issue together. Teachers have a possibility to work on the curriculum and our education programs in order to facilitate a development for the students that can foster a community spirit, and a sense of responsibility for more than one's own academic and personal development. We also have the possibility to include the students in the planning of both the curriculum and ways of teaching and learning in order to foster a spirit of shared responsibility on the educational dimensions of university life. And we can, as representatives of faculty and as academics, on intramural and extramural boards and other positions, support and secure student representation and organization.

The Structure of Epistemic Practices Acute for Academic Bildung

The research universities have held a particular position in our societies and, in northern parts of Europe, the dual role of research and education has been the prominent trait, in the spirit of Wilhelm von Humboldt. The academic freedom of the institutions and of each researcher has been a guarantee for the independence of research, due to a freedom from the dominance of both government and market. The free chase for truth and new descriptions, and the goal of development of new knowledge, undertaken by able minds, have been conceived of as vital for development of our societies. Another purpose for the research universities has been the transmission of knowledge to the young such that, through the education of the students, we further the existing, thereby also grounding the development of new knowledge. The most important deliverables from the universities to society have thus been both new knowledge and educated students. Such is it today and it is hard to see that this will change in the future.

If we can agree that also the future university should facilitate development of citizens of academia who strive towards autonomy and authenticity, who have independence and personal engagement in their academic pursuits, and a willingness to take part in civic academic citizenship, what kinds of knowledge practices need to be pursued? This is not the place for turnings to details, but I will suggest that the creative use of one's intellect and sensibility toward common and communal human interests is vital. This is the kind of activity that Immanuel Kant (1724–1804) describes in his variant of the human sensus communis, describing the not only common but also communal sense of men.

According to Kant, all human beings are equally equipped for using their own intellect. To make use of one's own intellect means, according to Kant, to think for yourself. However, a notion of self-thinking built on Kant is not subjective. A Kantian notion of self-thinking can best be seen as based in his idea of sensus communis, and this is put in the following words in his *Critique of Judgment* from 1790:

> ..we must take sensus communis to mean the idea of a sense shared, i.e., a power to judge that in reflecting takes account (a priori), in our thought, of everyone else's way of presenting [something], in order as it were to compare our own judgment with human reason in general... Now we do this as follows: we compare our judgment not so much with the actual as rather with the merely possible judgments of others, and [thus] put ourselves in the position of everyone else... (Kant 1790/1987, § 40: 160)

Sensus communis is here seen as a general faculty for judgment that all humans have, and the main point is that we relate our own thinking to the potential thinking of others. He notes that there are three maxims (rules of action) that are part of the common human understanding.

> They are the following:

1. To think for oneself;
2. To think in the position of everyone else;
3. Always to think in accord with oneself.

> The first is the maxim of the unprejudiced way of thinking, the second of the broad-minded way, the third that of the consistent way. (Kant 1790/1987, § 40: 161)

The *Critique of Judgment* is Kant's critique on aesthetics, and he notes that the maxims "do not belong here, to be sure, as parts of the critique of taste, but can nevertheless serve to elucidate its fundamental principles." It is the movement from the specific to the general that, according to Kant, is distinctive for intersubjectively valid judgments. This has inspired several interpreters of Kant, among them Hannah Arendt, to see the potential of Kant's version of the sensus communis as not only characteristic for aesthetic judgment but also for political judgment. A politically reflective judgment can favorably be described as a movement from the sensibility of the individual agent to a community of agents. It is based in the faculties of all men; it is an evenly distributed capacity. This means that this particular form of enlarged thinking is an egalitarian source for cultivation of our thinking.

Can this way of cultivating the thinking towards intersubjectively valid judgment be informative for the kind of teaching and learning that should take place in higher education? How can the student know whether the acquired understanding of a phenomenon holds good academic standard? I have, loosely inspired by Kant's understanding of the sensus communis, together with my own experiences from three decades of teaching and research in higher education, suggested the following rule of thumb for my students: Think with, think against, and think for yourself (Solberg 2010: 61). In Norwegian: Tenke med, tenke mot, tenke selv. To think with, think against, and think for yourself could mean:

(a) Inform yourself of all the best ways of understanding a point (a critical endeavor).
(b) Find all the best reasons you can to hold against it (a critical endeavor).
(c) Let this be the basis for your own thinking (a creative endeavor).

This movement can also be seen in a familiar three-phase process in teaching and learning that make explicit distinctions between:

(a) Information acquisition (understanding)
(b) Knowledge consolidation (evaluation – pros/cons)
(c) Application of theory to practice (creation)

Anyhow, according to Kant, I must include the possible judgment of others, in my own judgment, in order to reach intersubjectively valid judgments. In order to make this into a habit I must practice, together with others. This is the basis for being a skilled thinker. In order to truly think for yourself, as a student at a university, you cannot start from own intellect alone. You must think on the basis of the well-established knowledge in your discipline, and thus you need to be acquainted with this knowledge base. You must further be able to train your thinking skills in conjunction with your peers and the previous and present authorities in your field. This means that self-thinking requires a community. The lack of Bildung thus will show as lack of active and independent use of one's intellect and a lack of inclusion of the possible judgment of others.

The Student in a Future Higher Education

Due to the growing number of students seeking higher education, higher education has an even more important role to play now in the shaping of the life of the students and, indirectly, in the shaping of society, as a consequence of the formation of students. The original idea of the university as a community of teachers and scholars may need reinterpretation in light of marketization. However, students may see teachers as either delivering the goods or not, but teachers and students still have common interests in the development of higher education. Students and teachers should unite in the endeavor of making and maintaining higher education as a place for academic freedom, for creative re-construction, and new development of knowledge.

If we imagine future ideals for student formation in higher education, will academic Bildung, in the sense of a striving for autonomy and authenticity, still be a realistic or even possible ideal to chase? Will academic citizenship be possible to foster in the students if they see themselves first and foremost as customers on a global education market? My contention is that we who already are within higher education need to do what we can to invite students in, in order to build our education programs together in such a way as to foster students and future researchers that have the courage to challenge, the ability for resistance, and the capacity to create. Subjects who see themselves as taking part in a common and communal endeavor. Academic Bildung describes presuppositions for inner freedom and human flourishing. Academic Bildung, as seen through the lens of a Kantian and politicized version of sensus communis, is a vital prerequisite for truth seeking at the outskirts of what is already known. It is also a platform for fostering academic citizenship and societal responsibility.

References

Arthur, J., & Bohlin, K. E. (2005). *Citizenship and higher education. The role of universities in communities and society.* Oxon: Routledge.
Arthur, J. (2005). Student character in the British university. In J. Arthur & K. E. Bohlin (Eds.), *Citizenship and higher education. The role of universities in communities and society.* Oxon: Routledge.
Barnett, R., & Peters, M. A. (2018). *The idea of the university. Contemporary perspectives.* New York: Peter Lang.
Biesta, G. (2011). How useful should the university be? On the rise of the global university and the crisis in higher education. *Qui Parle: Critical Humanities and Social Sciences, 20*(1), 35–47.
Canaan, J., & Shumar, W. (Eds.). (2008). *Structure and agency in the neoliberal university.* New York: Routledge.
Fossland, T., Mathiasen, H., & Solberg, M. (Eds.). (2015). *Academic Bildung in net-based higher education: Moving beyond learning.* London: Routledge.
Furedi, F. (2011). Introduction to the marketisation of higher education and the student as consumer. In M. Molesworth, R. Scullion, & E, Nixon, (Eds.), *The marketisation of higher education and the student as consumer* (pp.1–7). Oxon: Routledge.
Giroux, H. A. (2002). Neoliberalism, corporate culture, and the promise of higher education: The university as a democratic public space. *Harvard Educational Review, 72*(4), 425–463.
Hagtvet, B. & Ognjenovic, G. (2011). *Dannelse: Tenkning, modning, refleksjon. Nordiske perspektiver på allmenndannelsens nødvendighet i høyere utdanning og forskning.* Oslo: Dreyer Forlag.
Hellesnes, J. (1975). *Sosialisering og teknokrati: Ein sosialfilosofisk studie med særleg vekt på pedagogikkens problem.* Oslo: Gyldendal.
Horlacher, R. (2016). *The educated subject and the german concept of Bildung. A comparative cultural history.* New York: Routledge.
Humboldt, W. (2016 [1903]). «Teori om menneskets danning: Et bruddstykke», oversatt av Tomas Stølen,.i *Norsk filosofisk tidsskrift, 51*(3–4), 179–183.
Humboldt, W. (1988 [1841]). *Gesammelte Werke* (ed. Brandes C, Vol. 1). Berlin: G. Reimer. Reprint 1988, Berlin: De Gruyer.
Kant, I (1987 [1790]). *Critique of judgment* (trans. Pluhar 1978). Indianapolis: Hackett.
Kjeldstadli, K. (2010). *Akademisk kapitalisme.* Oslo: Res Publica.
Koselleck, R. (2002). On the anthropological and semantic structure of Bildung i. In *The practice of conceptual history* (pp. 170–207). Stanford: Stanford University Press.
Kuntz, A. M. (2006). Academic citizenship: The risks and responsibility of reframing faculty work. *Journal of College and Character, 7*(5), 1–9.
Løvlie, L. (2003). Teknokulturell danning. In R. Slagstad, O. Korsgaard, & L. Løvlie (Eds.), *Dannelses forvandlinger* (pp. 347–371). Pax Forlag: Oslo.
Løvlie, L., & Standish, P. (2002). Introduction: Bildung and the idea of a liberal education. *Journal of Philosophy of Education, 36*(3), 317–340.
Macfarlane, B. (2007). Defining and rewarding academic citizenship: The implications for university promotions policy. *Journal of Higher Education Policy and Management, 29*(3), 261–273.
Macfarlane, B., & Burg, D. (2018). *Rewarding and recognising academic citizenship.* London: Leadership Foundation for Higher Education.
Marginson, S. (2016). *Higher education and the common good.* Melbourne: Melbourne University Publishing.

Molesworth, M., Nixon, E., & Scullion, R. (2011). *The marketisation of higher education: The student as consumer*. London: Routledge.

Nixon, J. (2012). *Higher education and the public good. Imagining the university*. London: Bloomsbury.

Readings, B. (1996). *The university in ruins*. Cambridge, MA: Harvard University Press.

Rorty, R. (1979). *Philosophy and the mirror of nature*. Princeton: Princeton UniversityPress.

Shumar, W. (1997). *College for sale: A critique of the commodification of higher education*. London: Falmer Press.

Siljander, P., Kivelä, A., & Sutinen, A. (Eds.). (2012). *Theories of Bildung and growth. Connections and controversies between continental educational thinking and American pragmatism*. Rotterdam: Sense Publishers.

Solberg, M. (2010). Om akademisk danning med utgangspunkt i Kants sensus communis og "Hva er opplysning?". In L. Dybdal & F. Nilsen (Eds.), *Festskrift til Hjørdis Nerheim i anledning 70-årsdagen* (pp. 51–68). Unipub forlag: Oslo.

Solberg, M., & Hansen, F. T. (2015). On academic Bildung in higher education – A Scandinavian approach. In T. Fossland, H. Mathiasen, & M. Solberg (Eds.), *Academic Bildung in net-based higher education, moving beyond learning* (pp. 28–54). London: Routledge Research in Higher Education.

Solberg, M., Grepperud, G., & Hansen, F. T. (2015). Pedagogical considerations: A new discourse based on Academic Bildung. In T. Fossland, H. Mathiasen, & M. Solberg (Eds.), *Academic Bildung in net-based higher education: Moving beyond learning* (pp. 163–176). London: Routledge.

Standish, P. (2013). Transparency, accountability and the public role of higher education. In O. Filippakou & G. L. Williams (Eds.), *Higher education as a public good: Critical perspectives on theory, policy and practice*. New York: Peter Lang.

Straume, I. S. (Ed.). (2013). *Danningens filosofihistorie*. Oslo: Gyldendal Akademisk.

Universitets og høgskolerådet. (2011). *Dannelsesaspekter i utdanning. Rapport fra en arbeidsgruppe nedsatt av UHRs utdanningsutvalg*. Available online at http://www.uhr.no/aktuelt_fra_uhr/dannelsesaspekter_i_utdanning

Mariann Solberg is Professor of Pedagogy at UiT The Arctic University of Norway and head of the research group Philosophy of Education. She gained her M.A. and her Dr. Art. in philosophy. She is editor-in-chief of Uniped, the Norwegian journal for university pedagogy. Her research interests centers on knowledge and Bildung with a particular focus on higher education. Further areas of interest is philosophical anthropology, philosophical naturalism, transformative learning, information literacy, academic development and education policy. She has published on philosophy of education, teaching and learning in higher education, philosophy of social science, epistemology, and philosophy in the working life.

Chapter 13
Creating Experimenting Communities in the Future University

Sarah Robinson, Klaus Thestrup, and Wesley Shumar

Introduction

The connected global world brings groups of people together, who are otherwise separated by geographical distances, time and economic constraints to play, learn, experiment and work together. The potential of the internet and digital technologies are enormous regarding informal learning. Digital technologies provide a myriad of platforms and formats for informal learning to take place in a range of communities where common interests are held and outcomes are not predetermined. Given the connectedness of everything around us and the potential for a global learning environment where anything is possible, we are interested in exploring what kinds of pedagogies could harness the enormous potential of digital technology in order to equip students to take a critical stance and take action in an uncertain future. Harnessing the potential of the digital in meaningful and creative ways and integrating these into formal modes of learning at the university, however, have not been particularly successful. Often strong institutional practices, led by neoliberal discourses, bend and manipulate digital learning technologies into particular kinds of managerial and performative strategies.

The purpose of the university has been narrowed down to be about delivering knowledge, products and services to a paying public. And it is at this point that teaching and learning came to mean knowledge transfer with digital technology becoming just another strategy to be accountable and efficient in that transfer

S. Robinson (✉) · K. Thestrup
Aarhus University, Aarhus, Denmark
e-mail: srobin@au.dk

W. Shumar
Department of Communication, Drexel University, Philadelphia, PA, USA
e-mail: shumarw@drexel.edu

(Newfield 2016; Nussbaum 2010; Marginson 1997). There is a real sense that the university needs to be re-thought, and that knowledge has been watered down to mean something that can be packaged and measured. Bengtsen and Barnett (2018: 3) suggest that there are important purposes embedded in the thinking and thoughtful university as well as being able to think deeply about and inquire into the world, but also to be able to engage with and imagine different outcomes. As the global pandemic took hold in 2020, it has changed the world in ways that were unimaginable to us and bring home the realization that the society we live in is no longer predictable and foreseeable. An unpredictable and unknown future awaits. Today, in an uncertain and in some ways unstable environment, new pedagogies are needed if a university education is to equip students for new challenges. Barnett (2004: 258) argues that student 'being-for-uncertainty' is a challenge for universities which can only be met by rethinking how teaching and learning are designed through new pedagogies. This argument for a different stance on learning links strongly to rethinking the design of teaching for learning that might support thinking and being in uncertainty. Nevertheless, some universities are seeking to pioneer notions of a connected curriculum that will allow students to combine active inquiry with current research engagement to push the boundaries of disciplines and reach across different fields (Fung 2017).

In this chapter, we explore how we can begin to talk about what being-for-uncertainty means for student learning and ask how can pedagogies that harness the potential of the digital to support learning for an unknown future be designed. We question the survival of a neoliberal institution, where standardization and packaging of knowledge for the consumer is challenged. This critique leads us to investigate the potential for opening learning environments to make these meaningful and to move away from pre-defined outcomes to focus on learning processes that include the potential of digital technology as it is seen in informal learning. We briefly present a pedagogical model that provides a potential structure for shaping meaningful learning through critical reflection where the digital experimenting community is central. The notion of an experimenting community is seemingly simple, based on asking questions one does not know the answer to. We discuss how the experimenting community links to developing knowledge and skills. In conclusion, we suggest that open pedagogies linked to digital technologies, such as the experimenting community, could be a way forward to new paths that support learning-for-being in an unpredictable world.

The University, Lost and Found

By this point in time, many researchers and philosophers of higher education have pointed out that the university has lost its way (Barnett 2013; Collini 2012, Nixon 2011; Readings 1996). Neoliberal economic ideology, and the audit culture it has inspired, have greatly changed the way that universities operate and the way that learning and knowledge are understood. In this framework, knowledge is seen as a product that can be transferred to students (in the case of classroom learning) or capitalized (in the sense of economic capital and to take advantage of) upon in terms of the products of research. One problem with this view of knowledge and learning is that it tends to obscure what these processes really are. Both learning and knowledge production are social processes. They are the ways that faculty and students work together to produce meaning (Bruner 1996). It is a sensemaking process that discovers "truths" with a small "t". That is to say, that we learn about the nature of the natural world, the social world, our sense of what is right and wrong and ultimately what we value. This learning is always partial and always in process, and it is the job of universities and the people who work within them to discuss, debate and challenge our understanding of the world and how society should be as well as our place in it.

A more contemporary and social view of learning and knowledge leads directly to the question of what the purpose of the university is. And the question of purpose directly connects with our concern with "creating experimenting communities". Knowledge production is a process of exploration that students and faculty engage in together. They seek not only knowledge but are also always questioning the value of the knowledge they seek. This ethical priority means that what we must come to understand that learning and knowledge are processes that need to be supported, evaluated and judged for the good of all. Knowledge and learning are not products to be sold and we cannot audit the efficient production of learning and knowledge as things.

Many researchers have attempted to address this more basic question of the purpose of the university. Rider (2018) looks to the philosopher Ortega y Gasset in order to think about the purpose of the university. Rider (2018: 18–20) shows how Ortega separated intellectual endeavor into two directions. One direction might seek specialization and scientific or professional knowledge. The other direction would focus on the well-being of people and the support of a common culture with this education being geared toward a general public. While technical expertise is important, a society needs a people that can understand its history and be ready to discuss and come up with a shared belief of what is true and good. While Rider points out that this is a complex and difficult task, in effect our society has done that already. It is just that we have left it to the elites to decide that what is true and good is the accumulation of capital and the social games associated with that accumulation whatever the cost. What is needed rather is a university that helps citizens focus on a more public good. Nixon (2011: 29) reminds us that the path toward deciding on a common cause and the public good is a dialogic process that involves the creative collaboration of people with each other, held on an equal footing. For Nixon, doing the right thing is at the core of a higher education.

The goal of educating citizens for a common good dovetails with much contemporary learning theory. What we have learned about learning over the last century is that it is as Dewey (1938) would say, rooted in experience. People learn whether we want them to or not, learning is not something that has to be taught. Indeed formal education has to take responsibility for building upon pro-social (educative) experiences and making room for further learning. Learning is done through interaction.

People will discuss and make meaning out of their experiences and then build upon that meaning. A good educator is someone who can steer people toward a goal of what would be good for people to learn, and then make the space for that learning. Again, this could be scientific or technical learning, but most importantly, learning to be an active and thoughtful citizen is central to the overall well-being of society. This means that the pedagogies we use to support and nurture learning need to be carefully considered if we are to equip students to cope with uncertainty and to imagine new ways of being together.

It is in this context that academic freedom becomes a meaningful concept and it is why the nineteenth century philosophers of the modern university saw academic freedom as something that was for both faculty and students. As faculty and students explore the world together, making sense of what they experience, they need the freedom to make sense of that experience in the ways that they see as best. Their interpretations will continue to be re-evaluated by themselves and by other scholars, that is the scholarly process and what allows us to say we have the current best understanding of whatever is being explored. But as Rider (2018) points out, this means that there is a responsibility to academic freedom as well. As faculty and students explore together, they are responsible to make the best interpretations they can. They are responsible to "truth" even as that truth is necessarily partial and always in motion.

Learning Processes and Digital Technologies

Traditionally and in the early phases of learning, the undergraduate student gradually becomes a domain expert through the scaffolding of practices that are often controlled by the educator to support the student's development of knowledge and ability to apply critical thinking. However, as the students become more knowledgeable, the educator's role may change through facilitating and mentoring. As the graduate student progresses, their role also changes, and learning may even become a joint activity. In this case, the students are both learners and researchers equally and, as such, become participants and creative thinkers (Resnick 2017) in a learning process.

That shift, from novice to knowledgeable, supports all to move toward a more active process of learning. But these processes are very individual as well. While in general, many undergraduates are supported through learning strategies and graduate students move toward being more independent, self-motivated learners and producers of knowledge, some undergraduates may be independent at a much earlier stage. As such, the teacher has to constantly evaluate what kind of support is needed for which students as they progress. This progression allows students to become aware of their own potential, competences and skills and their ability to act on real-life issues. Consequently, students are able to move toward directing their own learning as active citizens in an unpredictable world. This is what we might regard as an entrepreneurial mindset but, to get to this, we have to pay attention to how students understand who they are, what they can do and how they can work with others to create something of value. For the teaching faculty, this awareness about processes and learning maturity needs to be fine-tuned and reflected upon as students become more independent as they engage with their own learning. Creating learning environments where this is possible means that both faculty and students must understand learning as progression where learning will be different for each person. The work of universities is not only to impact on society but also through systematic inquiry to reveal what life in its fullness is. The latter appears to have been forgotten in the neoliberalism of an audit society. Therefore, the status of knowledge in the world is changing, which requires us to rethink 'the value that knowledge possesses' (Barnett and Bengtsen 2020: 30). This is a necessary starting point when we design new curricula and pedagogies for a new era and which will better society. The university must both be a productive place and a disruptive place and, charged with preparing the next generation to become active in a global world, the design of pedagogies must include creating communities that actively develop their learning together with a critical and ethical focus.

As digital tools and online access have come to be a regular part of university life, they have had an enormous impact on university work. The digital dramatically, and mostly positively, impacted university research. It made it possible for researchers to collaborate with more people more quickly. It allowed faculty to quickly disseminate ideas and research results (Sampath Kumar and Manjunath 2013). However, with regard to teaching and learning, there was a double failure of imagination. First and most importantly, the online was imagined as an analogue to the f2f classroom and, rather than taking advantage of the potential of digital to reorganize space and time in interesting ways, online classes were designed to be beholden to f2f classroom ideals. Second, learning was conceptualized as information flow, and that could be measured and marketized, much in line with neoliberal ideas about learning and knowledge. So, the digital was imagined as a potential profit center offering products to customers with lower production costs (Noble 2001). In this chapter, we see a very different way in which digital tools are used, and a very different imagination of the digital's potential. Here, the digital is used to bring the world outside and the university together. Further, the digital is used to enhance opportunities for sense-making among faculty and students.

Context and Background

This chapter draws on data gathered from four years of teaching the first semester module, taught by two of the authors, on Digital Learning Contexts of an online Masters program in ICT-based educational design at a Danish university. Students with backgrounds in educational settings, teachers, pedagogues, social workers, etc. take the course to explore and gain experience with how digital technologies can enhance learning in a range of informal and formal educational situations. The students may be located across the breadth of Denmark and may, for different reasons, be taking the course from countries outside of Denmark. Typically, the students chose the course as it provides an opportunity to learn online and offsite. Initially, many believe that the primary mode of learning will be to complete assignments and hand-ins after some kind of feedback. However, the course has been designed not to mimic a classroom where the lecturer delivers knowledge that the student acquires and reproduces. For example, the summative assessment is an oral examination that is supported by texts and visual material developed by the student themselves. While there is a core curriculum of texts to be covered, there is space for the students to suggest other relevant literature. The two teachers, researchers with backgrounds from drama and from entrepreneurship education, were concerned about 'getting more than the head involved'. They wanted to get away from 'what do I need to learn to get through the course' to 'what do I want to learn to change the (digital) practices that I am involved in?' A specific framework, called the changemaker model (Robinson 2020), was developed as the teachers found out what worked and what didn't when they met the students online. The framework is described briefly below. However, while the content and contexts vary from year to year depending on the student's own motivation and interest, the framework provides a process for establishing and setting up collaborative, experimenting communities that are central to the success of the course. The experimenting community relies on relationships being established around common issues or challenges and a need to make sense of the problem as well as an urgency to solve it. The experimenting community is therefore a group of people who share values around a set of interests and questions arise where the answers have not yet been found. More will be said about the experimenting community in the following section. At the beginning of the course, there is a two-day seminar where the students meet in a classroom face to face. This meeting is important for establishing and encouraging relationships and stimulating dialogues and discussions about experience, competence and ways of working. After this, the teaching and learning is carried out online and uses a range of digital media that allows for peer-feedback, interactions between individual students, between groups of students and between students and faculty. While none of these resources are innovative in themselves, the manner in which they are combined is and the development of an 'experimenting community' is both novel and powerful.

Experimenting Communities and Digital Media

Formal learning in higher education is often detached from real-life situations while, for the learner, meaning is created through the recognition of the attachment to life experiences. In order that meaningful learning can straddle theory and practice, knowledge and action, the ability to dwell within oneself and to critically reflect with others, pedagogical frameworks are needed that allow the learner to imagine what does not yet exist. The experimenting community represents such a possibility as this kind of community is driven by the experiment and the question and not the repetition of the existing result and the already given answer.

The rapidly changing state of technical knowledge, coupled with a world that has so many problems that demand intelligent thoughtful solutions is the background for the notion of the experimenting community. In principle, the experimenting community is formed from a group of people who have similar interests, goals and values. The culture of the group has, at its core, the experiment itself, driven by curiosity they seek new answers. The goal of the experimenting community is to investigate, analyse and make decisions about the actions they will take to meet a challenge and find potential solutions. These actions draw on the actual skills, competences and experiences of the community members and link to the resources and networks that they have access to in order to expand their existing knowledge. The experimenting community is therefore constantly evolving and is ever refocusing and qualifying the knowledge and experiences that they need in order to bring change (Caprani and Thestrup 2010; Thestrup 2013).

Social media gives the possibility to exchange and engage but, even so, it is not given what form the experimenting community might take. The production process and the methods of enquiry are up for experiments themselves in the community. A way this can be achieved is to understand the way the experimenting community uses digital media and digital technologies as an open laboratory, to open the world to new imaginaries (Thestrup and Robinson 2016: 153). The digital and the analogue, the physical and the virtual, the synchronous and asynchronous are all intertwined in the sense that digital media do not act alone or are screen-based and stationary. The communication, experimenting, playing and producing together through and with digital media are seen as mediated by the chosen platforms. However, as it learns to reflect on how media shapes interaction, the experimenting community looks for openings that will allow the media to be re-shaped for the purpose of the user. The users of a platform become not only users, they are also producers of content and meaning, which can be framed as 'prod-users' (Bruns 2008). In this case, they not only produce content for a platform defined for others, but that they, in principle, change the platform. The community consists of a group of individuals exchanging experiences and a curiosity and will to go in new directions. The experimenting community reaches out from itself using the abilities and the questions, the community asks. This is, in principle, a never-ending process as it all the time challenges itself and the world around it.

The term the open laboratory was framed in 2011 (Thestrup 2013), but actually builds upon discussions inside theatre and drama research (Lehmann and Szatkowski 2001), where the term the open theatre was used to indicate, that no theatre or drama traditions in advance could be discarded from the theatre laboratory when experimenting to find new processes of production. In these processes, digital media were included, so it was possible to go to the next step and frame the open laboratory as a place where, in principle, all media and all materials could be brought into a process of transformation and exchange. The open laboratory was born out of a situation, where the use and choice of tools, processes and materials were at stake.

The notion of an open laboratory opens up new combinations, but is also open to the world to seek inspiration, challenges, information and knowledge (Thestrup and Pedersen 2020). The open laboratory is, as such, a pedagogical method that potentially allows the participants to be open in three different ways: (i) open to combining the analogue and the digital, (ii) open to the world outside the experimenting community through the internet and (iii) open to cooperation and collaboration to such an extent, that the members of community might change their views upon what interests them, what questions to ask and how to ask (ibid 2020). At the same time, the community also has a lot to offer, that might influence others. The openness is connected to the understanding of culture, as a group of people who, at the core of their culture, make meaning in their everyday life and as part of that are creative (Gauntlett and Thomsen 2013). One can also say that every culture has the potential to change (Hastrup 2004) and that culture is something that is actively conducted by the participants in it (Jantzen 2005, 2013; Nielsen et al. 2019). This understanding of a group of people as some who might change part of their behavior or keep it, advances the possibility to meet other groups of people through a creative exchange. This exchange can take form through constructing a flexible meeting place (Gislev et al. 2020) or platforms of creativity (Culpepper and Gauntlett 2020), where the experimenting community continually (re)constructs the actual use of chosen digital media, so that shared creativity might be possible.

The experimenting community that seeks to create an open laboratory draws on Caprani and Thestrup (2010) whose interest in how teachers and children learn and play in a pre-school setting over a period of several years looked at how they experimented with scrapped computers, took them apart and made new toys out of them using narratives as well. During the experiments, children also used mobile phones and LEGO Scouts that were small robots. As none of the researchers, practitioners or the children in question had tried this before, both pedagogical methods and principles had to be tested. The experimenting community was born out of a situation, where the pedagogy itself was at stake.

A third source of inspiration has been the notion of play. The research on children's play culture offers an understanding of play, where children are all the time interchanging between copy and change. They can both maintain a given play practice and are capable of changing this practice when needed or desired (Mouritsen 2002). Therefore, the question of process and product are constantly interchangeable as any practice can be seen as a product of a process and any practice can be seen as a process that might lead to a new practice. One must also point at Resnick's work on the learning spirale, where play is part of an experimenting process and where any education system on all levels should be inspired by the pedagogy taking place in a kindergarten (Resnick 2017) and where play can be an important part of design processes and not limited to children (Gudiksen and Skovbjerg 2020). Finally play, tinkering and experimenting are part of actual discussions and recommendations on how the educational system could include play (Zosh et al. 2018). The experimenting community seems to have something to offer in these developments. Recently, experiences and discussions arising from the origins of the experimenting community and the open laboratory have been tested as an innovative way to teach some courses at Aarhus University.

In summary, the experimenting community can exist both locally and globally using the internet to connect internally and connect with others externally. The experiments that as the basis for establishing the group can both be on the digital media themselves, the subject in question and the challenges the group encounters during its journey of continuous and experience-based discoveries and experiments. All media and all materials can in principle be made to encounter each other, which may lead to new processes, new knowledge and new actions and definitely to new experiments.

A Framework for Supporting Experimenting Communities

In the Masters course reported in this chapter, the notion of the experimenting community has been inspired and expanded through the change-maker model (Robinson 2020). The model was used as a pedagogical framework, even though there are many other pedagogies that can be used to support experimenting communities. The change-maker model draws on entrepreneurship education theories where the aim was to create value, understood in the broad sense, i.e., social, cultural, environmental, and so on. The model mimics in some respects an entrepreneurial process and moves through five phases with the student being central to learning, rather than the discipline or knowledge being the starting point. These five phases are; me, we, discovery, experimentation and consolidation.

Briefly, in the first phase, the student is asked to explain who they are in terms of what they are good at, what they like to do, what skills and competences they have and also who they know who has useful resources. A makerspace-inspired workshop is set up and the students are asked to construct a representation of themselves using a range of materials available from the workshop within a time limit. Students are asked to sit beside people they do not know and after a time lapse are asked to move to another part of the workshop and sit with other people they do not know and continue construction. This initial exercise is crucial in setting up the atmosphere of the experimenting community, its dynamics and founding social relations. It is important that the students for example, see and hear the extroverts and notice the introverts. The students present their images to the rest of the group within a given time limit and are asked to talk about what is important to them, what is it they value. During the presentations, the students are asked to note down who has skills that they admire that they do not possess themselves and who talks about values that ring true with their own. These are possible members for their future experimenting community.

The next phase is about finding people who want to work with the same issues, to create the same kind of value or who are interested in a similar challenge. Here the focus is rather on who we are, what we want to do together, what our skills and competences are and who we know who might be of help to us. Often the new communities are given a short exercise that requires them to take photos and make short videos of an event happening in the city that same day. This exercise allows them to analyse their roles and relationships internally. The video is presented to the cohort the following day demonstrating the extent of their technical and creative skills. However, the faculty also scaffold critical reflection and mimic and model discussion, debate and academic argument for the students when the videos are presented. The first online task is for each community to set up a blog where they present themselves as an experimenting community and also decide on what common context they would like to focus on. They have a relatively short time to do this as the communication goes online. From this point on, the communication will be online between members, but also between the groups and the teachers using the preferred technology, for example, Google hangout, Zoom or Skype. The media ecology of the course develops according to the preferences of the cohort and availability of different tools. The community's blog post is the platform for written and visual communication between them. Other groups are encouraged to meet, discuss and comment on each of the other's blog posts. Faculty comment on the blog post but will also refer to comments made by others.

The next phase, discovery, focuses on research and exploration of the identified issue in real life practices with stakeholders who are practitioners and recognize the challenge. In the discovery phase, the experimenting community begins to find out what it means to work together, to pull resources, networks and expertise. The students are required to use ethnographic methods to investigate the context that they have chosen over a short period of time (Robinson 2020). Examples of different contexts are digital technology used by library visitors, by the elderly and specifically in Care and Nursing homes, iPads in the kindergarten, for vulnerable children of school age, etc. The groups gather and analyse the data from their specific context and identify challenges to the practices they observe. The whole cohort meets with the teachers online, with each group allotted a limited time to present the challenges that they have identified. Allotting time for discussion to each group is prioritized. This is followed by a joint discussion where the teachers may introduce literature relevant to the topics arising from the discussion. The groups are asked to re-analyse their context challenge and, through a short video and a short text that demonstrates how the literature has helped them gain a deeper understanding of the field, present this on their blog. Again, there is a comment period allocated in which both the groups and the teachers comment on each combined video and text post. At the end of the commenting period, they meet again and take stock of what comments they have received, but also what others have inspired them to reflect on. The teachers introduce new literature following these presentations. The discovery period is relatively long with a number of iterations to allow the students to go back to the field to talk to stakeholders, e.g., the library staff, but also to library visitors of different generations, at different time periods, and to different sections in order to gather more robust data and to re-analyse. The groups are asked to qualify the challenge and to begin to think about what might be needed to solve it.

The fourth phase is about experimenting. The experimenting communities work towards finding solutions to the identified challenge by closely working with their stakeholders, their networks and using their resources. At the end of this phase, they are required to showcase and demonstrate their solutions for others on a prearranged weekend in a public setting. The chosen setting is in the cultural center and has thousands of visitors in the course of a weekend. A central area through which many people move is made available for the demonstrations. The public, of all ages and backgrounds, are asked to come and try out the prototypes. The learning from this public event is always phenomenal. Immediately following the demonstrations, the teachers and students gather for an onsite debrief which provides them with the opportunity to ask for literature that could help them understand what they have witnessed.

The final phase consolidates and brings new knowledge and experience together. Firstly, in the product or service development, but also relates to an academic understanding of what has happened and why this has happened. The individual student is now equipped to talk from experience about digital media and learning processes in a range of contexts and from a range of positions. This is the learning process that they take with them to the oral exam where they reflect on their learning, not only on the product itself, but on the mistakes that have been made, what they would do differently and how their current knowledge has changed their approach to future practices.

Discussion

Developing experimenting communities of students may in principle sound easy but students come with preconceived ideas about how they should learn and the goals of their education. Getting the students to take ownership of their own learning, to set goals for their learning and to seek ways of mirroring themselves against others, in order to understand what they can do and what they can achieve, are central issues that must be tackled before setting up experimenting communities. The experimenting community that results from the above pedagogical process is a powerful group engaged and motivated to work together to answer important questions. They are bound by their identification of a common set of values and the ongoing discussion about what constitutes these values. At the center of the community are individuals who, through their reflection and action, can contribute to not only their own learning but to how a shared understanding of knowledge about a particular practice comes about. This is the power of the experimenting community.

What makes the experimenting community interesting is that it does not necessarily reach out through observations and interviews and informal conversations, but can do it through narratives or experiments, which have been produced and investigated by the community. The community might get to know each individual in the group and the group through producing narratives and experiments. The community can be discovering other narratives or experiments through their own attempt to make, solve and tell about a narrative or an experiment in a given context. The community might try to find solutions and framework for further work though the experimental phase originally designed to be just that. And when it comes to consolidation, the same might happen. The community is already consolidated through the many phases, the members of it have been through. It might have found a solution, an answer to the questions asked, if such a one exists, or a way to conduct and conclude on an experiment. But it is in the very essence of the experimenting community that it wants to evolve and at the very least not to be reliant on reproducing existing knowledge or actions.

The experimenting community is as such a societal and cultural entity, as it acts in the world with the attempt to encounter it and change it if need be. It is more of a socio-culturally-based pedagogy than anchored in abstraction and distance to the world outside school or university. It is a real community of practice, where the members learn from each other on a regular basis, where critical reflection on practice and sharing of experiences and knowledge become visible (Lave and Wegner 1991; Wenger-Trayner and Wenger-Trayner 2015). All in all, the experimenting community can reach out, navigate and investigate through digital media and digital technologies.

The consequence of such an endeavor is also a distinct new possibility for the roles of teaching staff. One does not only deliver knowledge and answers and check that the students can copy it all in a sort of echo room (Tække and Paulsen 2017). In addition, the teacher is more than a facilitator, who takes care that the learning processes challenge and engage the students. In order to establish experimenting communities, the teacher has to be able to reflect on how they design teaching for learning that opens up explorative spaces to question what knowledge is and how it is shaped by practice, what is true and what is valued. Designing such learning processes resulted in 'engaging the self' (Barnett 2004: 257). The experimenting community presents a way in which to engage students with their own learning, with others in a learning process and to explore and investigate authentic practices that present real life issues.

Conclusion

As we have seen in this paper, the rise of neoliberalism and the decline of state support for universities, worldwide, has led universities to seek to become entrepreneurial in particular ways. On the one hand, this makes universities more nimble and responsive to their environments. But on the other hand, it has led to a crisis of legitimacy as universities have prioritized market demand for knowledge and training to the detriment of a clear vision of what the university should be. Further, the pressures of neoliberal ideology have led to an emphasis on measurable assessment, even before we understand clearly what is being assessed.

Experimenting communities focus on active learning, collaborative learning, and arise from the interests and the experiences of the students as they move forward and the learning becomes deeper. In the experimenting community, the internet and digital tools are used to connect students, faculty, and community members in hybrid spaces that are both physical and virtual. Learning can be guided and enhanced, without dumbing things down to pure information flow. Through sharing, collaboration, creativity, critical reflection is nuanced and student-being is rooted in purposeful action. The tools enhance communication and interaction and make it easier for the group to both discuss and store ideas. This is rather like the way university researchers use digital tools as discussed at the beginning of the chapter. The digital experimenting community is a more authentic model for incorporating the digital into contemporary learning spaces and has the potential to bring the university out of survival mode to be productive and disruptive.

In this chapter, we present experimenting communities as an approach to include in the design of new pedagogies for a university that is immersed in an uncertain environment. With this emphasis on real world learning and community-engaged learning, students are encouraged to become involved in real world problems and work toward a solution for these problems. Further, it encourages genuine knowledge production in a collaborative process among students, the university faculty, and community members, in which spaces are created for ethical and critical reflection. The experimenting community has the potential to return us to the dialogical process that the university is based on and the values that underlie a common cause and public good (Nixon 2011).

Furthermore, the experimenting community is perhaps reminiscent of the values of the Humboldt University, but in a modern way. Here, the liberal arts are the core of learning as students work to figure out how to, in a small way, make the world a better place in which they seek to "disclose new worlds" (Spinosa et al. 1997; Heidegger 1962 (1927)). To use their imagination for what could be and to find out what it takes to achieve those ends. So this kind of knowledge production process is a process that requires academic freedom that includes both faculty and students working, exploring and creating knowledge together in academic communities willing to experiment (Shumar and Robinson 2018). In designing teaching this way, the students become engaged in their own learning process of being and becoming, and gain experience of acting in an uncertain and unpredictable world.

References

Barnett, R. (2004). Learning for an unknown future. *Higher Education Research & Development, 23*(3), 247–260.
Barnett, R. (2013). *Imagining the university*. Milton Park/New York: Routledge.
Barnett, R., & Bengtsen, S. (2020). *Knowledge and the university; reclaiming life*. Oxon: Routledge.
Bengtsen, S., & Barnett, R. (2018). Introduction; considering the thinking university in. In S. Bengtsen & R. Barnett (Eds.), *The thinking university; a philosophical examination of thought and higher education* (pp. 1–12). Springer.
Bruner, J. (1996). *The culture of education*. Cambridge, MA: Harvard University Press.
Bruns, A. (2008). *Blogs, Wikipedia, second life, and beyond*. New York: Peter Lang Publishing.

Caprani, O., & Thestrup, K. (2010). Det eksperimenterende fællesskab – Børn og voksnes leg med medier og teknologi (The experimenting community – children and grown-ups playing with media and technology). *LOM, 3*(5), 1–39.

Collini, S. (2012). *What are universities for?* London: Penguin Group.

Culpepper, M. K., & Gauntlett, D. (2020). Making and learning together: Where the makerspace mindset meets platforms for creativity. *Global Studies of Childhood, 10*(3), 265–274.

Dewey, J. (1938). *Experience and education*. New York: Macmillan.

Fung, D. (2017). *The connected curriculum for higher education*. London: UCL Press.

Gauntlett, D., & Thomsen, B. S. (2013). *Cultures of Creativity Project Report*. Denmark: The LEGO Foundation.

Gislev, T., Thestrup, K., & Elving, P. R. (2020). The flexible meeting place: Connecting schools through networked learning. *Global Studies of Childhood, 10*(3), 275–288.

Gudiksen, S., & Skovbjerg, H. M. (2020). *Framing play design*. Amsterdam: BIS Publishers.

Hastrup. (2004). *Det flexible fællesskab (The flexible community)*. Denmark: Aarhus Universitetsforlag.

Heidegger, M. (1962, 1927). *Being and time*. New York: Harper and Row.

Jantzen, C. (2005). Tertium Datur. Kampen om kulturbegrebet (The Battle over the understanding of culture). In K. K. Povlsen & A. S. Sørensen (Eds.), *Kunstkritik og Kulturkamp* (pp. 40–49). Aarhus: Klim.

Jantzen, C. (2013). Det pragmatiske kulturbegreb (The pragmatic understanding of culture). *Gjallerhorn, 17*, 40–49.

Lave, J., & Wegner, E. (1991). *Situated learning legitimate peripheral participation*. Cambridge: Cambridge University Press.

Lehmann, N., & Szatkowski, J. (2001). Creative pragmtics – A manifesto for the open theatre. In B. Rasmussen, T. Kjølner, V. Rasmussen, & H. Heikkinen (Eds.), *Nordic voices in Drama, theatre and education* (pp. 59–72). Bergen: IDEA Publications.

Marginson, S. (1997). Steering from a distance: Power relations in Australian higher education. *Higher Education 34*, 63–80.

Mouritsen, F. (2002). Child culture – Play culture. In F. Mouritsen & J. Qvortrup (Eds.), *Childhood and children's culture*. Odense: University Press of Denmark.

Newfield, C. (2016). Aftermath of the MOOC wars: Can commercial vendors support creative higher education? *Learning and Teaching, The International Journal of Higher Education in the Social Sciences, 9*(2), 12–41.

Nielsen, K. W., Jerg, K., Kallehauge, P., Kier, D., & Burgård, M. (2019). *Vi gør kultur (We do culture)*. Frederikshavn: Dafolo.

Nixon, J. (2011). *Higher education and the public good: Imagining the university*. London/New York: Continuum International Publishing Group.

Noble, D. F. (2001). *Digital diploma mills: The automation of higher education*. New York: Monthly Review Press.

Nussbaum, M. C. (2010). *Not for profit: Why democracy needs the humanities*. Princeton: Princeton University Press.

Readings, B. (1996). *The university in ruins*. Cambridge, MA: Harvard University Press.

Resnick, M. (2017). *Lifelong kindergarten*. Cambridge MA: MIT Press.

Rider, S. (2018). Truth, democracy, and the mission of the university. In S. S. E. Bengtsen & R. Barnett (Eds.), *The thinking university: A philosophical examination of thought and higher education*. Cham: Springer.

Robinson, S. (2020). Ethnography for engaging students with higher education and societal issues in. In C. Weiser & A. Pilch-Ortega (Eds.), *Ethnography in higher education*. Wiesbaden: Springer.

Sampath Kumar, B. T., & Manjunath, G. (2013). Internet use and its impact on the academic performance of university teachers and researchers: A comparative study. *Higher Education, Skills and Work-Based Learning, 3*(3), 219–238. https://doi.org/10.1108/HESWBL-09-2011-0042.

Shumar, W., & Robinson, S. (2018). Universities as societal drivers; entrepreneurial interventions for a better future. In S. Bengtsen & R. Barnett (Eds.), *The thinking university a philosophical examination of thought and higher education* (pp. 31–46). New York: Springer.

Spinosa, C., Flores, F., & Dreyfus, H. L. (1997). *Disclosing new worlds: Entrepreneurship, democratic action and the cultivation of solidarity*. Cambridge, MA: MIT Press.

Thestrup, K. (2013). *Det eksperimenterende fællesskab* (The experimenting community). Denmark: VIA Systime. Ph.d. thesis from Aarhus University finished in 2011 printed in 2013.

Thestrup, K., & Robinson, S. (2016). Towards an entrepreneurial mindset; empowering learners in an open laboratory. In P. Papadopolous, R. Burger, & A. Faria (Eds.), *Innovation and entrepreneurship in education* (Vol. 2, pp. 147–168). Bingley: Emerald Publishing.

Thestrup, K., & Pedersen, H. L. (2020). Makeative makerspaces: When the pedagogy is makeative. In A. Blum-Ross, K. Kumpulainen, & J. Marsh (Eds.), *Enhancing digital literacy and creativity – Makerspaces in the early years* (pp. 24–37). London/New York: Routledge.

Tække, J., & Paulsen, M. (2017). *Digitalisation of education: The theory of the three waves Center for Internet Research* (29p).

Zosh, J. M., Hirsh-Pasek, K., Hopkins, E. J., Jensen, H., Liu, C., Neale, D., Solis, L., & Whitebread, D. (2018). Accessing the inaccessible: Redefining play as a spectrum. *Frontiers in Psychology, 9*, 1124.

Wenger-Trayner, E., & Wenger-Trayner, B. (2015). *Introduction to communities of practice*. Located 12.06.2020 on http://wenger-trayner.com/introduction-to-communities-of-practice

Sarah Robinson is an Associate Professor in the Center for Educational Development at Aarhus University, Denmark. She is an Educational Anthropologist interested in the role of higher education and the purpose and future of the university. Her research spans curriculum reform, policy in practice, ethnographic methods, teacher agency and enterprise education. She has a strong international profile and has published in *The Thinking University; A Philosophical Examination of Thought and Higher Education* Springer (Bengtsen and Barnett 2018) and *The Idea of the University: Volume 2 – Contemporary Perspectives*. Peter Lang (Peters and Barnett 2018), as well as being a co-author on *Teacher Agency; An ecological approach* Bloomsbury (Priestley et al. 2015). Sarah is on the board of the Philosophy and Theory of Higher Education Society (PaTHES) and arranges conferences, webinars, and online discussions that bring together a range of international scholars interested in Higher Education and its reforms. Currently she is working to design 'a pedagogy for change' by combining an exploration of academic identity with learning from enterprise education.

Klaus Thestrup is an associate professor at The Danish School of Education, Aarhus University in Denmark, where he teaches on the online MA program *ICT-Based Educational Design*, where digital media and pedagogy are combined. He is also a social educator from University College South Denmark, a dramaturg from Aarhus University and holds a professional master in children's- & youth culture and digital media from the University of Southern Denmark. He has taught drama and media for many years and has over the years written many articles on pedagogy, culture and media. He has his own YouTube channel and a blog. He is through practical research developing and formulating a pedagogy based on experimenting communities, open laboratories, global communication, online teaching, media play and children's culture.

Wesley Shumar is a professor in the Department of Communication at Drexel University. His research focuses on higher education, mathematics education, and entrepreneurship education. His recent work in higher education focuses on the spatial transformation of American universities within the consumer spaces of cities and towns. From 1997 to 2018 he worked as an ethnographer at the Math Forum, a virtual math education community and resource center. He continues to do research into the use of online spaces to support mathematics education. He is author of *College for Sale: A Critique of the Commodification of Higher Education*, Falmer Press, 1997, and *Inside Mathforum.org: Analysis of an Internet-based Education Community*, Cambridge University Press, 2017. He co-edited, with Joyce Canaan, *Structure and Agency in the Neoliberal University*, Routledge/Falmer, 2008. He also co-edited, with K.Ann Renninger, *Building Virtual Communities: Learning and Change in Cyberspace*, Cambridge, 2002.

Chapter 14
Coda: *Perpetuum Mobile*

Ronald Barnett

'The university becoming' – what a perplexing idea; and yet what a brave idea, especially at this time. After all, becoming is both real and imaginative; both fact and value; both a description and a hope. Becoming suggests a journey on the way to realizing an entity's true being, becoming itself fully, realising its full potential. There is the university, changing before our eyes, and despite the travails that it has been encountering, somehow it is finding the resources, the will, and the space in the world to become itself; to achieve what always lay within itself. There are the facts of the matter and *there* is value, much value, that we impute to the university now becoming itself.

Is this fantasy? Is it hubris, on somebody's part, at least? The belief that the university can become itself, and all that entails, not least that it can be discerned just what it is for the university to become itself. Nobody can become the university for it; the university will have to do it largely by and for itself. And, in any event, can we be sure – can the university be sure – just what it is for the university to become itself?

Let us get down – as they say – to brass tacks. Derrida spoke of the university without condition: *there* was fantasy! Show me a university without condition and I will show you a mirage. There is no such university; but especially in the twenty-first century. Across the world, albeit to different degrees, the university is caught in multiple conditions, of power and direction that are imposed upon it, of systems and audits that wield enormous influence, of hierarchies of knowledge, and of ideologies of markets and of nationalism.

So much so obvious. The university cannot evade the many conditions that come its way and that are stipulated for it. But the university also imposes conditions upon

---

R. Barnett (✉)
University College London Institute of Education, London, UK
e-mail: ron.barnett@ucl.ac.uk

© The Author(s), under exclusive license to Springer Nature Switzerland AG 2021
S. S. E. Bengtsen et al. (eds.), *The University Becoming*, Debating Higher Education: Philosophical Perspectives 6,
https://doi.org/10.1007/978-3-030-69628-3_14

itself. In its external engagements and its internal activities, it slides into roles that are cast for it in cognitive capitalism, signing up to questionable contracts with corporations, but it also turns a blind eye to ways in which the academic community at large exhibits the enclosed tendencies that its separate academic tribes can exhibit, in enforcing their own internal rules and procedures.

Becoming, then, takes its place amid multiplicities of forces, tempi, rules, and ideologies; and it is bound to be a struggle. But those struggles, as this volume testifies, are taking place in departments, in teaching situations, in students' efforts (on and beyond the campus), in civic engagements, and in reaching out to the disempowered. The university can never fully become itself, it seems, but it can struggle always towards its own becoming.

Is that it, then; that the university's becoming is always before it and never quite reached? Is the university's becoming a mirage, then? No matter how much it listens to and opens itself to the dispossessed, and the invisible; no matter how much it identifies a set of counter-values which it tries to live out in its entanglements with the world; and no matter how much it seeks to go beyond 'learning outcomes' to enable students to become themselves, still the university cannot evade the conditions of its existence. It cannot *ever* fully become itself.

Perhaps, the situation is a matter of attitude: the glass is both half empty and half full and there is no objective way of determining the matter. And many in universities today show both low morale while others seem to be content with their lot. Again, it may be felt that it is a matter of particular contexts. Those who experience problems - of social injustice, of race, gender, social class, religion or nationality, or less obvious but still painful conditions of epistemic injustice, where one's cognitive efforts are being downplayed - can quite legitimately form dismal perceptions of academic life. And it is hardly surprising if those in dominant positions, whether of hierarchy or rankings or gender or favoured discipline, have a much more sanguine sense of matters. There can be no universal account of the university's becoming, it appears; only the particularities of circumstance and position.

But is not struggle for the university's becoming a permanent and universal condition of the university? The world has been experiencing a global virus that plays out differentially across social class, ethnicity, location, and age. It does, however, point up what we should have learnt from the ecological crisis, namely, that the world is totally interconnected. Understood in this way, the university's becoming has no shape: the assemblage that constitutes each university – values, networks, knowledges, communities, identities – can be entered at any point. Interventions of some kind or other are normally possible. Becoming can take a multitude of paths. And now, the situation is no longer entirely wayward. If the world is interconnected, the university becomes itself by being evermore interconnected.

But now huge challenges open for the university. Its knowledges have to connect with each other; and we are witnessing a resurgence of interest in trans-disciplinarity. Its students can be encouraged to see tangible and rooted connections between their studies and the wider world. Its faculty members might recognize each other across their disciplines as colleagues in a joint enterprise rather than as strangers. And the university as such might try to connect itself to the wider world, both the human and the natural worlds. In turn, the university would be setting itself on a path where it displaces itself so that it is in the world, paying attention to and listening to the world; almost losing itself in the world.

And so becoming becomes the university, but only if it turns itself inside out. It becomes itself by exercising a self-denying ordinance. It avoids its natural hubris, seeing itself at the centre of matters, and instead works with the world. 'World', though, now takes on its own character. It is the whole world that is in question, not the positions of power and domination. There would be here a promise within the university's becoming in this way, that the university promises to the world that it will go on struggling, with, for and from the world. In this sense, the university will never let the world down, no matter what its circumstances; and the world will be able to trust the university on this account.

Of course, in this perpetual motion, there is a continuous struggle in front of the university, but that is part of the university's becoming. The future is always ahead of the university's becoming. Just as truth is never met but still is worth struggling for, so too the university's becoming. And, as they say, it is better to travel than to arrive.

Ronald Barnett is Emeritus Professor of Higher Education at University College London Institute of Education, where he was a Dean and a Pro-Director. He is a past Chair of the Society for Research into Higher Education (SRHE), was awarded the inaugural prize by the European Association for Educational Research for his 'outstanding contribution to Higher Education Research, Policy and Practice' and has been elected as the inaugural President of the Philosophy and Theory of Higher Education Society. He is a Fellow of the Academy of Social Sciences, the SRHE and the Higher Education Academy, has published 35 books (several of which have been prize-winners), has written over 150 papers, has given 150 keynote talks across the world and is a consultant in the university sector. He has been cited in the literature over 20,000 times and can fairly be regarded to have established the philosophy of higher education as a serious field of study. For nearly 40 years, he has been advancing ideas, and creating concepts and practical principles to transform universities and academic life for the twenty-first century. He has been described as 'the master scholar of the university'.

Index

A
Aaen, J.H., 104
Absence, 117, 131–132
Academic bildung, 9, 173–183
Academic freedom, 15, 18, 26, 33, 67, 72, 74, 82, 126, 180, 182, 188, 197
Academics, 1–3, 5–9, 19–21, 25, 26, 38, 67–70, 72–75, 82, 83, 87, 96–99, 101, 103–106, 117, 132, 141, 142, 144, 147, 151, 153, 154, 158, 159, 161, 173–183, 194, 195, 197, 202
Accelerated university, 141, 143, 154
Accumulation, 31, 32, 39–42, 45, 62, 125, 164, 166, 187
Actions, 39, 52, 54–57, 62, 67, 71, 72, 74, 82, 86, 89, 91, 92, 111, 114, 116, 120–122, 130, 132, 147, 149, 151, 159, 168, 181, 185, 190, 191, 193, 195–197
Adams, R., 101
Adler, M.J., 44
Affective, 29, 47, 169, 173
Agencies, 2, 25, 26, 55, 56, 68, 71, 87, 101, 105, 118, 163
Alexander, F.K., 38
Alien, 87, 133–135
Althusser, L., 31
Andersen, H.L., 99, 100
Anderson, Z., 38
Angeli, C., 119
Anthropological, 82, 129, 159–161, 169
Anxieties, 33, 34, 36, 37, 41, 42, 45, 46
Applebaum, A., 62

Arendt, H., 51–63, 73, 85
Aristotle, 93
Arthur, J., 175, 178
Arvanitakis, J., 6
Assemblages, 19, 93, 134, 202
Attention, 8, 24, 34, 54, 68, 69, 81–93, 106, 168, 169, 188, 203
Authenticity, 72, 74, 142, 174, 177, 180, 182
Autonomous, 73, 74, 76, 86, 87, 113, 123
Autonomy, 8, 15, 69, 72, 93, 114, 116, 173–177, 180, 182

B
Bad faith, 71, 76
Baez, B., 43
Baker, R., 142
Balibar, E., 31
Ball, S.J., 125
Barnacle, R., 75
Barnett, A., 61
Barnett, R., 2–7, 15–27, 34, 52, 97, 104–106, 112–114, 119, 127, 128, 132, 134, 141, 153, 154, 173, 186, 189, 196, 201–203
Barnett, R.A., 74
Bataille, G., 32, 44
Batchelor, D., 8, 112
Baudrillard, J., 43, 45
Becker, G., 36
Becomings, 2–8, 15–27, 43, 47, 51, 76, 111–113, 117–119, 122, 123, 125, 128, 130, 135, 162, 176, 185, 197, 201–203

© The Author(s), under exclusive license to Springer Nature Switzerland AG 2021
S. S. E. Bengtsen et al. (eds.), *The University Becoming*, Debating Higher Education: Philosophical Perspectives 6, https://doi.org/10.1007/978-3-030-69628-3

Beings, 3–5, 7, 8, 16–20, 22–26, 31, 34, 40, 42–44, 53–55, 57, 58, 61, 67, 68, 70–72, 74, 76, 84, 86, 89–93, 95, 98, 102, 103, 106, 107, 111–123, 128, 130–132, 141, 144, 145, 147, 149–151, 153, 154, 159, 168, 174–177, 180, 182, 186–188, 190, 193, 196, 197, 201, 202
Bengtsen, S., 1–9, 95–107, 132–134, 186, 189
Bengtsen.S.S.E., 141
Bergson, H., 97, 103, 104
Bergsten, S.S.E., 52
Bernstein, R.J., 58
Besley, T., 4
Bhaskar, R., 19, 22, 26
Biesta, G., 173
Biesta, G.J.J., 97, 131, 132
Bildung, 9, 17, 147, 174–179, 182
Biopolitical, 9, 160–163, 165, 166
Bird, S,J, 68
Blenker, P., 128
Blenkinsop, S., 76
Bohlin, K.E., 178
Bok, D., 68
Bologna Process, 96, 98, 100
Boutang, Y.M., 21
Bruner, J., 187
Bruns, A., 191
Buber, M., 82
Burg, D., 178, 179
Burgård, M., 192
Burke, E., 58
Bustamante, L., 161

C

Caillois, R., 144, 148
Canaan, J., 125, 173
Capitalism, 30, 36, 40, 42, 44–47, 141
Caplan, B., 35
Caprani, O., 191, 192
Care, 70, 71, 75, 76, 114, 131, 134, 151, 194, 196
Cassirer, E., 82
Categorical imperative, 112
Citizens, 6, 9, 38, 41, 55, 56, 60, 90, 158, 162, 164, 173–183, 187, 188
Clark, B.R., 22, 127
Cognitive, 19, 23, 87, 88, 173, 202
Cognitive capitalism, 21, 202
Collaboration, 4, 160, 187, 192, 197
Collaborative, 5, 190, 196, 197
Collini, S., 3, 63, 68, 186

Communality, 144, 150–154
Communities, 4, 6, 8, 9, 25, 52, 63, 67, 74, 106, 118, 130–132, 144, 150, 151, 159–162, 164–169, 175, 176, 178–182, 185–197, 202
Considine, M., 34, 127
Constanti, P., 71
Consumers, 9, 31, 36, 54, 69, 102, 160, 173–183, 186
Consumption, 30–33, 40, 44, 168
Contextual, 149
Cooper, M.A., 39
Creates, 38, 41, 58, 130, 132, 134, 143, 145, 146, 148–152, 182, 189, 192, 193
Creating, 9, 23, 29, 38, 54, 72, 128, 130, 147, 148, 185–197
Creation, 2, 5, 38, 90, 105, 106, 126, 128, 131–136, 149, 182
Creative, 4, 9, 63, 97, 103, 105, 126, 151, 161, 180–182, 185, 187, 188, 192, 194
Creativity, 9, 37, 74, 103, 104, 134, 141, 142, 144–154, 192, 197
Critical, 2, 4, 6–8, 26, 42, 53, 54, 59, 60, 68, 70, 73, 74, 85, 86, 119, 128, 130, 135, 161, 174, 181, 185, 186, 188, 189, 194, 196, 197
Critical realism, 19
Cruz, C., 164
Culpepper, M.K., 192
Cultures, 3, 19, 20, 59, 90, 91, 106, 125, 129, 131, 133, 136, 141, 142, 144, 145, 147, 149–152, 159, 162, 175, 179, 186, 187, 191, 192
Curiosity, 5, 59, 144–147, 150–154, 191
Curricula, 2–6, 8, 9, 15, 17, 68, 82, 97, 99, 105, 106, 117, 134, 186, 189, 190
Curriculum, 143, 157, 180
Curzon-Hobson, A., 73

D

Dall'Alba, G., 75, 104, 105
Darkness, 104, 105
Deci, E.L., 142
Deleuze, G., 47
Democratic, 2, 35, 41, 53, 56, 58, 61, 130, 131, 158, 177, 179
Derrida, J., 23
de Sousa Santos, B., 5, 21
Dewey, J., 129, 131, 187
Digital, 9, 18, 20, 26, 70, 73, 83, 106, 142, 143, 177, 185, 186, 188–197

Digitalization, 1
Disciplines, 4, 17, 19–22, 24, 53, 70, 74, 81, 82, 87, 103, 129, 148, 173, 175–177, 182, 186, 193, 202
Discourses, 33, 34, 36, 37, 39–43, 45, 53, 59, 69, 84, 92, 98, 100–102, 126, 127, 136, 153, 160, 164, 174, 177–178, 185
Disharmonies, 130
Donato, R., 161
Dreyfus, H., 197
Duties, 67, 68, 70, 74, 75, 114–116, 121, 143, 150, 178

E
Eberly, T.E., 61
Ecological, 4, 25, 106, 107, 136, 202
Ecologies, 7, 8, 27, 105, 128, 130, 133, 194
Economics, 3, 7, 8, 19–21, 23, 24, 30–35, 39–46, 51, 53, 72, 76, 96, 102, 106, 125–129, 135, 158, 160, 162, 163, 185–187
Economies, 7, 24, 30–35, 40, 42–44, 47, 48, 98, 101, 126, 127, 129, 135, 136, 141, 161, 164
Edelman, L., 40
Education, 3, 7, 17, 23, 26, 34–36, 38, 41, 43–46, 48, 51–63, 67, 69, 71–73, 75, 76, 85–87, 90–92, 125, 126, 128, 142–145, 149, 153, 160, 166, 167, 174, 175, 178–180, 182, 186, 187, 190, 192, 193, 195
Elving, P.R., 192
Empathy, 9, 74, 116, 120
Entrepreneurial, 8, 127, 128, 130, 131, 135, 188, 193, 196
Entrepreneurship, 126–128, 130–136, 190, 193
Epistemic injustice, 21, 202
Epistemological, 5, 19, 23, 25, 97, 134
Epistemological diversity, 19, 20, 22
Espino, M., 167
Ethical, 5, 8, 52, 61, 75, 97, 131, 132, 135, 174, 187, 189, 197
Ethics, 8, 128, 131, 158, 169
Ethnographic, 159, 166, 194
Existential, 8, 59, 69, 74, 146, 174
Experiences, 15, 17, 18, 37, 45–48, 53, 55, 56, 58, 73, 74, 86, 92, 93, 101, 103, 104, 106, 111, 112, 114, 120, 122, 129, 132, 142–144, 146, 148–150, 157, 163, 176, 180, 181, 187–192, 195–197, 202
Experimenting, 9, 151, 160, 185–197

Experiments, 61, 133, 147–149, 185, 191–193, 195–197
Expulsions, 163–168

F
Fekete, E., 61
Filippakou, O., 95–107
Fine, B., 43
Fink, E., 144, 149–151
Flores, F., 197
Formation, 2, 8, 9, 26, 29, 30, 85, 96, 103, 105, 111, 112, 119, 131, 133, 134, 173, 175, 177, 182
Formulae, 92, 111–123
Fossland, T., 173, 176
Foucault, M., 21, 160
Foucault, P., 75
Francis, J., 141, 143, 151
Fraser, N., 42
Frederiksen, J.T., 99, 100
Freedoms, 5, 7, 30, 33, 34, 37, 38, 40, 44, 45, 47, 48, 51, 54, 57, 60, 68, 70, 73, 106, 111, 114–116, 123, 144, 146, 147, 149, 151, 153, 163, 167, 169, 180, 182, 188
Fung, D., 186
Furedi, F., 69
Futures, 2–9, 25, 32, 34–48, 57–59, 62, 70, 75, 89, 95, 97, 103, 106, 113, 118, 133–136, 141, 151–154, 158, 160–162, 167, 176, 180, 182–183, 185–197, 203

G
Gadamer, H., 144, 146
Gadamer, H.-G., 85
Galston, W.A., 59
Gamification, 142
Gamified, 8, 141–144, 148, 151, 152, 154
Garcia, M., 161, 167
Gary, R., 36, 48
Gauntlet, D., 192
Gellner, E., 21
Gessen, M., 61
Gibb, A., 128
Gibbs, P., 2, 4, 7, 8, 67–76, 96, 97
Gibson, C., 161
Gildersleeve, R.E., 5, 9, 133, 157–169
Giroux, H.A., 178
Gislev, T., 192
Global marketplace, 41
Global spaces, 17
Global systems, 17, 19

Good
    common, 4, 6, 74, 187, 197
    public, 6, 179, 187
Governance, 53, 96, 97
Graeber, D., 129, 130, 135
Graham, B., 149
Gramlich, J., 161
Grammar, 74, 89, 98, 100, 105
Grant, B., 6, 134
Graziano, M., 59
Greene, M., 151
Grenberg, J., 120
Grepperud, G., 177
Grondin, J., 146
Guattari, F., 22, 46, 47
Gudiksen, S., 192
Guyer, P., 114, 115, 123

H
Halfon, M., 117, 120, 121
Hansen, F.T., 174, 176, 177
Harding, L., 61
Harman, G., 19
Hastrup, 192
Hausman, D., 43
Hayden, P., 54
Heidegger, M., 130, 131, 197
Hellesnes, J., 175
Hernández, S., 159, 164
Higher education, 1–9, 15–18, 25–27, 29, 30, 33–48, 51, 52, 63, 68–76, 81–93, 96–106, 111–113, 117, 119, 121, 123, 126, 127, 133–136, 141–154, 157–169, 173–179, 181–183, 186, 187, 190
Homo Ludens, 144, 145, 147, 151–153
Horlacher, R., 173, 174
Hornsby, D., 6
Huizinga, L., 144, 149–151
Humanities, 2, 22, 23, 33, 43, 52, 53, 55, 59, 75, 82, 90, 103, 111–119, 121–123, 158, 177
Humboldt, W., 126, 173, 175, 177, 178, 180, 197
Hunt, E.K., 31
Hutchins, R.M., 34
Hyvönen, A.-E., 52

I
Identities, 47, 71, 88, 96, 103, 105, 117–119, 122, 131, 143, 166, 176, 177, 202
Ideologies, 3, 36, 53, 61, 62, 97, 126, 127, 186, 196, 201, 202

Imagination, 6, 52, 57, 73, 104, 122, 126, 130, 131, 134, 141, 145–148, 189, 197
Imagines, 8, 112, 130, 150, 167, 182, 186, 188, 190
Institutions, 3–6, 8, 15–19, 22, 23, 26, 33, 34, 37–39, 41, 45, 47, 51, 53, 57, 62, 68–70, 72, 74–76, 83, 89, 90, 95, 96, 100, 104–106, 112, 117, 126–129, 132–134, 136, 141, 143, 153, 157–169, 177–180, 186
Integrity, 2–4, 8, 55, 68, 111, 112, 116–123
Intellectual, 4, 5, 20, 33, 38, 52, 53, 55, 56, 58, 59, 61, 81, 85–89, 105, 126, 151, 187
Intensity, 101–104, 106

J
Jackson, A.Y., 159
Jacobsen, L.L., 99
James, A., 143, 147
Jameson, J., 68
Jantzen, C., 192
Jayasuriya, K., 141
Jerg, K., 192
Judgements, 18, 21, 26, 52, 54, 56, 57, 61, 62, 67, 69, 73, 85, 88, 91, 129
Judt, T., 52
Justice, 5, 16, 26, 56, 57

K
Kallehauge, P., 192
Kant, I., 22, 34, 82, 85–87, 89, 111–116, 119–121, 123, 180–182
Katz, J., 128
Keiding, T.B., 100
Kelso, L.O., 44
Kerr, C., 22
Keynes, J.M., 31
King, M.L., 62
Kinopolitics, 159, 162–165, 167–169
Kirby, C.C., 149
Kivelä, A., 175
Kjeldstadli, K., 173
Kleinhesselink, K., 5, 133
Knowledge, 2, 16–24, 26, 27, 43, 44, 62, 68–72, 74, 81, 82, 87–90, 93, 97, 101, 104–106, 119, 125–127, 132, 133, 141, 145, 147, 148, 150, 153, 154, 158–162, 169, 173, 178, 180, 182, 185–193, 195–197, 201, 202
Koeners, M.P., 141–143, 151
Koestner, R., 142
Kohler, L., 56

Index

Kohn, J., 55, 56
Koro-Ljungberg, M., 159
Korsgaard, C.M., 113–115, 118
Koselleck, R., 174
Kramer, E., 5
Kuntz, A.M., 158, 160, 161, 178

L

Labour, 18, 54, 72, 105
Laches, P., 70
Lackéus, M., 128
Land, R., 17
Langan, M., 141, 151
LaRouche, Jr., 44
Latinx, 159–162, 164–169
Lave, J., 196
Leadership, 1, 15, 26, 51, 178
Learner motivation, 142
Learners, 84, 86, 102, 104, 105, 107, 132, 143, 153, 188, 190
Learning, 1, 7, 8, 15, 16, 25, 26, 51–63, 71, 73, 76, 81–93, 95–101, 103–107, 119, 125, 126, 132–136, 142, 143, 150, 151, 173–177, 179–182, 185–190, 192, 193, 195–197, 202
Lehmann, N., 191
Levinas, E., 131, 135
Levitsky, S., 61
Liberal, 17, 24, 51, 52, 58, 62, 68, 69, 71, 73–75, 90, 174, 197
Lingis, A., 131, 132, 135
Lipman, P., 158, 160, 161
List, C., 25
Løvlie, L., 174, 177
Lyndon, H., 44
Lysgaard, J.A., 133

M

Macfarlane, B., 117, 178, 179
MacIntyre, A., 25
Madriz, D., 164
Madsen, S.R., 97–100
Manathunga, C., 102
Manjunath, G., 189
Marginson, S., 4, 34, 102, 127, 173, 179
Marketization, 173, 179, 182
Markets, 2, 3, 18, 32, 33, 35, 38, 69, 70, 97, 102, 106, 126, 127, 129, 165, 174, 180, 182, 196, 201
Marsh, J., 36

Marx, K., 31
Marxism, 29, 53
Maslow, A.H., 33
Masschelein, J., 6
Massey, D., 47
Mathiasen, H., 176
Mauss, M., 129
Maxwell, N., 23, 25
Mazzei, L.A., 159
Mazzucato, M., 129
McArthur, J., 5
McFall, L., 120
McGettigan, A., 125
Meaningful, 90, 118, 185, 186, 188, 190
Melendrez-Flores, C., 164
Metaphors, 6, 7, 16–18, 26, 52, 133
Methodological, 84, 158, 159
Meyer, J.F.H., 17
Migrants, 9, 157–169
Migrations, 157–169
Mimicry, 148
Minds, 18, 30, 33–35, 37, 38, 52, 56, 58, 59, 61, 81–83, 86–88, 91, 115, 174, 180
Molesworth, M., 173, 179
Mor, Y., 97, 141
Moral, 8, 20, 41, 52, 55, 59, 61, 67, 74–76, 116, 118–122, 132, 147, 158
Mouritsen, F., 192
Müller, J.-W., 59
Multiversity, 22
Muñoz, S., 167

N

Nail, T., 19, 159, 162–165, 168, 169
Nash, M., 164
Natality, 7, 54, 55
Neiwert, D., 61
Neoliberal, 6, 46, 75, 96, 97, 125–127, 134, 135, 141, 158, 160–162, 164, 165, 185, 186, 189, 196
Neoliberalism, 24, 30, 36, 51, 125, 127, 158, 161, 189, 196
Nerantzi, C., 143
Newfield, C., 125, 185
Newman, J.H., 34
Nielsen, G.B., 97, 98, 106
Nielsen, K.W., 192
Nietzsche, F., 133, 135
Nixon, E., 173, 179
Nixon, J., 4, 7, 51–63, 179, 186, 187, 197
Noble, D.F., 189

Nørgård, R.T, 97, 141–154
Nussbaum, M., 3
Nussbaum, M.C., 125, 185

O
O'Boyle, L., 126
Olafson, F.A., 75
O'Neill, O., 67, 68, 70
Ontological interconnectedness, 20
Ontologies, 19, 20, 97, 162, 168
Orlando, S., 37
Ortega y Gasset, J., 90

P
Pandemic, 1, 2, 29, 35, 42, 46, 95–97, 106, 126, 127, 133, 186
Papastephanou, M., 119
Paulsen, M., 196
Pawlett, W., 43
Pedagogical, 17, 18, 24, 52, 69, 71, 83–85, 153, 174, 180, 186, 190, 192, 193, 195
Pedagogies, 17, 73, 143, 145, 169, 179, 185, 186, 188, 189, 192, 193, 196, 197
Pedersen, H.L., 192
Pedetic, 165, 166, 168, 169
People, 1, 3, 5, 35, 38, 42, 44, 52, 56, 57, 60–62, 67, 68, 84, 91, 111, 113–119, 121–123, 126, 128–131, 146, 149–151, 153, 160, 164, 174, 175, 177, 185, 187–193, 195
Peters, M., 73, 75
Peters, M.A., 2, 4, 21, 173
Pettit, P., 26
Philosophies, 5–7, 15, 18, 20, 22, 58, 81–83, 85, 91, 92, 97, 103, 104, 141–154, 158, 162, 163, 169
Plato, 58, 84
Playful, 8, 9, 141–154
Playfulness, 9, 142–147, 150, 151, 153, 154
Plays, 4, 15, 18, 19, 22, 45, 46, 51, 57, 98, 100, 101, 142–154, 182, 185, 192, 202
Plumb, J.H., 22
Plurality, 7, 54, 56, 57, 60, 61
Polanyi, K., 129, 135
Policies, 4, 24, 27, 37, 42, 51, 63, 69–72, 76, 96–98, 100, 104, 106, 126, 159, 164, 165
Polis, 55, 56, 60, 61
Political, 2–5, 7, 20, 21, 23, 24, 30–33, 35–37, 40–46, 53, 54, 57, 59, 61, 68, 73, 85, 89, 97, 99, 101–103, 105, 106, 130, 135, 161–166, 168, 169, 178, 179, 181
Political economy, 30–33, 40, 47
Powers, 5, 19–21, 23, 25, 30, 31, 34, 41, 42, 51, 54–57, 61, 62, 68–70, 73, 75, 91, 115, 122, 127, 133, 134, 143, 162, 163, 165, 166, 168, 179, 181, 195, 201, 203
Press, E., 38
Prestige maximization, 38, 39, 43
Problems, 30, 31, 33, 37, 39, 41–43, 46, 81–85, 87, 89, 93, 102, 127, 134, 145, 153, 160, 162, 176, 187, 190, 191, 197, 202
Processes, 5–8, 15, 17, 19, 24, 26, 41, 52–56, 61, 69, 74, 76, 86, 97, 98, 100, 103–107, 115, 117, 118, 120, 121, 125, 126, 130–132, 134, 145, 146, 159, 162, 163, 174, 175, 178, 182, 186–193, 195–197
Public, 2, 4, 6, 18, 19, 24, 34–36, 42, 52–54, 57, 59, 68, 71, 73–75, 95, 97, 99, 117, 119, 125, 134, 160, 161, 169, 178, 179, 185, 195
Public good, 4–7, 15, 18, 27, 32, 179, 187, 197
Public sphere, 18, 60, 61
Purposes, 2, 34, 35, 39, 42–45, 57, 60, 62, 68, 69, 75, 82, 102, 105, 113, 115–117, 122, 126–128, 130, 144, 145, 151, 161, 180, 185–187, 191

R
Rational, 31, 39, 58, 69, 71, 87, 104, 111, 113–116, 118, 129
Readings, B., 6, 48, 173, 186
Realities, 29, 36, 43, 56, 67, 71, 73, 74, 103, 105, 106, 116, 127, 132, 143, 146, 149, 150, 152–154, 162, 168
Realpolitik, 53
Reasons, 26, 59, 67, 70, 71, 85–92, 96, 106, 112–117, 123, 127, 181, 189
Rebellion, 165, 167
Reiff, M.R., 35
Research, 1, 2, 7, 17, 18, 23, 25, 26, 35, 38, 58, 68, 70, 74, 90, 96, 97, 104, 117, 118, 126, 127, 132, 136, 142, 143, 158, 159, 161, 164, 174–176, 178–181, 186, 187, 189, 191, 192, 194
Resistances, 47, 120, 165, 167–168, 182
Resnick, M., 188, 192
Respects, 3, 26, 60, 68, 72, 74, 75, 87, 89, 90, 113, 116, 118, 121–123, 193

Responsibilities, 5, 6, 8, 19, 27, 52, 55, 58, 60, 62, 71, 72, 74, 76, 89, 91, 101, 107, 117, 136, 141, 174, 175, 179, 180, 183, 187, 188
Restricted economy, 32–34, 40, 42, 48
Revolt, 165–167, 169
Rhizome, 16, 17
Rhoades, G., 36, 43
Ricoeur, P., 82
Rider, S., 3, 8, 67, 90, 187, 188
Risks, 4, 15–27, 60, 61, 70, 73, 74, 83, 113, 114, 120, 142, 146
Robinson, S., 1–9, 128, 185–197
Rogers, C., 114
Rolfe, G., 48
Rorty, R., 175
Ryan, R., 142

S
Said, E.W., 58
Sampath Kumar, B.T., 189
Saner, H., 56
Sarauw, L.L., 95–107
Sartre, J.-P., 71
Saunders, N., 54
Scheler, M., 82
Scherkoske, C., 119
Schier, S.E., 61
Schildermans, H., 6
Schiller, F., 144, 147, 150
Sciences, 20, 21, 30, 33, 38, 43, 53, 63, 73, 82, 83, 90, 101, 103, 142, 148, 157, 158, 160
Scruton, R., 113, 114, 116
Scullion, R., 173, 179
Self-deception, 8, 68, 70–73, 76
Self-determination, 175
Sheila, S., 36, 43
Sherman, H.J., 31
Shoho, A.R., 69
Shore, C., 125
Shore, C.N., 125
Shumar, W., 1–9, 125, 128, 141, 173, 185–197
Sicart, M., 145–149
Siljander, P., 174
Simons, M., 6
Skills, 2, 44, 75, 83, 97, 99, 101, 103, 113, 141, 148, 173, 177, 182, 186, 188, 191, 193, 194
Skovbjerg, H.M., 192
Slaughter, S., 36, 43
Smith, P.A., 69
Snyder, T., 51, 61

Social, 3–8, 19, 20, 30, 31, 33, 35–37, 39, 42, 43, 45–47, 53, 68, 70–74, 91, 102, 103, 105–107, 118, 126, 128–136, 143, 150, 151, 157–165, 167, 169, 179, 187, 189, 191, 193, 202
Social Justice, 5, 7, 15, 25–27, 42
Societies, 1–9, 16, 18, 20, 23, 25, 29, 30, 32, 40–44, 46, 51, 54, 58, 62, 63, 67, 68, 70, 74, 75, 82, 90, 95, 103, 106, 127–131, 133–136, 141, 142, 151, 160, 161, 163, 164, 175, 177–180, 182, 186–189
Sockett, H., 68
Solberg, M., 9, 173–183
Sørensen, A., 5
Sovereignty, 30, 44–48, 69, 149
Spaces, 6, 7, 16, 26, 27, 31, 47, 53, 54, 57, 59, 60, 92, 95, 96, 100, 104–106, 112, 114, 117, 130, 131, 134, 146, 147, 149–151, 153, 161, 168, 188–190, 196, 197, 201
Spinosa, C., 197
Standish, P., 134, 173, 174
Stensaker, B., 127
Steyaert, C., 128
Stiegler, B., 23
Stoller, A., 5
Straume, I.S., 173, 174
Students, 1, 2, 4, 5, 8, 9, 15, 17, 18, 24–26, 33–35, 38, 39, 42, 55, 56, 59, 67–76, 86, 87, 89, 91–93, 95–107, 111–115, 117–119, 121, 123, 130, 132–134, 141, 142, 151, 157–161, 163–169, 173–183, 185–190, 193–197, 202
Sutinen, A., 174
Sutton-Smith, B., 144
Szadkowski, K., 6, 135
Szatkowski, J., 191

T
Tække, J., 196
Taylor, C., 112
Teaching, 15, 17, 23, 26, 39, 55, 58, 70, 71, 73, 74, 85, 87, 96, 100–103, 106, 117, 136, 143, 159, 174–177, 179–182, 185, 186, 189, 190, 196, 197, 202
Temporalities, 8, 95–98, 103–107
Thestrup, K., 185–197
Thinking, 2, 3, 8, 26, 30–32, 37, 42, 43, 52–57, 61, 62, 73, 82–93, 96–98, 103, 105, 106, 111, 114, 116, 119, 126, 128, 142, 144, 147, 150, 151, 153, 154, 157, 158, 162, 176, 177, 181, 182, 186, 188
Thompson, G.F., 32

Thomsen, B.S., 192
Thoughts, 3, 6, 18, 30, 33, 37, 43, 45–48, 52, 54, 56, 57, 60–62, 71, 72, 81, 83–89, 91, 93, 104, 116, 119–122, 128, 129, 131, 132, 134, 144, 147, 149, 181
Tierney, W.G., 74
Time
  functional, 95–98, 100, 102–105
  lived, 8, 96, 97, 103, 105
Toft-Nielsen, C., 142, 143, 147, 151, 153
Totalitarian, 58, 61
Trusts, 2, 7, 58, 67–70, 72–76, 101, 117, 151, 203
Truths, 3, 7, 26, 42, 43, 45, 51–53, 58–63, 67, 69–76, 89, 92, 93, 146, 151, 180, 182, 187, 188, 203
Tsai, K.C., 145
Tucker, A., 61

U
Ulriksen, L., 96, 106
Uncertain, 1, 106, 120, 185, 186, 197
Uncertainties, 8, 17, 29, 57, 81, 96, 102, 104, 105, 119, 134, 186, 188
Understandings, 4, 5, 8, 9, 17–19, 23, 30, 31, 37, 40, 45, 46, 54, 56, 62, 82, 85–88, 90, 92, 96–101, 103–105, 107, 111–113, 116–123, 128, 132, 135, 157, 159, 163, 174, 181, 182, 187, 188, 192, 194, 195
Universities, 1–9, 15–27, 34, 35, 37–39, 43, 47, 48, 51, 52, 55–58, 62, 63, 67–70, 73, 74, 76, 81, 83, 84, 87, 90, 93, 95–102, 105, 106, 114, 125–128, 130–136, 141–154, 157–169, 173, 175–180, 182, 185–197, 201–203
Utility, 7, 30–37, 39–45, 47, 48, 90

V
Vadeboncoeur, J.A., 147, 149
Values, 3–5, 7, 8, 21, 22, 24–26, 29–31, 35, 36, 40, 45, 46, 53, 62, 67–73, 75, 91, 101, 102, 111, 113–117, 125–136, 143, 145, 158, 160, 174, 175, 177, 187, 189–191, 193, 195, 197, 201
Veblen, T., 34
Villa, D., 56
Virtues, 17, 20, 56, 57, 60, 75, 112, 113, 115–123
Voices, 3, 22, 53, 56, 60, 112, 119, 123, 131, 132, 135, 175

W
Waddington, T., 76
Washburn, J., 34, 38
Watson, D., 114, 117
Wegner, E., 196
Weil, C., 70
Weil, S., 91, 92
Wenger-Trayner, B., 196
Wenger-Trayner, E., 196
Weyl, H., 85
Whitton, N., 141–143, 146, 147, 151, 153
Williams, B., 117
Williams, R., 29, 36, 39
Wittgenstein, L., 81, 88, 90
Worlds, 1, 3–5, 7, 16, 18–26, 35, 37, 39, 41, 44, 46, 47, 52, 54–62, 70, 73–75, 86, 88–92, 95, 106, 125–128, 130, 132, 134, 135, 144–151, 153, 154, 164, 174, 175, 177, 185–189, 191, 192, 196, 197, 201–203
Wright, S., 6, 105, 125

Y
Young-Bruehl, E., 55, 56

Z
Zafirovski, M., 31
Ziblatt, D., 61
Zosh, J.M., 192

Lightning Source UK Ltd.
Milton Keynes UK
UKHW021028270622
405018UK00004B/333